The University of Chicago School Mathematics Project

Transition Mathematics

Solution Manual for Student's Text

This Solution Manual contains answers for all exercises in the lessons, Progress Self-Tests, and Chapter Reviews of the Scott, Foresman UCSMP Transition Mathematics student's text. The answers in this manual are correct for the questions in both the 1990 Edition and the 1992 Edition. Questions that were changed in or added to the 1992 Edition are designated with an asterisk (*).

Most answers include only one method of solving that particular exercise. Remember, however, there is often more than one way to find an answer. Answers that involve measures are often approximations, as are computations with decimals. In some cases, even though the equal sign is used, the answer is an approximation.

Scott, Foresman
Editorial Offices: Glenview, Illinois Regional Offices: Sunnyvale, California • Tucker, Georgia • Glenview, Illinois • Oakland, New Jersey • Dallas, Texas

ISBN :   0-673-45262-X

678910-MAL-959493

CHAPTER 1 DECIMAL NOTATION

LESSON 1-1 (pp. 4-7)

1. the first letter of their alphabet (α)
2. II denotes the number two.
3. V stands for five.
4. X stands for 10.
5. the Hindus
6. around 600 to 900 A.D.
7. the number zero (0)
8. Fibonacci (Leonardo of Pisa) was an Italian mathematician who translated Arabic mathematics documents into Latin in the year 1202 A.D. These documents contained decimal arithmetic.
9. the late 1400s (the last part of the 15th century)
10. 10 whole numbers have one digit, namely: 0, 1, 2, 3, 4, 5, 6, 7, 8, and 9.
11. 90 whole numbers from 10 through 99 have two digits.
12. There are 900 3-digit numbers in the decimal system; namely, 100 through 999.

In the number 568,249, the digit in the
13. thousands place is 8;
14. ones place is 9;
15. hundreds place is 2;
16. tens place is 4;
17. ten-thousands place is 6;
18. hundred-thousands place is 5.
19. No
20. Numbers as decimals are shorter.
21. whole number
22. Many possible answers. Sample: the U.S. population (226,545,806 in 1980)
23. a. 226,545,806 is the count;
    b. "people" is the counting unit.
    *1992 Edition: a. 248,239,010 is the count;
    b. "people" is the counting unit.
24. Many possible answers. Sample: the 1980 world population.

25. a. 50 is the count;
    b. "stars" is the counting unit.
26. 46,500
27. a. Appleton-Oshkosh, Wisconsin
    b. McAllen-Edinburg, Texas
28. Population counts are always estimates because it is impossible to get an exact count. While the count is being taken (which could last many weeks) people are out of town, born, or die.
29. 600,000,000   30. 10,000
31. 506
32. 10,000   33. 9999
34. In Europe, the number 7 is frequently written with a horizontal slash to help distinguish it from the numeral 1.

LESSON 1-2 (pp. 8-13)

1. 21.83 is between 21 and 22.
2. The digit in the tenths place is 8;
3. hundredths place is 3.
4. 21.83 seconds measure Evelyn Ashford's time in the 200-meter dash.

In the number 654,987.123456789, the digit in the
5. thousandths place is 3;
6. tenths place is 1;
7. hundredths place is 2;
8. ten thousandths place is 4;
9. millionths place is 6;
10. hundred thousandths place is 5.
11. In π, the digit in the millionths place is 2.
12. Many possible answers. Sample: computer speed
13. Simon Stevin invented the idea of extending decimals to the right in the year 1585.
14. Many possible answers. Sample: Decimals are easier to order and compare.
15. 0.033   largest
    0.015   smallest
    0.024

16. 6.783

   .6783   smallest

   67.83   largest

17. 0.98   largest

   0.8   smallest

   0.9

18. 4.398   smallest

   4.4

   4.4001   largest

19. **a.** Pi (π) is the circumference of a circle with diameter 1.

   b. The first five decimal places of π are 14159.

20. E

21. K

22. N

23. S

24. S

25. none; 64.08 is between the numbers that correspond to K and L.

26. Measures can be split; counts cannot.

27. five and nine tenths

28. three hundred twenty-four and sixty-six hundredths

29. twenty-four thousandths

30. one and four hundred fourteen thousandths

31. 2 zeros

32. Many possible answers. Samples: 44.61, 44.69 are between 44.60 and 44.70.

33. $3.20

34. 10.39 seconds

From smallest to largest, the numbers are

35. three millionths, three thousandths, four thousandths;

36. sixty-five thousandths, sixty-five, sixty-five thousand.

37. Florence Griffith-Joyner's speed of 21.77 seconds is faster than Evelyn Ashford's speed of 21.83 seconds.

38. 400,000,000

39. 31.068

40. In the number 587,402,139, the digit in the

   a. thousands place is 2;

   b. hundred thousands place is 4;

   c. ten millions place is 8;

   d. ones place is 9.

41. Miami

   1992 Edition: Seattle, Washington

42. 6 zeros

43. 76 is the count and "trombones" is the counting unit.

44. **a.** Answers will vary from 7 to 10.

   b. Several possible answers. Samples:
   3.1415927, 3.141592653

LESSON 1-3 (pp. 14-17)

1. Many possible answers. Sample: An estimate of the number attending an outdoor concert should be preferred over the exact value.

2. (1) Exact values may not be worth the trouble it takes to find them. (2) Estimates are often easier to use. (3) Estimates may be safer than exact values. (4) Exact values may change from time to time. (5) Exact values may be impossible to obtain.

3. The most common way of estimating is by rounding.

4. The three types of rounding are up, down, and to the nearest.

5. at least 1800 labels

6. at least 40 pencils

7. 34¢   **8.** 55¢

9. 0.012345

10. When a decimal is truncated, it is cut off or rounded down to a particular decimal place.

11. 0.97531246

12. **a.** $1800   **b.** $1790

13. **a.** 6000   **b.** 5000

14. **a.** 30.5   **b.** 30.4

15. **a.** $40   **b.** $30

16. **a.** 1.610   **b.** 1.609

*These are solutions to questions changed in or added to the *1992 Edition.*

To play it safe, use a

17. high estimate for the size of a birthday cake;

18. high estimate for the amount of money to take on a trip;

19. low estimate for the weight an elevator can carry;

20. high estimate for the time it will take to do your math homework.

21. From smallest to largest, the numbers are 5.001, 5.01, 5.1.

22. From smallest to largest the numbers are .07, .29, 0.3

23. .086 does not equal 0.86.

24. Many possible answers. Samples: 5.81, 5.88 are between 5.80 and 5.90.

25. Many possible answers. Samples: 5.91, 5.99 are between 5.90 and 6.00.

26. 0.2

27. **a.** Q   **b.** R   **c.** Y

28. 4,030,000

29. three minutes, forty-six and thirty-two hundredths seconds

30. Many possible answers. Sample: Truncate means to cut off a part of.

31. **a.** 4

b. The computer rounds the number inside the parentheses down to the nearest integer.

LESSON 1-4 (pp. 18-21)

1. The number 43
   a. rounded up to the next ten is 50;
   b. rounded down to the preceding ten is 40;
   c. rounded to the nearest ten is 40. 43 is nearer to 40 than to 50.

2. The number 0.547
   a. rounded up to the next hundredth is 0.55;
   b. rounded down to the preceding hundredth is 0.54;
   c. rounded to the nearest hundredth is 0.55. 0.547 is nearer to 0.55 than to 0.54.

3. The number 88.8888 rounded to the nearest

a. hundredth: 88.89 (because 88.8888 is between 88.88 and 88.89 and is nearer to 88.89);

b. tenth: 88.9 (because 88.8888 is between 88.8 and 88.9 and is nearer to 88.9);

c. one: 89 (because 88.8888 is between 88 and 89 and is nearer to 89);

d. ten: 90 (because 88.8888 is between 80 and 90 and is nearer to 90);

e. hundred: 100 (because 88.8888 is between 0 and 100 and is nearer to 100)

4. $4.70 ($4.69 is between $4.60 and $4.70 and is nearer to $4.70.)

5. $5.00 ($4.69 is between $4.00 and $5.00 and is nearer to $5.00.)

6. $120 ($19.95 rounded to the nearest dollar is $20, and 6 × $20 = $120.)

7. 200,000 miles per second (186,281.7 is between 100,000 and 200,000 and is nearer to 200,000.)

8. When the first digit to the right of the place to be rounded to is a 5 and there are no other digits to the right, there is a choice in rounding.

9. 0.0525 may be rounded to either 0.053 or 0.052.

10. It is sensible to round up half the time, down the other half.

11. **a.** $89
   b. $166 (because half dollars must be rounded up)
   c. $101
   d. $5324

12. 2.5

13. 328

14. **a.** 3.7   **b.** 3.67
   c. 3.667   **d.** 3.6667

15. 12.53

16. **a.** $20.97
   b. $5 + $7 + $9 = $21, only 3¢ off.

17. **a.** 3 + 8 = 11

   b. Many possible answers. Sample: Round to the nearest tenth or hundredth.

18. 6 × $4 = $24

19. $12 divided by 2 = $6

20. 921 − 0 = 921

21. 2 + 3 = 5

22. When rounded to the nearest hundred, 9550 can be rounded to either 9500 or 9600, and 9650 can be rounded to either 9600 or 9700. So

   a. 9550 is the smallest value;

   b. 9650 is the largest value.

23. Many possible answers. Samples: 3.25, 3.32 are between 3.20 and 3.40.

24. Many possible answers. Samples: 6.291, 6.299 are between 6.300 and 6.290.

25. There are none. These numbers are equal.

26. 1506.3

27. 12 (a dozen) is the count; "eggs" is the counting unit.

28. $1.54

29. **a.** 1.01   **b.** 1.00

30. 3.7   **31.** 7 zeros

32. **a.** By Condition 2, the number is one of the numbers from 570 to 579. By Condition 3, the number must be 4 less than a multiple of 10. Hence, the number is 576.

   b. Conditions 1 and 4 are not needed.

LESSON 1-5 (pp. 22-25)

1. negative four, opposite of four; ("Minus four" is correct but can be confused with subtraction.)

2. negative

3. behind

4. Negative numbers are usually to the left of positive numbers on a horizontal line.

5. Negative numbers are usually below positive numbers on a vertical number line.

6.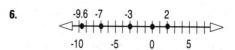

7.

8. losing yardage: negative; gaining yardage: positive; no gain: zero

9. tomorrow: positive; yesterday: negative; today: zero

10. no change: zero; gain: positive; loss: negative

11. . . . , −3, −2, −1, 0, 1, 2, 3, . . . are integers.

12. .5 is not an integer.

13. Natural number is another name for positive integer.

14. 0 (zero)

15. Many possible answers. Samples: −1.5, −π, −2.36 (Any negative number other than −1, −2, −3, −4, . . . is not an integer.)

16. **a.** −1 stands for yesterday;

   b. 1 stands for tomorrow;

   c. −2 stands for the day before yesterday;

   d. 2 stands for the day after tomorrow.

17. **a.** 3 stands for a guess 3 points too high;

   b. −10 stands for a guess 10 points too low;

   c. 0 stands for a perfect guess.

18. J   **19.** Q   **20.** K

21. none

22. −43.3 and −43.30 are equal.

23. −1, 0, $\frac{1}{2}$ are not natural numbers.

24. -2 (-1.75 is between -1 and -2 and is nearer to -2.)

25. -4 (-3.9 is between -3 and -4 and is nearer to -4.)

26. -43 (-43.06 is between -43 and -44 and is nearer to -43.)

27. -1 (-0.53 is between 0 and -1 and is nearer to -1.)

28. From smallest to largest, the numbers are 349, 394, 439, 493.

29. 5.67, 5.067, 5.607, 5.60
From smallest to largest the numbers are 5.067, 5.60, 5.607, 5.67.

30. 462,000.1

31. In the number 24,680.13579, 4 is in the thousands place.

32. In the number 24,680.13579, 5 is in the thousandths place.

33. $28.47
  a. rounded up to the next dollar is $29;
  b. rounded down to the preceding dollar is $28;
  c. rounded to the nearest dollar is $28.
    ($28.47 is between $28 and $29 and is nearer to $28.)

34. 1.2

35. Death Valley; -282 represents the elevation of Death Valley (about 282 feet below sea level.)

36. Many possible answers. Samples: East is positive, west is negative; clockwise is positive, counterclockwise is negative.

LESSON 1-6 (pp. 26-29)

1. Many possible answers. Samples: It is helpful to compare counts when comparing numbers of births or comparing heights.

2. is less than   **3.** is greater than

4. $-5 < -3$ **5.** $6 > -12$

6. $4'11'' < 5'$

7. $-2 < 0 < 2$ or $2 > 0 > -2$

8. $2.1 > 2$ **9.** $0 < 18$

10. $0.44 > 0.432 > 0.43$

11. Negative three is less than three.

12. Seventeen is greater than negative one and five tenths.

13. Negative three is between negative four and negative two. (Or negative three is greater than negative four and less than negative two.)

14. $-6°F < 15°F$

15. $7'4'' > 7'2''$
  1992 Edition: $7'4'' > 7'1''$

16. $125 > 119$

17. Larger numbers are to the right of smaller numbers on a horizontal number line.

18. Larger numbers are above smaller numbers on a vertical number line.

19. $8000 > -$2000$

20. -300 ft > -400 ft

21. $>$ (Write .305 as .3050. Then compare .3050 and .3046: .3050 > .3046)

22. $<$ (Write 0.008 as .0080. Then compare .0008 and .0080: .0008 < .0080)

23. $>$ (Write 6.01 as 6.010000. Then compare 6.010000 and 6.000001: 6.010000 > 6.000001)

24. $>$ (-14 is to the right of -14.5 on a horizontal number line.)

25. $<$ (-99.5 is to the left of 9.95.)

26. $=$

27. $0.621 < 6.21 < 62.1$ (The arrangement of these numbers from left to right is 0.621, 6.21, 62.1.), or $62.1 > 6.21 > 0.621$

28. $-41 < -4.1 < 4.1$ (The arrangement of these numbers from left to right is -41, -4.1, 4.1); or $4.1 > -4.1 > -41$

29. $99.2 < 99.8 < 100.4$ (The arrangement of these numbers from left to right is 99.2, 99.8, 100.4), or $100.4 > 99.8 > 99.2$

30. In the number 8249.0351, the digit in the
  a. thousands place is 8
  b. thousandths place is 5

c. hundreds place is 2;

d. hundredths place is 3.

31. From smallest to largest, the numbers are 0.07243, 0.07249, 0.0782.

32. 0, 1, 2, 3, and 4 are the whole numbers less than 5.

33. −3, −2, −1, 0, 1, and 2 are the integers between −4 and 3.

34. **a.** 1   **b.** − 1

c. 21 (in 1989, or 20 in 1990, etc.)

d. −64 (in 1989, or −65 in 1990, etc.)

35. 70 + 7 = 77

36. $15 + $3 + $8 = $26

37. 6.283 (6.28318 . . . is between 6.283 and 6.284 and is nearer to 6.283.)

38. 22.95

39. Many possible answers. Sample: Harriot was sent by Sir Walter Raleigh in 1585 to survey and map what is now called North Carolina.

LESSON 1-7 (pp. 30-33)

1. A key sequence is a set of instructions for entering numbers and operations into a calculator.

2. False; different calculators may give different answers for the same key sequence.

3. On a scientific calculator, the display will show 8, 8, 7.2, 7.2, 10, 80. On a non-scientific calculator, the display will show 8, 8, 7.2, 15.2, 10, 152.

4. 15 $\boxed{-}$ 27 $\boxed{=}$

5. If the calculator displays 3.1415926 or 3.141592653, it truncates. If it displays 3.1415927 or 3.141592654, it rounds to the nearest. If it displays 3.14159265, you can't tell.

6. −87

7. Many possible answers. (On many truncating calculators, the number of decimal places equals the last digit in the display after completing this calculation.)

8. 1824 (Key sequence: 3.5625 $\boxed{\times}$ 521 $\boxed{=}$)

9. 2.889 (Key sequence: 0.9 $\boxed{+}$ 0.99 $\boxed{+}$ 0.999 $\boxed{=}$)

10. 18.849555 (Key sequence: 6 $\boxed{\times}$ $\boxed{\pi}$ $\boxed{=}$)

11. 206 (Key sequence: 412 $\boxed{\pm}$ $\boxed{\div}$ 2 $\boxed{\pm}$ $\boxed{=}$)

12. 38.62 (Key sequence: 8.3 $\boxed{\times}$ 5.1 $\boxed{-}$ 3.71 $\boxed{=}$)

13. Answer depends on the calculator. Samples: 99,999,999 or 9,999,999,999.

14. Answer depends on the calculator. Samples: 0.0000001 or 0.000000001

15. Answer is usually the opposite of the answer to Question 13. Sample: −99,999,999.

16. 10 ($\pi \times \pi$ is about equal to 9.8696044)

17. $\boxed{C}$, $\boxed{CE}$, or $\boxed{CE/C}$ is usually the key used to correct a mistake in an entry.

18. A new calculation is usually handled with $\boxed{C}$, $\boxed{AC}$, or $\boxed{C}$ $\boxed{C}$.

19. **a.** From smallest to largest, the numbers are −2, −1.5, −1. (The arrangement of these numbers from left to right on a horizontal number line is −2, −1.5, −1.)

b. −2 < −1.5 < −1 or −1 > −1.5 > −2

20. **a.** .3

.33

.303

From largest to smallest, the numbers are .33, .303, .3.

b. .33 > .303 > .3 or .3 < .303 < .33

21. > (−4 is to the right of −10.)

22. 53.5 seconds

23. 54 seconds (53.7 is between 53 and 54 and nearer to 54.)

24. 900 − 0 = 900

25. Many possible answers. Samples: −4.6315, −4.6319 (Write −4.632 as −4.6320 and −4.631 as −4.6310. −4.6315 and −4.6319 are between −4.6320 and −4.6310.)

26. three million, four hundred twelve thousand, six hundred seventy

27. 5 zeros

28. $300,000 - 3 = 299,997$

29. **a.** An error message is shown.

   b. There is an error in the attempted calculation.

   c. Division by zero is undefined.

30. **a.** Division by zero error message is shown.

   b. same message as in part a

   c. any number divided by zero

LESSON 1-8 (pp. 34-38)

1. In the fraction $\frac{15}{8}$

   a. 15 is the numerator.

   b. 8 is the denominator.

   c. — is the sign for division.

   d. The fraction is equal to $\frac{15}{8}$.

   e. No, it is not equal to $8 \div 15$.

   f. Yes, it is equal to $15 \div 8$.

   g. 8 is the divisor.

   h. 15 is the dividend.

   i. It is equal to 1.875.

2. Before the 1500s, the Arabs used the fraction bar.

3. The slash symbol was first developed by Manuel Antonio Valdes in 1784.

4. **a.** $\frac{15}{8}$ is a simple fraction.

   b. $\frac{-7}{1}$ is a simple fraction.

   c. $\frac{3.5}{2.3}$ is not a simple fraction.

   d. $6\frac{2}{3}$ is not a simple fraction.

   e. $-5/6$ is a simple fraction.

5. Decimals are easier to order, round, add, and subtract.

6. .15 ($3 \div 20 = .15$)

7. 1.15 ($23 \div 20 = 1.15$)

8. −1.15 (Do work as in Question 7 and add negative sign.)

9. .5714286

10. $.\overline{037}$ ($1 \div 27 = .037037037 \ldots$)

11. 27 is the repetend.

12. 8 is the repetend.

13. 9.8777777777

14. 0.1428571428

15. −5.4444444444

16. **a.** .1   **b.** .2   **c.** .3

   d. .4   **e.** .5   **f.** .6

   g. .7   **h.** .8   **i.** .9

   j. .2   **k.** .4   **l.** .6

   m. .8   **n.** .5   **o.** .25

   p. .75   **q.** .375   **r.** .625

   s. .875   **t.** $.\overline{3}$ **u.** $.\overline{6}$

   v. $.\overline{6}$ **w.** $.1\overline{6}$ **x.** $.8\overline{3}$

17. $\frac{2}{5}$ or $\frac{4}{10}$ **18.** $\frac{1}{4}$ **19.** $\frac{1}{3}$

20. $\frac{3}{5}$ or $\frac{6}{10}$ **21.** $\frac{7}{10}$ **22.** $\frac{2}{3}$

23. 23 is a factor of 92.

24. 4 is a factor of 12.

25. The factors of 30 are 1, 2, 3, 5, 6, 10, 15, and 30.

26. **a.** .1875 in. ($3 \div 16 = .1875$)

   b. shorter ($3/16 = .1875$ and $1/5 = .2$. Write .2 as .2000. Then compare .1875 and .2000: $.1875 < .2000$.)

27. .071 ($1 \div 14 = .0\overline{714285}$)

28. From smallest to largest, the numbers are $3/10$, .33, $1/3$. (Write $3/10$ as .3, $1/3$ as .333 . . . . Then order .3, .333 . . . , and .33 from smallest to largest: .3, .33, .333 . . . .)

29. From smallest to largest, the numbers are $\frac{2}{11}, \frac{2}{9}, \frac{2}{7}$.

   $(\frac{2}{11} = 0.\overline{18}; \frac{2}{9} = .\overline{2}; \frac{2}{7} = .\overline{285714})$

30. Many possible answers. Samples: 0.03591, 0.03599 (Write 0.036 as 0.03600 and 0.0359 as 0.03590. 0.03591 and 0.03599 are between 0.03600 and 0.03590.)

31. 34.000791

34.0079

The larger number is 34.0079.

32. $-2 > -3$

33. $99.6°$

34. 9.8979 (9.8978675645 is between 9.8978 and 9.8979 and is nearer to 9.8979.)

35. a. $.\overline{1}$ $(1 \div 9 = .1111 \ldots);$

$.\overline{2}$ $(2 \div 9 = .2222 \ldots);$

$.\overline{3}$ $(3 \div 9 = .3333 \ldots);$

$.\overline{4}; .\overline{5}; .\overline{6}; .\overline{7}; .\overline{8}$

b. $.\overline{9}$

c. yes; $.\overline{9} = 1.0$ $(\frac{9}{9} = .\overline{9}$ and $\frac{9}{9} = 1)$

36. a. $.5, .\overline{3}, .25, .2, .1\overline{6};$

b. $.\overline{142857}, .125, .\overline{1}, .1, .\overline{09}, .08\overline{3}$

c. 0 (The decimals are getting smaller and smaller.)

37. $1/7 = 0.142857142857 \ldots;$

$2/7 = 0.285714285714 \ldots;$

$3/7 = 0.428571428571 \ldots;$

$4/7 = 0.571428571428 \ldots;$

$5/7 = 0.714285714285 \ldots;$

$6/7 = 0.857142857142 \ldots;$

(All these decimals repeat digits in the same order.)

LESSON 1-9 (pp. 39-41)

1. a. $10\frac{3}{4}$ is between 10 and 11.

b. 10 is the integer part.

c. 10.75 $(\frac{3}{4} = .75; 10 + .75 = 10.75)$

d.

2. a. $4\frac{2}{3}$ is between 4 and 5.

b. 4 is the integer part.

c. $4.\overline{6}$ $(\frac{2}{3} = .\overline{6}; 4 + .\overline{6} = 4.\overline{6})$

d.

3. Fourths are quarters, a term used in money.

4. 2.5

5. 7.4

6. 1.3

7. $17.8\overline{3}$

8. 5.125 $(\frac{1}{8} = .125)$

9. 12.1875 $(\frac{3}{16} = .1875)$

10. $4.\overline{09}$ $(\frac{1}{11} = .\overline{09})$

11. $20.5\overline{3}$ $(\frac{8}{15} = .5\overline{3})$

12. -1.8 $(\frac{4}{5} = .8)$

13. \$4.25 $(\frac{1}{4}$ of a dollar is \$.25.)

14. $-\$1.875$ $(\frac{1}{8}$ of a dollar is \$.875.)

15. From smallest to largest, the numbers are $2\frac{3}{5}, 3\frac{2}{5}, 5\frac{2}{3}$. (Compare the integer parts: $2 < 3 < 5$.)

16. Mouse A is longer. (Write $2\frac{3}{10}$ as 2.3 and $2\frac{1}{4}$ as 2.25. Compare 2.3 and 2.25; 2.3 > 2.25)

17. 12.53$\overline{3}$ $(\frac{8}{15} = .53333 \ldots)$

18. 1.1875 miles $(\frac{3}{16} = .1875)$

19. $35\frac{11}{32}$ in. is longer than $35\frac{1}{3}$ in. $(\frac{11}{32} = .34375;$ $\frac{1}{3} = .333 \ldots; .34375 > .333 \ldots)$

20. a. $.1\overline{6}$ $(1 \div 6 = .1666 \ldots)$

b. $.\overline{3}$ $(2 \div 6 = .333 \ldots)$

c. .5 **d.** .6 **e.** .8$\overline{3}$

f. .125 **g.** .25 **h.** .375

i. .5 **j.** .625

21. 1 is in the ten thousands place.

22. **a.** 27 and 206 are the counts.

    b. The counting units are "small bones" and "bones."

23. 1,000,000 − 1 = 999,999

24. Many possible answers. Sample: Decimals are easier to order.

25. **a.** −4.3 (−4.3 is to the right of −4.4.)

    b. Many possible answers. Samples: −4.31, −4.38 (Write −4.3 as −4.30 and −4.4 as −4.40. −4.31 and −4.38 are between −4.30 and −4.40.)

26. Many possible answers. Samples: 2.01, 2.04 (Write 2 as 2.00 and 2.1 as 2.10. 2.01 and 2.14 are between 2.00 and 2.10.

27. 16 + 84 = 100

28. Zero is greater than negative six.

29. −9.99 < 9 < 9.99 (The arrangement of these numbers from left to right is −9.99, 9, 9.99.)

30. True, 5 = 5.0

31. 4 (7.$\overline{8142}$ = 7.814281428142 . . .)

32. The factors of 36 are 1, 2, 3, 4, 6, 9, 12, 18, and 36. (All of these numbers divide evenly into 36.)

33. The factors of 39 are 1, 3, 13, and 39.

34. Many possible answers. (To arrive at a good estimate, choose 1 inch of 1 column on the page and count the mixed numbers in that inch. Then multiply that count by the length of the column, and multiply that answer by the total number of columns.)

35. **a.** Answers will vary.

    b. Answers will vary. If the last digit shown is 7, the computer rounds to the nearest. If the last digit is 6, it rounds down.

    c. The computer will usually show more places for $\frac{1}{7}$.

LESSON 1-10 (pp. 42-46)

1. b, $\frac{8}{12}$ is not equal to $\frac{3}{4}$. ($\frac{8}{12}$ can be reduced to $\frac{2}{3}$ by dividing the numerator and denominator by 3.)

2. Many possible answers. Samples: $\frac{14}{4}$, $\frac{21}{6}$, $\frac{28}{8}$ (Multiply the numerator and denominator by the same number.)

3. All are equal. (Each fraction reduces to $\frac{2}{3}$.)

4. $\frac{8}{12}$ is not equal to the other fractions. ($\frac{8}{12}$ reduces to $\frac{2}{3}$. The other fractions each reduce to $\frac{3}{4}$.)

5. Many possible answers. Sample: $\frac{42}{24}$ (Multiply the numerator and denominator by 2.)

6. A fraction is in lowest terms when there is no whole number greater than 1 that is a factor of both the numerator and the denominator.

7. **a.** 1, 2, 3, 4, 6, 8, 12, 16, 24, and 48 are the factors of 48.

    b. 1, 2, 3, 4, 5, 6, 10, 12, 15, 20, 30, and 60 are the factors of 60.

    c. 1, 2, 3, 4, 6, and 12 are factors of both 48 and 60.

    d. 12 is the greatest common factor of 48 and 60.

    e. $\frac{4}{5}$ (Divide the numerator and denominator by 12.)

8. **a.** 3 is a common factor. (1 is also a common factor, but it is not helpful to identify it when reducing fractions.)

    b. $\frac{7}{4}$ (Divide the numerator and denominator by 3.)

9. **a.** 5 is a common factor.

b. $\frac{3}{4}$ (Divide the numerator and denominator by 5.)

10. a. Several possible answers. Sample: 4 is a common factor.

b. $\frac{45}{4}$ (Divide the numerator and denominator by 4.)

11. a. Several possible answers: Samples: 12 and 24 are common factors.

b. $\frac{10}{3}$ (Divide the numerator and denominator by 24.)

12. Many possible answers. Sample $11\frac{10}{24}$ (Multiply the numerator and denominator of $\frac{5}{12}$ by 2 to get $\frac{5}{12} = \frac{10}{24}$.)

13. Many possible answers. Sample: $37\frac{6}{14}$ (Multiply the numerator and denominator of $\frac{3}{7}$ by 2 to get $\frac{6}{14}$.)

14. $\frac{2}{8} = \frac{1}{4}$

15.

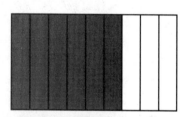

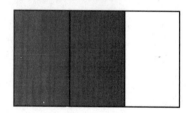

16. Many possible answers. Sample: $\frac{26}{2}, \frac{39}{3}, \frac{52}{4}$ (Multiply the numerator and denominator of $\frac{13}{1}$ by 2 or 3 or 4.)

17. $\frac{24}{3}$ (Multiply the numerator and denominator of $\frac{8}{1}$ by 3.)

18. $\frac{14}{8} = \frac{7}{4}$ (Divide the numerator and denominator by 2.)

19. $\frac{75}{100} = \frac{3}{4}$ (Divide the numerator and denominator by 25.)

20. 4.12 ($\frac{2}{17} = .1176 \ldots$)

21. .01

22. .86 ($\frac{43}{50} = .86$; .86 is already rounded to hundredths. No further rounding is necessary.)

23. Many possible answers. Samples: $-\frac{1}{2}$, −.2, −.05

24. $\frac{4}{7}$ is larger. ($\frac{9}{16} = .5625$; $\frac{4}{7} = .5714 \ldots$)

Questions 25-27 are easily handled on a calculator.

25. 12.2 ($4062 \times .003 = 12.186$; 12.186 rounded to the nearest tenth is 12.2.)

26. −1782.4 ($\pi \times -567.34 \approx -1782.3512$. −1782.3512 rounded to the nearest tenth is −1782.4.)

27. 19.6 ($18 + 1.8 - 0.18 = 19.62$. 19.62 rounded to the nearest tenth is 19.6.)

28. 5.8125 ($\frac{13}{16} = .8125$)

29. a. .4   **b.** .625   **c.** .75
   d. $.\overline{3}$ **e.** $.8\overline{3}$

30. 1, 2, 3, 4, 6, 8, 12, and 24 are the factors of 24.

31. 1, 3, 17, and 51 are the factors of 51.

32. True, 16 and 20 are both factors of 80. (80 can be divided evenly by both 16 and 20.)

33. **a.** 2 is a factor of an integer if and only if the ones digit of the integer is even (0, 2, 4, 6, or 8).

b. 5 is a factor of an integer if and only if the ones digit of the integer is 0 or 5.

c. 4444 is not divisible by 3. (4 + 4 + 4 + 4 = 16; 16 is not divisible by 3.)

d. 267 is not divisible by 9. (2 + 6 + 7 = 15; 15 is not divisible by 9.)

e. Many possible answers. Samples: 49,995 and 83,115 are both divisible by 5 and 9, but not by 2. (They are divisible by 5 because the ones digit in each number is 5. They are divisible by 9 because the sum of the digits in each number is 9. They are not divisible by 2 because the ones digit in each number is not even.)

CHAPTER 1 PROGRESS SELF-TEST (p. 48)

1. 700,000

2. 45.6

3. 0.25 (1 ÷ 4 = .25)

4. $15\frac{13}{16} = 15 + \frac{13}{16} = 15 + 0.8125 = 15.812$

5. 6 is in the hundredths place in the number 1234.5678.

6. three thousandths

7. .6
.66
.6666 . . .
.606
The largest number is .6666 . . . , or $.\overline{6}$.

8. $\frac{3}{10}$ is the smallest number. ($\frac{1}{2}$ = .5, $\frac{2}{5}$ = .4, $\frac{3}{10}$ = .3, and $\frac{1}{3}$ = .333 . . .)

9. 98.7

10. 99 (98.76 is between 98 and 99 and is nearer to 99.)

11. −80 ft > −100 ft (The negative numbers stand for distances below sea level and the > sign means "is higher than.")

12. M is $\frac{1}{2}$. (Each tick mark to the right of 0 is $\frac{1}{4}$. So M is $\frac{2}{4}$ or $\frac{1}{2}$.)

13. F corresponds to −1.25. (Each tick mark to the left of 0 is a decrease of $\frac{1}{4}$ or 0.25.)

14. Many possible answers. Samples: 16.52, 16.55, 16.58 (Write 16.5 as 16.50 and 16.6 as 16.60. 16.52, 16.55, and 16.58 are between 16.50 and 16.60.)

15. Many possible answers. Samples: −2.3901, −2.3904 (Write −2.39 as −2.3900 and −2.391 as −2.3910. −2.3901 and −2.3904 are between −2.3900 and −2.3910.)

16. 0.45 < 0.4500000001

17. $-9.24 = -9.240$ (Zeros written to the right of the digits that are to the right of the decimal point do not affect the value of the number.)

18. $-4 > -5$ (-4 is to the right of -5 on a horizontal number line.)

19. $\frac{6}{10}$ or $\frac{3}{5}$

20. Many possible answers. Samples: $\frac{1}{2}$, 0.43, or 7.6 (Any number other than . . . $-3, -2, -1$, 0, 1, 2, 3 . . . is not an integer.)

21. The store will probably round up. You will pay 18¢.

22. $3 + 9 = 12$

23. 3.456 $\boxed{\times}$ 2.345 $\boxed{=}$

24. 19. (6 $\boxed{\times}$ $\boxed{\pi}$ $\boxed{=}$ is a calculator sequence that will yield 18.8495 . . . . 18.8495 . . . rounded to the nearest integer is 19.)

25. 7 is the repetend.

26. On the graph below each tick mark represents 0.1.

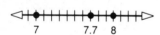

27.

28. Many possible answers. Sample: the number of people who watched a particular TV program

29. Many possible answers. Sample: <u>Twelve elephants</u> marched in the circus parade.

30. 0.1 is the largest number. (The numbers are 0.1, 0.000001, 0.000000001, and .001.)

31. 1, 2, 3, 6, 9, and 18 are the factors of 18.

32. $\frac{30}{5}$ (Multiply the numerator and denominator of $\frac{6}{1}$ by 5.)

33. $\frac{4}{7}$ (3 is a factor of both 12 and 21. Divide the numerator and denominator by 3.)

34. b, The decimal system was developed around 800 A.D.

12

CHAPTER 1 REVIEW (pp. 49-51)

1. 4003   **2.** 0.75

3. 120,000,000   **4.** 3.006

5. five hundred thousand four hundred

6. one thousandth

7. 400,000,000
4000,000,001
      .40000 00000 0001
    0.4

The largest number is 400,000,001; the smallest is 0.4.

8. From smallest to largest, the numbers are $^-0.2$, 0, 0.19, 0.2. ($^-0.2$ is to the left of 0 on a horizontal number line. Write 0.2 as 0.20. Then $0.19 < 0.20$.)

9. From smallest to largest, the numbers are $^-586.363$, $^-586.36$, $^-586.34$. (These numbers, written with the same number of decimal places, are arranged from left to right as follows: $^-586.363$, $^-586.360$, $^-586.340$.)

10. From smallest to largest, the numbers are $\frac{1}{11}$, $\frac{1}{9}$, $\frac{1}{7}$. ($\frac{1}{11} = 1.0909 \ldots$, $\frac{1}{9} = .111 \ldots$, $\frac{1}{7} = .1428 \ldots$)

11. From smallest to largest, the numbers are $\frac{6}{10}$, 0.66, $\frac{2}{3}$. ($\frac{6}{10} = .6$, $\frac{2}{3} = .666 \ldots$)

12. From smallest to largest, the numbers are $2\frac{2}{3}$, $3\frac{1}{3}$, $4\frac{1}{6}$ (Only the integer parts need to be compared in this case.)

13. 4.33
5.3
5.333 . . .
From smallest to largest, the numbers are 4.33, 5.3, $5.\overline{3}$

14. Many possible answers. Samples: 73.01, 73.09 (73 = 73.00 and 73.1 = 73.10. 73.01 and 73.09 are between 73.00 and 73.10.)

15. Many possible answers. Samples: $^-1.4$, $^-1.7$

$(^-1 = ^-1.0$ and $^-2 = ^-2.0$. $^-1.4$ and $^-1.7$ are between $^-1.0$ and $^-2.0$.)

16. Many possible answers. Samples: 6.991, 6.995 (6.99 = 6.990 and 7 = 7.000. 6.991 and 6.995 are between 6.990 and 7.000.)

17. Many possible answers. Samples: 3.401, 3.402, 3.403 (3.4 = 3.400 and 3.40 = 3.404040 . . . . 3.401, 3.402, and 3.403 are between 3.400 and 3.404040 . . . .)

18. 345.7   **19.** 5.84   **20.** 30

21. 0.595959 (When a calculator truncates, it rounds down.)

22. 34,000 (34,498 is between 34,000 and 35,000 and is nearer to 34,000.)

23. 6.8 (6.81 is between 6.8 and 6.9 and is nearer to 6.8.)

24. 6 (5.55 is between 5 and 6 and is closer to 6.)

25. $59 + 3 = 62$ **26.** $6 \times 8 = 48$

27. 4402.912   **28.** 561.605

29. 69.8584 (On the calculator, $73 - \pi$ yields 69.858407. 69.858407 is between 69.8584 and 69.8485 and is nearer to 69.8584.)

30. 2.2 ($11 \div 5 = 2.2$)

31. $^-5.\overline{3}$ ($16 \div 3 = 5.333 \vdots \ldots$)

32. $6.57142\overline{8}$ ($4 \div 7 = .571428571428 \ldots$ or $.\overline{571428}$; $6\frac{4}{7} = 6 + .\overline{571428} = 6.57142\overline{8}$)

33. 5.25 ($1 \div 4 = .25$; $5\frac{1}{4} = 5 + .25 = 5.25$)

34. .75   **35.** $.\overline{6}$ **36.** .2

37. $.1\overline{6}$ **38.** $\frac{8}{10}$ or $\frac{4}{5}$ **39.** $\frac{1}{3}$

40. $\frac{1}{4}$ **41.** $2.0 > 0.2$

42. $0.1 < 0.\overline{1}$ ($0.\overline{1} = 0.1111 \ldots$)

43. $.6 < \frac{2}{3} < .667$, or $.667 > \frac{2}{3} > .6$

($\frac{2}{3} = .666 \ldots$ and $.6 = .600$)

44. 1 ($.\overline{1428} = .1428142814281428 \ldots$)

45. $468.5\overline{68}$

46. Many possible answers. Sample: $\frac{4}{14}$ (Multiply the numerator and denominator by 2.)

47. 1, 2, 3, 6, 7, 14, 21, and 42 are the factors of 42.

48. $\frac{4}{3}$ (Divide numerator and denominator by 20.)

49. 29,000 (29,451 is between 29,000 and 30,000 and is nearer to 29,000.)

50. Round $8.95 to $9

51. 50¢ (The store will round up to the next whole cent.)

52. Many possible answers. Sample: To be safe, give a low estimate for the weight load of a bridge.

53. Many possible answers. Sample: Exact values change from time to time, such as the number of minutes of travel time to school.

54. −350

55. −75,000 < 10,000

56. **a.** −25;   **b.** 40;   **c.** 0

57.

-4 -3 -2 -1 0 1 2 3 4 5

58.

6   6.4   7

59.

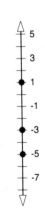

60. tenths

61. 4.6

62. fifths

63. $7\frac{1}{5}$

64. 5 $\boxed{\pm}$

65. 77 $\boxed{\div}$ 8.2 $\boxed{=}$

66. The Hindus invented the decimal system.

67. (c) (The symbols for 0, 1, 2, 3, 4, 5, 6, 7, 8, and 9 were developed in the late 1400s.)

CHAPTER 2   LARGE AND SMALL NUMBERS

LESSON 2-1   (pp. 54-57)

1. 10

2. 10 × 634 = 6340

3. 10 × 2.4 = 24

4. 10 × 0.08 = 0.8

5. 10 × 47.21 = 472.1

6. To multiply a decimal by 10, move the decimal point one place to the right.

7. To multiply a decimal by 100, move the decimal point two places to the right.

8. 100 × 113 = 11,300

9. 100 × .05 = 5

10. 100 × 7755.2 = 775,520

11. 100 × 6.301 = 630.1

12. To multiply a decimal by 1000, move the decimal point three places to the right.

13. To multiply a decimal by 10,000, move the decimal point four places to the right.

14. 1.43 × 10,000 = 14,300

15. 32 × 1000 = 32,000

16. 1000 × 46.314 = 46,314

17. 0.095 × 10,000 = 950

18. one thousand

19. one million

20. one billion

21. on trillion

22. one quadrillion

23. one quintillion

24. $2.02 \times 1{,}000{,}000{,}000 = 2{,}020{,}000{,}000$

25. $1.35 \times 1{,}000{,}000 = 1{,}350{,}000$

26. $88 \times 1{,}000{,}000 = 88{,}000{,}000$;
$\$22.2 \times 1{,}000{,}000{,}000 = \$22{,}200{,}000{,}000$;
$33.6 \times 1{,}000{,}000{,}000 = 33{,}600{,}000{,}000$

27. Round 46.314 to 46 or 47. The answer should be between 46,000 and 47,000.

28. 1000

29. World population in 1950: 2.5 billion or 2.6 billion; 2,500,000,000 or 2,600,000,000
1992 Edition: World population in 1950: 2.4 billion or 2.5 billion; 2,400,000,000 or 2,500,000,000

30. World population in 1960: 3.0 billion or 3.1 billion; 3,000,000,000 or 3,100,000,000
1992 Edition: World population in 1965: 3.3 billion or 3.4 billion; 3,300,000,000 or 3,400,000,000

31. World population in 1970: 3.6 billion or 3.7 billion; 3,600,000,000 or 3,700,000,000
1992 Edition: World population in 1980: 4.4 billion or 4.5 billion; 4,400,000,000 or 4,500,000,000

32. World population in 1980: 4.4 billion or 4.5 billion; 4,400,000,000 or 4,500,000,000
1992 Edition: World population in 1990: 5.2 billion or 5.3 billion; 5,200,000,000 or 5,300,000,000

33. 230 million   **34.** $15.6 million

35. 26.5 trillion   **36.** quadrillion

37. a. 0.5 (The interval between 0 and 1 is divided into tenths.);
b. 0.1
c. $G\left(\dfrac{3}{5} = 0.6\right)$

38. a. 0.125 ($1 \div 8 = 0.125$)
b. 0.1 (0.1 means "one tenth.")
c. 0.02 ($1 \div 50 = 0.02$)
d. 0.01 (0.01 means "one tenth.")

39. 2.6494 rounded down to thousandths is 2.649.

40. $-10 < 9$.

41. Answers will vary.

42. In England, "billion" often means 1,000,000,000,000.

LESSON 2-2   (pp. 58-61)

1. For the number 4^6,
a. 4 is the base
b. 6 is the exponent
c. and we say this number is 4 to the 6th power.

2. $3^2 = 3 \times 3 = 9$; $3^3 = 3 \times 3 \times 3 = 27$;
$3^4 = 3 \times 3 \times 3 \times 3 = 81$;
$3^5 = 3 \times 3 \times 3 \times 3 \times 3 = 243$;
$3^6 = 3 \times 3 \times 3 \times 3 \times 3 \times 3 = 729$

3. $2^2 = 2 \times 2 = 4$; $2^3 = 2 \times 2 \times 2 = 8$;
$2^4 = 2 \times 2 \times 2 \times 2 = 16$;
$2^5 = 2 \times 2 \times 2 \times 2 \times 2 = 32$;
$2^6 = 2 \times 2 \times 2 \times 2 \times 2 \times 2 = 64$

4. 117,649 (Key in: 7 $\boxed{y^x}$ 6 $\boxed{=}$)

5. 1,048,576 (key in: 2 $\boxed{y^x}$ 20 $\boxed{=}$);
400 ($20^2 = 20 \times 20 = 400$)

6. 1 (1^{984} means $1 \times 1 \times 1 \times 1 \times 1 \times \ldots \times 1$, such that there are 984 ones.)

7. $1.08^3 = 1.08 \times 1.08 \times 1.08 = 1.259712$

8. seven

9. a. 10^6 is a 1 followed by 6 zeros: 1,000,000;
b. one million

10. a. 1000   **b.** 10^3

11. a. 10^6 **b.** 10^9 **c.** 10^{12}

12. $10^1 = 10$

13. 500 (Write 5 as 5. and move the decimal point 2 places to the right.)

14. 37,000 (Move the decimal point 4 places to the right.)

15. To multiply by a positive integer power of 10, move the decimal point to the right the same number of places as the value of the exponent.

16. one

17. **a.** 4; **b.** 4^4, 4^3, 4^2, ____ or 2^8, 2^6, 2^4, ____

18. 999 ($10^3 = 1000$)

19. 3^2 ($2^3 = 8$; $3^2 = 9$)

20. 10^4, ten thousand, 10,000; 10^5, hundred thousand, 100,000

21. seventh ($10,000,000 = 10^7$)

22. c, ($3^{10} = 59,049$; $2^{10} = 1024$)

23. **a.** 96 or 7776 (The answer depends on the type of calculator used.)

b. If the answer was 96, the calculator took the power first. If the answer was 7776, the calculator multiplied first.

24. true ($2^{10} = 1024$; $10^3 = 1000$)

25. Forty-three quintillion, two hundred fifty-two quadrillion, three trillion, two hundred seventy-four billion, four hundred eighty-nine million, eight hundred fifty-six thousand

26. 1,800,000,000

27. 3×7 (Round $6.95 to $7.)

28. **a.** 13; **b.** -1485; **c.** -459.67

29. $44.\overline{4}$ ($44.444444 \ldots = 44.\overline{4}$)

30. 2 ($15 \div 7 = 2.\overline{142857}$)

31. **a.** 1,000,000 **b.** 1,800,000 **c.** 8,000

32. A googol is 10^{100}, or 1 followed by 100 zeros.

33. **a.** Answers will vary depending on the computer.

b. 279936; The calculator and the computer give the same answer.

LESSON 2-3 (pp. 62-66)

1. 26,000,000,000,000 miles (Move the decimal point in 2.6 13 places to the right.)

2. 160,000 kg (Move the decimal point in 1.6 5 places to the right.)

3. one; ten; power

4. 8×10^2 (Write 8.00. The decimal point must move 2 places to the right to get 800, so the exponent of 10 is 2.)

5. 8.04×10^2 (Write 8.04. The decimal point must move 2 places to the right to get 804, so the exponent of 10 is 2.)

6. 3.5×10^6 (Write 3.5. The decimal point must move 6 places to the right to get 3,500,000, so the exponent of 10 is 6.)

7. 5.88×10^{21} (Write 5.88. The decimal point must move 21 places to the right to get 5,880,000,000,000,000,000,000, so the exponent of 10 is 21.)

8. 5.754×10^7 (57.54 million is 57,540,000. Write 5.754. The decimal point must move 7 places to the right to get 57,540,000. So the exponent of 10 is 7.)

*1992 Edition: 5.922×10^7 (59.22 million is 59,220,000. Write 5.922. The decimal point must move 7 places to the right to get 59,220,000. So the exponent of 10 is 7.)

9. 1.2×10^{12} (One trillion $= 10^{12}$, so 1.2 trillion $= 1.2 \times 10^{12}$.)

10. 6.321×10^1 (Write 6.321. The decimal point must move 1 place to the right to get 63.21, so the exponent of 10 is 1.)

11. 7.654×10^2 (Write 7.654. The decimal point must move 2 places to the right to get 765.4, so the exponent of 10 is 2.)

12. 6.75 $\boxed{\text{EE}}$ 11 or 6.75 $\boxed{\text{Exp}}$ 11

In 13-15, answers may vary depending on the calculator used.

13. $\boxed{4.9 \qquad 15}$

14. $\boxed{6. \qquad 13}$

15. $\boxed{3.8 \qquad 12}$

16. about 5.8746×10^{12} mi (key in: 1.60947 $\boxed{\text{EE}}$ 10 $\boxed{\times}$ 365 $\boxed{=}$)

17. 31,536,000 sec (key in: 60 $\boxed{\times}$ 60 $\boxed{\times}$ 24 $\boxed{\times}$ 365 $\boxed{=}$)

18. Several possible answers, depending on the calculator. Sample:
a. 9.9999×10^{99} **b.** -9.9999×10^{99}

19. 1×10^{10} ($1 \times 10^{10} = 1 \times 10,000,000,000$ $= 10,000,000,000$; $9 \times 10^{9} =$ $9 \times 1,000,000,000 = 9,000,000,000$)

20. $8^{1} = 8$; $8^{2} = 8 \times 8 = 64$; $8^{3} = 8 \times 8 \times 8 = 512$

21. 6 (Move the decimal point 4 places to the right.)

22. 52,300 (Move the decimal point 2 places to the right.)

23. From smallest to largest the numbers are $14\frac{3}{5} = 14.6$, $14.\overline{61}$, $14.\overline{6}$. ($\frac{3}{5} = .6$ so $14\frac{3}{5} = 14.6$; $14.\overline{61} = 14.616161 \ldots$; $14.\overline{6} = 14.6666 \ldots$)

24. Many possible answers. Samples: $\frac{9}{10}$, $\frac{90}{100}$ (0.9 means "nine tenths.")

25. a. Q **b.** E **c.** S
d. C (The interval is one tenth.)

26. a. 0.329 ($202 \div 614 = 0.32899 \ldots$)
b. 0.329 ($186 \div 566 = 0.32862 \ldots$)
c. Johnson, since $0.3290 > 0.3286$ (To the nearest thousandth, the "averages" are equal. Round $0.32899 \ldots$ and $0.32862 \ldots$ to the nearest ten thousandth and then compare the numbers.)

27. a. 1,000,000,000   **b.** one billion

28. a. $\frac{2}{17} = 0.117647 \ldots$

$\frac{3}{17} = 0.176470 \ldots$

$\frac{4}{17} = 0.235294 \ldots$

$\frac{5}{17} = 0.294117 \ldots$

$\frac{6}{17} = 0.352941 \ldots$

$\frac{7}{17} = 0.411764 \ldots$

$\frac{8}{17} = 0.470588 \ldots$

$\frac{9}{17} = 0.529411 \ldots$

$\frac{10}{17} = 0.588235 \ldots$

$\frac{11}{17} = 0.647058 \ldots$

$\frac{12}{17} = 0.705882 \ldots$

$\frac{13}{17} = 0.764705 \ldots$

$\frac{14}{17} = 0.823529 \ldots$

$\frac{15}{17} = 0.882352 \ldots$

$\frac{16}{17} = 0.941176 \ldots$

b. $.\overline{0588235294117647}$

c. No, only up through $\frac{10}{17}$ (Since $\frac{10}{17}$ is 10 times greater than $\frac{1}{17}$, the decimal point in the decimal for $\frac{10}{17}$ is 1 place to the right of the decimal point in the decimal for $\frac{1}{17}$. $\frac{10}{17} = 0.588235 \ldots$, so $\frac{1}{17} = 0.0588235 \ldots$. The rest of the digits in the repetend are found in the patterns of the other decimals, such as those for $\frac{6}{17}$, $\frac{7}{17}$, and $\frac{2}{17}$.)

29. a. $\boxed{5.31 \quad 22}$
b. The number has been converted to scientific notation. (The number 531×10^{20} written in scientific notation is 5.31×10^{22}.)

30. a. 6; multiplying 2×3 **b.** 60
c. Answers will vary depending on the computer. Sample: $6E + 09$ stands for 6×10^{9}.
d. Answers will vary. Sample: 99,999,999

LESSON 2-4 (pp. 67-69)
1. 1   **2.** .01
3. .001   **4.** .0001
5. To multiply a decimal by .1, move the decimal point one place to the left.

6. To multiply a decimal by $\frac{1}{10}$, move the decimal point one place to the left.

7. To multiply a decimal by .01, move the decimal point two places to the left.

8. To multiply a decimal by $\frac{1}{10,000}$, move the decimal point four places to the left.

9-12. 4.6 (Move the decimal point in 46. one place to the left.)

13. .06 (Move the decimal point in 6. two places to the left.)

14. .0593 (Move the decimal point in 5.93 two places to the left.)

15. 7.7 (Move the decimal point in 770. two places to the left.)

16. .00003 (Move the decimal point in .03 three places to the left.)

17. .0052 (Move the decimal point in 52. four places to the left.)

18. 25 (Move the decimal point in 250,000. four places to the left.)

19. $\frac{1}{10}$

20. .001

21. $\frac{1}{10000} \times 15.283 = 0.0015283$

$\frac{1}{100000} \times 15.283 = 0.00015283$

$\frac{1}{1000000} \times 15.283 = 0.000015283$

22. $12345 \times .00001 = .12345$

23. Many possible answers. Sample: $7 \times 10 = 70$ and $70 \times .1 = 7$.

24. .01 (Multiplying a decimal by .01 moves the decimal point two places to the left.)

25. 9 lb ($\frac{1}{10} \times 87.5 = 8.75$; 8.75 rounded to the nearest whole number is 9.)

26. .04387 ($\frac{1}{10^3} = \frac{1}{1000}$, so move the decimal point in 43.87 three places to the left.)

27. 9,690,000; 14,670,000; 12,500,000

($12\frac{1}{2}$ million = 12.5 million = 12,500,000)

28. 9.69×10^6 (Write 9.69. The decimal point must move 6 places to the right to get 9,690,000, so the exponent of 10 is 6.); 1.467×10^7 (Write 1.467. The decimal point must move 7 places to the right to get 14,670,000, so the exponent of 10 is 7.); 1.25×10^7 (Write 1.25. The decimal point must move 7 places to the right to get 12,500,000, so the exponent of 10 is 7.)

29. **a.** 59 and 60

b. $59.\overline{45}$ ($\frac{5}{11} = .454545 \ldots$)

c. 59.454545 (59.45454545 . . . is between 59.454545 and 59.454546 and is nearer to 59.454545.)

30. **a.** $-14, -1.4, .14$

b. $-14 < -1.4 < .14$ or $.14 > -1.4 > -14$

c. On a horizontal number line, smaller numbers are on the left.

31. 3.9×10^7 (39 million = 39,000,000. Write 3.9. The decimal point must move 7 places to the right to get 39,000,000, so the exponent of 10 is 7.)

1992 Edition: 4.15×10^7 (41.5 million = 41,500,000. The decimal point must move 7 places to the right to get 41,500,000, so the exponent of 10 is 7.)

32. 8^3 ($8 \times 3 = 24$; $8^3 = 8 \times 8 \times 8 = 512$)

33. **a.** .2 ($1 \div 5 = .2$)

b. .5 ($1 \div 2 = 5$)

c. .6 ($3 \div 5 = .6$)

d. $.8\overline{3}$ ($5 \div 6 = .8333 \ldots$)

*These are solutions to questions changed in or added to the *1992 Edition.*

34. **a.** 1,000,000,000,000,000,000

35. **a.** 1,000,000,000,000,000,000,000,000, 10^{21}

    b. 1,000,000,000,000,000,000,000,000,000,
       10^{27}

    c. 1,000,000,000,000,000,000,000,000,000,000,
       10^{30}

    d. 1,000,000,000,000,000,000,000,000,000,
       000,000, 10^{33}

36. .00000 00000 00000 00000 00000 06

LESSON 2-5 (pp. 70-73)

1. The symbol % is read percent.

2. The symbol % means hundredths.

3. To change a % to a decimal, multiply the number in front of the % symbol by .01 (or $\frac{1}{100}$).

4. Many possible answers. Sample: "Save 25% on our clearance sale!"

5. $80\% = 80 \times .01 = .8$

6. $50\% = 50 \times .01 = .5$

7. $5\% = 5 \times .01 = .05$

8. $2\% = 2 \times .01 = .02$

9. $1.5\% = 1.5 \times .01 = .015$

10. $5.75\% = 5.57 \times .01 = .0575$

11. $300\% = 300 \times .01 = 3$

12. $150\% = 150 \times .01 = 1.5$

13. $105\% = 105 \times .01 = 1.05$

14. $10.6\% = 10.6 \times .01 = .106$

15. $8\frac{1}{2}\% = 8.5\% = 8.5 \times .01 = .085$

16. $8\frac{1}{3}\% = 8.\overline{3}\% = 8.\overline{3} \times .01 = .08\overline{3}$

17. $25\% = 25 \times .01 = .25; .25 = \frac{25}{100} = \frac{1}{4}$

18. $75\% = 75 \times .01 = .75; .75 = \frac{75}{100} = \frac{3}{4}$

19. $20\% = 20 \times .01 = .2; .2 = \frac{2}{10} = \frac{1}{5}$

20. $10\% = 10 \times .01 = .1; .1 = \frac{1}{10}$

21. $33\frac{1}{3}\% = 33.\overline{3} \times .01 = .333 \ldots = .\overline{3};$
    $.\overline{3} = \frac{1}{3}$

22. $66\frac{2}{3}\% = 66.\overline{6} \times .01 = .666 \ldots = .\overline{6};$
    $.\overline{6} = \frac{2}{3}$

23. $87\frac{1}{2}\% = 87.5\% = 87.5 \times .01 = .875;$
    $.875 = \frac{875}{1000} = \frac{7}{8}$

24. $40\% = 40 \times .01 = .4; .4 = \frac{4}{10} = \frac{2}{5}$

25. $\frac{2}{3}$ ($\frac{2}{3}$ is to the right of $\frac{5}{8}$.)

26. Many possible answers. Sample: $5\frac{1}{4}\%$

27. $\frac{1}{2} = 1 \div 2 = .5; .5 = .50 =$
    $50 \times .01 = 50\%$

28. $\frac{3}{5} = 3 \div 5 = .6; .6 = .60 =$
    $60 \times .01 = 60\%$

29. $\frac{7}{8} = 7 \div 8 = .875; .875 = .87\frac{1}{2} =$
    $87\frac{1}{2} \times .01 = 87\frac{1}{2}\%$ (or 87.5%)

30. $\frac{3}{10} = 3 \div 10 = .3; .3 = .30 =$
    $30 \times .01 = 30\%$

31. The symbol % is about 100 years old.

32. $\frac{7}{100}$ or .07 ($7\% = 7 \times \frac{1}{100} = \frac{7}{100} = .07$);
    $\frac{1}{25}$ or .04 ($4\% = 4 \times \frac{1}{100} = \frac{4}{100} =$
    $\frac{1}{25} = .04$)

33. $\frac{3}{2}$, $1\frac{1}{2}$ or 1.5 $(150\% = 150 \times \frac{1}{100} = \frac{150}{100} =$

$\frac{3}{2} = 1\frac{1}{2} = 1.5)$

1992 Edition: $\frac{3}{2}$, $1\frac{1}{2}$ or 1.5; $\frac{34}{5}$, $6\frac{4}{5}$, or 6.8

$(680\% = 680 \times \frac{1}{100} = \frac{680}{100} = \frac{34}{5} = 6\frac{4}{5} =$

6.8)

34. b, $(.3 = .30 = 30 \times .01 = 30\%)$

35. b, $(.\overline{3} = .333 \ldots = 33.\overline{3} \times .01 =$

$33\frac{1}{3} \times .01 = 33\frac{1}{3}\%$

36. 2 and 3 $(250\% = 250 \times .01 = 2.5)$

37. 0 and 1 $(5.625\% = 5.625 \times .01 = .05625)$

38. $0.1\% = 0.1 \times .01 = .001; .001 = \frac{1}{1000}$

39. $\frac{1}{25} = 1 \div 25 = .04 = 4 \times .01 = 4\%$

40. **a.** Hyundai (56% increase), **b.** GM
(21% decrease), **c.** Nissan (5% increase)
d. Toyota and Ford (.6% and 1% decrease)
e. 0% (no increase or decrease)
1992 Edition: **a.** Honda (15% increase);
b. Hyundai (29% increase); **c.** VW (1%
increase); **d.** VW and Mazda (1% and 3%
increase); **e.** 0% (no increase or decrease)

41. **a.** 2300, **b.** 23, **c.** 23,000, **d.** .023, **e.** .00023

42. 7.24×10^7 (Write 7.24. The decimal point
must move 7 places to the right to get
72,400,000, so the exponent of 10 is 7.)

43. 9×10^4 is smallest. $(9 \times 10^4 = 90,000;$
$8.2 \times 10^5 = 820,000; 3.01 \times 10^9 =$
3,010,000,000)

44. Answers will vary. Samples for 1989:
  a. 8.5%   **b.** 9.75%   **c.** 5% to 8%

LESSON 2-6 (pp. 74-78)
1. The purpose of rewriting numbers is to give
   flexibility.
2. If two numbers are equal, then one may be
   substituted for the other in any computation
   without affecting the results of the computation.
3. **a.** true   **b.** true   **c.** true
4. **a.** The Substitution Principle is used when 30%
   is rewritten as .3
   b. $.3 \times 2000 = 600$
5. "100% of" means "all of;" "50% of" means
   "half of;" "0% of" means "none of."
6. 3000 (half of 6000 is 3000.)
7. 12 (All of 12 is 12)
8. 0 (None of 50 is 0)
9. 45 ("150% of" means "all of" plus "half of;"
   all of 30 plus half of 30 is 30 + 15, or 45.)
10. **a.** $900
    b. 30% of $900
       $= .3 \times \$900$
       $= \$270$
         \$900 original price
     $-$ ___270 amount saved
         \$630 sale price
11. 25% of $11 = .25 \times \$11 = \$2.75$
12. We are with you totally.
13. Let's split it equally, half for you, half for me.
14. $10\% = \frac{1}{10}$, so to figure out 10% of
    250,000,000, move the decimal point one
    place to the left to get 25,000,000.
    a. 50,000,000   **b.** 75,000,000
    c. 100,000,000   **d.** 125,000,000
15. 1.6% of 250,000,000 people
    $= .016 \times 250,000,000$ people
    $= 4,000,000$ people

16. 10% of 365 days

= .1 × 365 days

= 36.5 days

About 36 or 37 days

17. Store A:

25% of $600

= .25 × $600

= $150

$600 original price

− $\underline{\quad 150}$ amount saved

$450 sale price

Store B:

20% of $575

= .2 × $57.5

= $115

$575 original price

− $\underline{\quad 115}$ amount saved

$460 sale price

Store A has the lower price.

18. lose (48% < 50%, so Team E wins less than half of its games.)

19. half price (Since 50% > 40%, half price is a greater amount saved.)

20. 250% of 10   300% of 8

= 2.5 × 10   = 3 × 8

= 25   = 24

250% of 10 is larger

21. 1.5% of $1000

= .015 × $1000

= $15

22. 1800% of 100,000 people

= 18 × 100,000 people

= 1,800,000 people

23. **a.** 29,028 feet (Distances "above sea level" are represented by positive number.)

  b. 29,000 feet (29,028 is between 29,000 and 29,100 and is nearer to 29,000.)

  c. 29,000 feet (29,028 is between 29,000 and 30,000 and is nearer to 29,000.)

  d. 30,000 feet (29,028 is between 20,000 and 30,000 and is nearer to 30,000.)

24. **a.** 3,000,400,000

  b. 625 ($5^4 = 5 \times 5 \times 5 \times 5$)

  c. 8,300,000

  d. 256,000,000 (Move the decimal point 8 places to the right.)

  e. 4.8 $\left(\dfrac{4}{5} = .8 \right)$

25. .7853 $\left(\dfrac{\pi}{4} = .78539 \right)$

26. **a.** 56

  b. 5.6 (Move the decimal point 1 place to the left.)

  c. .56 (Move the decimal point 2 places to the left.)

  d. .056 (Move the decimal point 3 places to the left.)

27. **a.** $\dfrac{1}{4} = 1 \div 4 = .25 = 25 \times .01 = 25\%$;

  b. $\dfrac{1}{3} = 1 \div 3 = .333 \ldots = 33.\overline{3} \times .01 = 33\dfrac{1}{3} \times .01 = 33\dfrac{1}{3}\%$;

  c. $\dfrac{5}{4} = 5 \div 4 = 1.25 = 125 \times .01 = 125\%$

28. **a.** 10^{15} (One quadrillion is 1,000,000,000,000,000.)

  b. 10^4 (One ten thousand is 10,000.)

29. $\dfrac{12}{25}$ (Divide numerator and denominator by 4.)

30. Answers will vary.

LESSON 2-7 (pp. 79-82)

1. **a.** eight and twenty-seven hundredths;

  b. $8\dfrac{27}{100}$ or $\dfrac{827}{100}$

2. **a.** six hundred thirty and five tenths;

  b. $630\dfrac{1}{2}$ or $\dfrac{1261}{2}$

3. **a.** one thousandth;

   b. $\frac{1}{1000}$

4. 52% (Move the decimal point 2 places to the right.)

5. 72.4% (Move the decimal point 2 places to the right.)

6. 800% (Move the decimal point 2 places to the right.)

7. $3.14 = 3\frac{14}{100} = 3\frac{7}{50}$ (Divide numerator and denominator by 2.)

8. $2.35 = 2\frac{35}{100} = 2\frac{7}{20}$ (Divide numerator and denominator by 5.)

9. $\frac{1}{4} = .25 = 25\%$

10. $3\frac{1}{3} = 3.333 \ldots = 333\frac{1}{3}\%$

11. $\frac{4.2}{1.04} = \frac{420}{104} = \frac{105}{26}$ (First multiply numerator and denominator by 100. Then divide the new numerator and denominator by 4.)

12. $\frac{6.5}{12} = \frac{65}{120} = \frac{13}{24}$ (First multiply the numerator and denominator by 10. Then divide the new numerator and denominator by 5.)

13. $6.75\% = .0675 = \frac{675}{1000} = \frac{27}{40}$ (Divide numerator and denominator by 25.)

14. $\frac{49}{500}$; .098 ($9.8\% = .098 = \frac{98}{100} = \frac{49}{500}$)

15. $3\frac{1}{5}$; 320% ($3.2 = 3\frac{2}{10} = 3\frac{1}{5}$; $3.2 = 320\%$)

16. .3125; 31.25% ($\frac{5}{16} = .3125 = 31.25\%$)

17. $\frac{27}{100}$; 27% ($.27 = \frac{27}{100}$; $.27 = 27\%$)

18. 12% of 10,000
    $= .12 \times 10,000$
    $= 1200$

19. $\frac{1}{3}$ off ($\frac{1}{3} = 33\frac{1}{3}\%$. Since $33\frac{1}{3}\% > 30\%$, $\frac{1}{3}$ off is a greater amount off.)

20. 19,183,700 (Move the decimal point 4 places to the right.

21. 14% of 231
    $= .14 \times 231$
    $= 32.34$

22. 243 ($3^5 = 3 \times 3 \times 3 \times 3 \times 3$)

23. one billion

24. on quadrillion

25. $1/10 = .1$ and $1/100 = .01$; from smallest to largest, the numbers are 1/100, .011, 1/10.

26. 3.32×10^6 (Write 3.32. The decimal point must move 6 places to the right to get 3,320,000, so the exponent of 10 is 6.)

27. 2.78784×10^7 (Write 2.78784. The decimal point must move 7 places to the right to get 27,878,400, so the exponent of 10 is 7.)

28. 5.256×10^5 (Write 5.256. The decimal point must move 5 places to the right to get 525,600, so the exponent of 10 is 5.)

29. 30% of $5.00
    $= .3 \times \$5.00$
    $= \$1.50$

30. 50,000,050

31. 240,000 (Move the decimal point 5 places to the right.)

32. 32 (Move the decimal point 2 places to the left.)

33. **a.** Each number is .5 times the one above;
    b. 0.00097,65625 (Multiply 0.001953125 $\times$ .5.)

LESSON 2-8 (pp. 83-86)

1. 7^3 is written in exponential form.

2. $10 \times 10 \times 10 \times 10$ can be written as 10^4.

3. **a.** 10^5: hundred thousands
   b. 10^4: ten thousands
   c. 10^3: thousands

d. 10^2: hundreds

e. 10^1: tens

4. a. 10^0: ones

b. 10^{-1}: tenths

5. $10^0 = 1$

6. a. $10^{-2} = .01$

b. $10^{-3} = .001$

7. a. positive ($10^0 = 1$)

b. positive ($10^{-1} = .1$)

8. $10^{-7} = $ one ten-millionth

9. one thousandth $= 10^{-3}$

10. one millionth $= 10^{-6}$

11. one trillionth $= 10^{-12}$

12. .03 (Move the decimal point 2 places to the left.)

13. .000345 (Move the decimal point 4 places to the left.)

14. 41.3 ($10^0 = 1$; $41.3 \times 1 = 41.3$)

15. .004

16. .00000 0060

17. .000005

18. To multiply a decimal by a negative power of 10, move the decimal point to the left as many places as indicated by the exponent.

19. (f) (They are all equal.)

20. a. $81 = 3 \times 3 \times 3 \times 3 = 3^4$ or

$81 = 9 \times 9 = 9^2$

b. $144 = 12 \times 12 = 12^2$

c. $32 = 2 \times 2 \times 2 \times 2 \times 2 = 2^5$

21. .00001 (Move the decimal point 7 places to the left.)

22. a. 1 ($10^4 \times 10^{-4} = 10,000 \times 10^{-4}$. Move the decimal point in 10,0000 4 places to the left.)

b. 1

c. When ten to a power is multiplied by ten to the opposite of that power, the product is 1.

23. From smallest to largest, the numbers are 0, 10^{-5}, 1, 10^2. ($10^{-5} = .00001$; $10^2 = 100$.)

24. .0012 m (To write 1.2×10^{-8} as a decimal, move the decimal point 8 places to the left. To multiply this quantity by 10^5, move the decimal point 5 places to the right.)

25. a. $12.45 = 12\frac{45}{100} = 12\frac{9}{20}$

b. $12.45 = 1245\%$

26. a. $0.1875 = \frac{1875}{10,000} = \frac{3}{16}$ (Divide numerator and denominator by 625.)

b. $0.1875 = 18.75\%$

27. 30% of $50

$= .3 \times \$50$

$= \$15$

$\$50$ original price

$- \quad \underline{15}$ amount saved

$\$35$ sale price

The price is the same at both stores.

28. 42% of 365 days

$= .42 \times 365$ days

$= 153.3$ days

About 153 days

29. a. .3 (Move the decimal point 2 places to the left)

b. $\frac{3}{10}$

30. ninth ($2^9 = 2 \times 2 \times 2 \times 2 \times 2 \times 2 \times 2 \times 2 \times 2 = 512$)

31. 9.3×10^7 (Write 9.3. The decimal point must move 7 places to the right to get 93,000,000, so the exponent of 10 is 7.)

32. one billionth of a second

LESSON 2-9 (pp. 87-90)

1. one; ten; negative integer; ten

2. Small numbers are often written in scientific notation because they are easier to deal with.

3. Many possible answers. Sample: masses of atomic particles

4. 1.675 $\boxed{\text{EE}}$ 24 $\boxed{\pm}$ or 1.675 $\boxed{\text{Exp}}$ 24 $\boxed{\pm}$

5. 6.008×10^{-5}

In 6-8, remember that the first number must be greater than or equal to 1 and less than 10.

6. 8.052×10^{-5} (Write 8.052. The decimal point must be moved 5 places to the left to get 0.00008052, so the exponent of 10 is −5.)

7. 2.8×10^{-1} (Write 2.8. The decimal point must be moved 1 place to the left to get 0.28, so the exponent of 10 is −1.)

8. 3.96×10^{-22} (Write 3.96. The decimal point must be moved 22 places to the left to get 0.00000 00000 00000 00000 0396, so the exponent of 10 is −22.)

9. left

10. .00000 001 (Move the decimal point 8 places to the left.)

11. .00000 02 (Move the decimal point 7 places to the left.)

12. .00000 00000 282 (Move the decimal point 11 places to the left.)

13. .009803 (Find $1 \div 102$.)

14. .00000 04675 (This key sequence enters 4.675×10^{-7}.)

15. .05 (Key in: 3 $\boxed{\text{EE}}$ 8 $\boxed{\pm}$ $\boxed{\div}$ 6 EE 7 $\boxed{\pm}$ $\boxed{=}$)

16. $<$ (5.37×10^{-5} = .0000537; 5.37×10^{-4} = .000537)

17. = (49×10^{-9} = .000000049; 4.9×10^{-8} = .000000049)

18. 4.5×10^9 (Write 4.5. The decimal point must move 9 places to the right to get 4,500,000,000, so the exponent of 10 is 9.)

19. **a.** 10^6 **b.** 10^{-6}

20. 78,125 ($5^7 = 5 \times 5 \times 5 \times 5 \times 5 \times 5 \times 5$)

21. The team lost more often. (60% > 50%, so the team lost more than half of its games.)

22. **a.** $75\% = .75 = \frac{75}{100} = \frac{3}{4}$

b. 75% of 400
= .75 × 400
= 300

23. .03 (Move the decimal point 2 places to the left.)

24. −19.7 ($\frac{7}{10}$ = .7)

25. 1.5 (Move the decimal point 2 places to the left.)

26. 0 and 1 (3.4% = .034)

27. **a.** 10% of $0.01
= .1 × $0.01
= $.001

b. 1% of $0.01
= .01 × $0.01
= $.0001

c. $0.01
     .001
+   .0001
   $ .0111

d. $.01 ($.01 and $.02 and in nearer to $.01.)

28. **a.** 19 and 20

b. yes ($19\frac{5}{16} = 19 + \frac{5}{16} = 19 + .3125 =$ 19.3125; 19.3 < 19.3125)

29. A low estimate would be preferred (to ensure that the plane is not too heavy).

30. A high estimate would be preferred (to ensure that everyone has enough to eat).

31. From smallest to largest, the numbers are $-\frac{2}{3}$, −.666, −.66, −.656, −.6 ($-\frac{2}{3}$ = −.6666 . . .)

32. **a.** 7623% (Move the decimal point 2 places to the right)

b. $76\frac{23}{100}$

33. Answers may vary depending on the calculator used.

  a. 1×10^{-99}

  b. -1×10^{-99}

34. a. .075; multiplying

  b. .0075

  c. 7.5E-09 (for $7.5 \cdot 10^{-9}$)

  d. Several possible answers. Sample: .01

CHAPTER 2 PROGRESS SELF-TEST (p. 92)

1. 2,351,864,000 (Move the decimal point 9 places to the right.)

2. 34% of 600

  $= .34 \times 600$

  $= 204$

3. .00000 0032 (1 billionth $= 10^{-9}$)

4. .0082459 (Move the decimal point 5 places to the left.)

5. .077 (Move the decimal point 3 places to the left.)

6. 345,689,100 (Move the decimal point 5 places to the right.)

7. .002816 (Move the decimal point 3 places to the left.)

8. $10^{-7} = .00000 01$

9. .08 (Move the decimal point 2 places to the left, or calculate: $8\% = 8 \times .01 = .08$.)

10. 216 ($6^3 = 6 \times 6 \times 6$)

11. In the number 125^6, 125 is called the base and 6 is called the exponent.

12. 125 $\boxed{y^x}$ 6 $\boxed{=}$

13. 3.8147   12

14. 3,814,700,000,000 (The display in Question 13 means 3.8147×10^{12}, so move the decimal point 12 places to the right.)

15. 2.107×10^{10} (Write 2.107. The decimal point must move 10 places to the right to get 21,070,000,000, so the exponent of 10 is 10.)

16. 8×10^{-8} (Write 8. The decimal point must move 8 places to the left to get 0.00000 008, so the exponent of 10 is 8.)

17. 4.5 $\boxed{\text{EE}}$ 13 or 4.5 $\boxed{\text{Exp}}$ 13

18. 1.23456 $\boxed{\text{EE}}$ 7 $\boxed{\pm}$ or 1.23456 $\boxed{\text{Exp}}$ 7 $\boxed{\pm}$
($0.00000\ 01234\ 56 = 1.23456 \times 10^{-7}$)

19. From smallest to largest, the numbers are 5^3, 3^5, 4^4. ($4^4 = 256$; $5^3 = 125$; $3^5 = 243$)

20. 0 and 1 ($40\% = .4$)

21. a. $4.73 = \frac{4.73}{1} = \frac{473}{100}$ (Multiply numerator and

  denominator of $\frac{4.73}{1}$ by 100.)

  b. $4.73 = 473\%$ (Move the decimal point 2 places to the right, or refer to the answer to part a.)

22. $33\frac{1}{3}\% = 33.\overline{3}\% = .333\ldots = \frac{1}{3}$

23. 30% of 150 chefs

  $= .3 \times 150$ chefs

  $= 45$ chefs

24. 25% of $699

  $= .25 \times \$699$

  $= \$174.75$, or about \$175

  \$699 original price

  $-$ 175 amount saved

  \$524 sale price

25. 80% of 20 items

  $= .8 \times 20$ items

  $= 16$ items

  20 items in test

  $-$ 16 items answered correctly

  4 items missed

26. 22.4 is not between 1 and 10.

27. sixth ($10^6 = 1,000,000$)

28. $60\% - 10\%$ ($\frac{3}{5} = .6 = 60\%$; $\frac{1}{10} = .1 = 10\%$)

29. 2.5×10^{11} (250 billions $= 250,000,000$. Write 2.5. The decimal point must move 11 places to the right to get 250,000,000, so the exponent of 10 is 11.)

CHAPTER 2 REVIEW (p. 93-95)

1. 320,000 (Move the decimal point 4 places to the right.)
2. 750 (Move the decimal point 2 places to the right.)
3. 25,000 (Move the decimal point 6 places to the right.)
4. 1000 (The decimal point must move 3 places to the right.)
5. $10,000,000,000
6. .0000046
7. 64 ($4^3 = 4 \times 4 \times 4$)
8. About 429,980,000 (Key in: 12 $\boxed{y^x}$ 8 $\boxed{=}$. The display 4.2998 08 means 4.2998×10^8.)
9. $10^5 = 100,000$
10. 10^9 is one billion.
11. $10^{-4} = .0001$
12. 10^{-2} is one hundredth.
13. twelfth ($1,000,000,000,000 = 10^{12}$)
14. negative fourth ($0.0001 = 10^{-4}$)
15. .00000 00273 (Move the decimal point 8 places to the left.)
16. 49.5 (Move the decimal point 1 place to the left.)
17. .075 (Move the decimal point 3 places to the left.)
18. .021 (Move the decimal point 2 places to the left.)
19. 30,000,000 (Move the decimal point 7 places to the right.)
20. 42,000 (Move the decimal point 5 places to the right.)
21. 7.34 ($10^0 = 1$; $7.34 \times 1 = 7.34$)
22. .00683 (Move the decimal point 4 places to the left.)
23. 4.8×10^5 (Write 4.8. The decimal point must move 5 places to the right to get 480,000, so the exponent of 10 is 5.)

24. 9×10^{15} (Write 9. The decimal point must move 15 places to the right to get 9,000,000,000,000,000, so the exponent of 10 is 15.)
25. 1.3×10^{-4} (Write 1.3. The decimal point must move 4 places to the left to get 0.00013, so the exponent of 10 is −4.)
26. 7×10^{-1} (Write 7. The decimal point must move 1 place to the left to get 0.7, so the exponent of 10 is −1.)
27. .15 (Move the decimal point 2 places to the left, or calculate: $15\% = 15 \times .01 = .15$.)
28. .0525 (Move the decimal point 2 places to the left.)
29. .09 (Move the decimal point 2 places to the left.)
30. 2 (Move the decimal point 2 places to the left.)
31. $\frac{1}{2} = 50\%$
32. $\frac{4}{5} = .8 = 80\%$
33. $30\% = .3 = \frac{3}{10}$
34. $66\frac{2}{3}\% = .66\frac{2}{3} = .\overline{6} = \frac{2}{3}$
35. 75 (Half of 150 is 75.)
36. 3% of 3
    $= .03 \times 3$
    $= .09$
37. 6.2 (All of 6.2 is 6.2.)
38. 7.8% of 3500
    $= .078 \times 3500$
    $= 273$
39. $5.7 = \frac{5.7}{1} = \frac{57}{10}$ (Multiply numerator and denominator of $\frac{5.7}{1}$ by 10.)
40. $.892 = \frac{892}{1000} = \frac{223}{250}$ (Divide the numerator and denominator of $\frac{892}{1000}$ by 4.)

41. 86% (Move the decimal point 2 places to the right.)

42. 320% (Move the decimal point 2 places to the right.)

43. about 42.9% ($\frac{3}{7} = .\overline{428571}$, or about .429. Move the decimal point 2 places to the right.)

44. 137.5% ($\frac{11}{8} = 1.375$. Move the decimal point 2 places to the right.)

45. If two numbers are equal, one may be substituted for the other in any computation without changing the results of the computation.

46. .75 is substituted for 75%.

47. Many possible answers. Samples: .5 and $\frac{1}{2}$

48. 50; 15 ($\frac{1}{2} = .5 = 50\%; \frac{1}{4} = .25 = 25\%$)

49. 23 is not between 1 and 10

50. one; ten; integer

51. 40% of $26.50
 $= .4 \times \$26.50$
 $= \$10.60$
 $\$26.50$ original price
 $- \underline{\quad 10.60}$ amount saved
 $\$15.90$ sale price

52. 53.9% of 89,000,000 votes
 $= .539 \times 89,000,000$ votes
 $= 47,970,000$ votes

53. 34% of $64,000 $= .34 \times \$64,000 =$ $21,760. $64,000 value in 1980 $-$ $21,760 drop in value $=$ $42,240 value in 1988 *1992 Edition: 61% of 64,000 $= .61 \times$ $64,000 = \$39,040$. $64,000 value in 1980 $-$ $29,040 drop in value $=$ $24,960 $\approx$ $25,000 in 1990.

54. 3,000,000,000,000,000,000,000,000,000,000

55. 5×10^{-3} (Write 5. The decimal point must move 3 places to the left to get 0.005, so the exponent of 10 is −3.)

56. 3.2 $\boxed{\text{EE}}$ 10 (32 billion = 32,000,000,000 = 3.2×10^{10})

57. 1 $\boxed{\text{EE}}$ 12 $\boxed{\pm}$ (one trillionth = .00000 00000 01 = 1×10^{-12})

58. 2 $\boxed{y^x}$ 45

59. 3.5184 13 (Key in $\boxed{=}$ to display the number keyed in for Question 58.)

60. 473,000,000 (4.73 08 means 4.78×10^8.)

61. 3.3516×10^{13} (The display, 3.3516 13 means 3.3516×10.)

62. 1.1418×10^{-7} (Key in 2.5 $\boxed{\text{EE}}$ 3 $\boxed{\pm}$ $\boxed{\times}$ 4.567 $\boxed{\text{EE}}$ 5 $\boxed{\pm}$ $\boxed{=}$. The display, 1.1418 −07 means 1.1418×10^{-7}.)

63. 3 $\boxed{\text{EE}}$ 21

CHAPTER 3   MEASUREMENT

LESSON 3-1   (pp. 98-103)

1. The first units of length were based on lengths of the parts of a human body.

2. A hand was the width of a person's palm.

3. The yard was the distance from the tip of the nose to the tips of the fingers of King Henry I.

4. Today's foot is said to be based on Charlemagne's foot.

5. More accurate measurements were needed for scientific experimentation.

6. In about 1760 accurate lengths became needed everywhere.

7. False. (Thomas Jefferson proposed a system based on the number 10.)

8. True   9. True   10. True

11. U.S. system or customary system of measurement; England now uses the metric system.

12. The meter is the base unit of length in the metric system.

13. $2\frac{1}{8}$ in.   **14.** $1\frac{3}{8}$ in.   **15.** $\frac{3}{4}$ in.

16. **a.** 5.8 cm

   b. $2\frac{2}{8}$ in. or $2\frac{1}{4}$ in.

17. **a.** 10.1 cm   **b.** 4 in.

18. **a.** 3.9 cm

   b. $1\frac{4}{8}$ in. or $1\frac{1}{2}$ in.

19. 25.3 cm; 19.5 cm

20. **a.** Answers will vary.

   b. Answers will vary.

21. The vertical segment below has length 3.5 in.

22. The horizontal segment below has length 12.4 cm.

23. If two numbers are equal, one may be substituted for the other in any computation without changing the results of the computation.

24. Each interval is .01.

   a. 12.24   **b.** 12.33

   c. K   **d.** B and C

25. **a.** improve (57.6% > 50%, so more than half of the subjects improved.)

   b. 156 (57.6% of 271 = .576 × 271 = 156.096)

26. 5^6 (5^6 = 15,625; 6^5 = 7776)

27. 28,200,000

28. $\frac{80}{5}$ (Write 16 as $\frac{16}{1}$ and multiply numerator and denominator by 5.)

29. $\frac{7}{5}$ (Divide numerator and denominator by 5.)

30. $\frac{1}{3} = .33\frac{1}{3} = 33\frac{1}{3}\%$

31. (a) (35 − 6 = 29; 28.97 is very close to 29.)

32. **a.** A pica is a size of type $\frac{1}{6}$ in. high.

   b. An ell is a length of 45 in. used to measure cloth.

   c. A link is $\frac{1}{100}$ of a surveyor's chain. It is 7.92 in.

   d. A chain is a length of 66 ft used in surveying.

33. Answers will vary.

34. **a.** A fathom is 6 ft.

   b. A cubit is 18 in. or 45.72 cm.

LESSON 3-2 (pp. 104-107)

1. inch, foot, yard, mile
2. pint, quart, gallon
3. ounce, pound, short ton
4. 1 ft = 12 in.
5. 1 gallon = 4 quarts
6. 1 yd = 3 ft
7. 1 quart = 2 pints
8. 1 mi = 5280 ft
9. 1 lb = 16 oz
10. 1 short ton = 2000 pounds
11. $\qquad$ 1 mi = 5280 ft
    0.62×1 mi = 0.62×5280 ft
    $\qquad$ 0.62 mi = 3273.6 ft
12. $\qquad$ 1 yd = 3 ft
    4×1 yd = 4×3 ft
    $\qquad$ 4 yd = 12 ft
13. $\qquad$ 1 ton = 2000 lb
    7×1 ton = 7×2000 lb
    $\qquad$ 7 tons = 14,000 lb
14. $\qquad$ 1 lb = 16 oz
    2.2×1 lb = 2.2×16 oz
    $\qquad$ 2.2 lb = 35.2 oz
15. $\qquad$ 1 gal = 4 qt
    8.3×1 gal = 8.3×4 qt
    $\qquad$ 8.3 gal = 33.2 qt
16. $\qquad$ 1 mi = 5280 ft
    $\frac{1}{8} \times 1$ mi = $\frac{1}{8} \times 5280$ ft
    $\qquad \frac{1}{8}$ mi = 660 ft
17. $\qquad$ 1 yd = 3 ft
    5.5×1 yd = 5.5×3 ft
    $\qquad$ 5.5 yd = 16.5 ft
    $\qquad$ 1 rod = 16.5 ft
18. $\qquad$ 1 gross ton = 2240 lb
    $70,200 \times 1$ gross ton = $70,200 \times 2240$ lb
    $\qquad$ 70,200 gross tons = 157,248,000 lb
19. $\qquad$ 1 yd = 3 ft
    440×1 yd = 440×3 ft
    $\qquad$ 440 yd = 1320 ft

20. $\qquad$ 1 mi = 5280 ft
    $\qquad$ = 12×5280 in.
    $\qquad$ = 63,360 in.
21. $\qquad$ 1 gal = 4 qt
    10×1 gal = 10×4 qt
    $\qquad$ 10 gal = 40 qt
    $\qquad$ = 2×40 pt
    $\qquad$ = 80 pt
    Fill it 80 times.
22. **a.** yard or mile
    b. short ton or pound
    c. gallon
23. A gallon is not a unit of length; it is a unit of volume or capacity.
24. **a.** $3\frac{3}{8}$ in. $\qquad$ **b.** 9 cm
25. **a.** 6 in.
    b. $6\frac{1}{4}$ in.
    c. $6\frac{2}{8}$ in. or $6\frac{1}{4}$ in.
26. **a.** 1.05×10^8 (Write 1.05. The decimal point must be moved 8 places to the right to get 105,000,000, so the exponent of 10 is 8.)
    b. 1.3837×10^{-2} (Write 1.3837. The decimal point must be moved 2 places to the left to get 0.013837, so the exponent of 10 is -2.)
    1992 Edition: **a.** 1.18865×10^8 (Write 1.18865. The decimal point must be moved 8 places to the right to get 118,865,000, so the exponent of 10 is 8.) **b.** 1.3837×10^{-2}
27. **a.** 5.2 (Move the decimal point 2 places to the right.)
    b. .0003446 (Move the decimal point 4 places to the left.)
    c. 1.536 (Move the decimal point 1 place to the left.)
    d. 6,400,000 (Move the decimal point 4 places to the right.)
28. 0 (0% of 500 = $0 \times 500 = 0$)

29. a. $60 \times 60 = 3600$

b. $3600 \times 24 = 86,400$

c. $86,400 \times 365 = 31,536,000$

d. $60 \times 24 \times 365 = 525,600$

e. $70 \times 60 \times 24 \times 365 = 36,792,000$

f. $36,792,000 \times 78 \approx 2.8698 \times 10^9$

30. A peck is 8 dry quarts; a bushel is 4 pecks or 32 dry quarts; a barrel is 105 dry quarts. (A heap is an informal unit meaning a lot.)

LESSON 3-3 (pp. 108-112)

1. List two of these three weaknesses: The names of units do not help you to know how the units are related. The units are multiples of each other in no consistent way. The numbers are not as easy to work with as are powers of 10.

2. the international system

3. Several possible answers. Samples: kilometer, centimeter, millimeter, meter

4. Several possible answers: Samples: gram, kilogram, milligram

5. Several possible answers: Samples: liter, milliliter

6. 1000 (kilo-)

7. .001 or $\frac{1}{1000}$ (milli-)

8. .01 or $\frac{1}{100}$ (centi-)

9. cm (centimeter)

10. kg (kilogram)

11. mL (milliliter)

12. $90 \text{ cm} = 90 \times 1 \text{ cm}$
$= 90 \times .01 \text{ m}$
$= .9 \text{ m}$

13. $345 \text{ mL} = 345 \times 1 \text{ mL}$
$= 345 \times .001 \text{ L}$
$= .345 \text{ L}$

14. $5 \text{ kg} = 5 \times 1 \text{ kg}$
$= 5 \times 1000 \text{ g}$
$= 5000 \text{ g}$

15. $10 \text{ km} = 10 \times 1 \text{ km}$
$= 10 \times 1000 \text{ m}$
$= 10,000 \text{ m}$

16. $48 \text{ mm} = 48 \times 1 \text{ mm}$
$= 48 \times .001 \text{ m}$
$= .048 \text{ m}$

17. $60 \text{ mg} = 60 \times 1 \text{ mg}$
$= 60 \times .001 \text{ g}$
$= .06 \text{ g}$

18. Many possible answers. Samples:
a. quart of milk
b. aspirin
c. speck of sawdust

19. Many possible answers. Samples:
a. height of a doorknob
b. 9 football fields
c. thickness of a dime

20. Many possible answers. Sample: a quart of milk

21. 10^{-2} (centi-)

22. 10^{-3} (milli-)

23. 10^3 (kilo-)

24. (c) 50 kg

25. (b) 1.7 m

26. (d) 35 mm

27. Yes (A kilometer is less than a mile.)

28. 20,000 tons (Kilo- means 1000.)

29. 57,000,000 tons (Mega- means 1,000,000.)

30. $\frac{1}{1000}$ or .001 second (Milli- means $\frac{1}{1000}$.)

31. a. $.56 (Multiply by .01.)
b. 1349¢ (Multiply by 100.)
c. $76,000.00 (Multiply by .01.)

32. .002 cm

33. From smallest to largest, the numbers are 0, 10^{-4}; $\frac{1}{100}$. $(10^{-4} = \frac{1}{10000})$

34. From smallest to largest, the numbers are 10^1, 5^2, 2^5. $(10^1 = 10; 5^2 = 5 \times 5 = 25; 2^5 = 2 \times 2 \times 2 \times 2 \times 2 = 32)$

35. **a.** $<$ (4 qt $=$ 8 pt)

   b. $<$ (2 yd $=$ 6 ft)

   c. $<$ (1 mi $=$ 5280 ft)

   d. $=$ (1 lb $=$ 16 oz)

36. nearest $\frac{1}{16}$ ($\frac{1}{16} < \frac{1}{10}$)

37. 1.7 cm

38. **a.** 25 or 26 (85% of 30 $=$ .85 $\times$ 30 $=$ 25.5)

   b. 24 (80% of 30 $=$ .8 $\times$ 30 $=$ 24)

   c. 22 (72% of 30 $=$ .72 $\times$ 30 $=$ 21.6)

39. Other answers are possible.

   a. France   **b.** Mexico

   c. USSR   **d.** China

   e. Yugoslavia   **f.** India

   g. Ghana

40. **b.** WHAT IS LENGTH IN MILES?
   ? 5
   THE NUMBER OF FEET IS 26400

   c. Many possible answers. Samples:
   10, 52800; 3.4, 17952

LESSON 3-4 (pp. 113-116)

1. Many possible answers. Samples: scientist, nurse, photographer

2. Many possible answers. Samples: carpenters, plumbers

3. The symbol $\approx$ means "is approximately equal to."

4. kilogram

5. quart

6. 1 in. $=$ 2.54 cm

7. 2.2 lb $\approx$ 1 kg

8. 39.37 in. $\approx$ 1 m

9. 1.06 qt $\approx$ 1 L

10. .62 mi $\approx$ 1 km

11. **a.** If two numbers are nearly equal, then when one is substituted for the other in a computation, the results of the computations will be nearly equal.

   b. Example: using 2.2 lb instead of 1 kg

12. 6 m $=$ 6 $\times$ 1m

   $\approx$ 6 $\times$ 39.37 in.

   $\approx$ 236.2 in.

13. 1.8 L $=$ 1.8 $\times$ 1 L

   $\approx$ 1.8 $\times$ 1.06 qt

   $\approx$ 1.9 qt

14. 0.45 kg $=$ 0.45 $\times$ 1 kg

   $\approx$ 0.45 $\times$ 2.2 lb

   $\approx$ 1 lb

15. 5 in. $=$ 5 $\times$ 1 in.

   $=$ 5 $\times$ 2.54 cm

   $=$ 12.7 cm

16. kilogram (1 kg $\approx$ 2.2 lb)

17. liter (1 L $\approx$ 1.06 qt)

18. meter (1 m $\approx$ 39.37 in.; 1 yd $=$ 36 in.)

19. inch (1 in $=$ 2.54 cm)

20. mile (1 km $\approx$ 0.62 mi)

21. **a.** .3125 (5 $\div$ 16 $=$ .3125)

   b. .3125 in. $=$ .3125 $\times$ 1 in

   $=$ .3125 $\times$ 2.54 cm

   $=$ .79375 cm

   $\approx$ .8 cm or 8 mm

22. 1.5 kg $=$ 1.5 $\times$ 1 kg

   $\approx$ 1.5 $\times$ 2.2 lb

   $\approx$ 3.3 lb

   $\approx$ 3.3 $\times$ 16 oz

   $\approx$ 52.8 oz

23. 16.4 km $=$ 16.4 $\times$ 1 km

   $\approx$ 16.4 $\times$ 0.62 mi

   $\approx$ 10.2 mi

24. $\frac{4}{9} + \frac{7}{13} \approx \frac{1}{2} + \frac{1}{2} \approx 1$

25. $\frac{19}{20} + \frac{19}{18} \approx 1 + 1 \approx 2$

26. $\frac{1}{1000} + \frac{1}{100} \approx 0 + 0 \approx 0$

27. 1 yd $=$ 3 ft

   $=$ 3 $\times$ 1 ft

   $=$ 3 $\times$ 12 in.

   $=$ 36 in.

28. 8 gal = 8 × 1 gal
= 8 × 4 qt
= 32 qt

29. 5 lb = 5 × 1 lb
= 5 × 16 oz
= 80 oz

30. 4 kg = 4 × 1 kg
= 4 × 1000 g
= 4000 g

31. 80 mm

32. 1% (1 cm = .01 m; .01 is 1%.)

33. 25 (Half of 50 is 25.)

34. $0.136 = \frac{136}{1000} = \frac{17}{125}$ (Divide numerator and

denominator of $\frac{136}{1000}$ by 8.)

35. Answers will vary.

36. Several possible answers. Sample:

```
10 PRINT "WHAT IS LENGTH IN INCHES?"
20 INPUT NINCHES
30 NCM = 2.54 * NINCHES
40 PRINT "THE NUMBER OF CM IS" NCM
50 END
```

Sample output:
```
WHAT IS LENGTH IN INCHES?
? 15
THE NUMBER OF CM IS 38.1
```

LESSON 3-5 (pp. 117-121)

1. $\overrightarrow{CB}$ (or $\overrightarrow{CA}$) and $\overrightarrow{CD}$ (or $\overrightarrow{CE}$)

2. C

3. a, b, c, e, and g

4. The Babylonians' number system was based on 60.

5. time and angles

6. $\overleftrightarrow{AB}$ (or $\overleftrightarrow{AF}$ or $\overleftrightarrow{BF}$)

7. B

8. 114° (Read the outer scale because $\overrightarrow{BA}$ crosses this scale at 0.)

9. 66° (Read the inner scale becaue $\overrightarrow{BF}$ crosses this scale at 0.)

10. m ∠AVB stands for the measure of angle AVB.

11. 151°

12. 40°

13. 90°

14. 75°

15. William Oughtred first used the symbol ∠ in 1657.

16. true

17. ∠JGH has the largest angle measure.

18. 6 (The angles are: ∠DEC, ∠CEB, ∠BEA, ∠DEB, ∠CEA, and ∠DEA.)

19.

20.

21.-24.

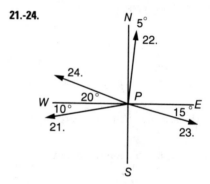

25. 150 km = 150 × 1 km
≈ 150 × 0.62 mi
≈ 93 mi

26. 12 L = 12 × 1 L
≈ 12 × 1.06 qt
≈ 12.72 qt

27. 82 mm = 82 × 1 mm
= 82 × .001 m
= .082 m

28. liters

29. quarts or gallons

30. 4.16×10^7 (41.6 million = 41,600,000. Write 4.16. The decimal point must move 7 places to the right to get 41,600,000, so the exponent of 10 is 7.)

31. $\frac{51}{68} = \frac{3}{4}$ (Divide numerator and denominator of $\frac{51}{68}$ by 17.)

32. A radian is about 57.3°; a grad is exactly 0.9°.

LESSON 3-6 (pp. 122-125)

1. An acute angle is an angle whose measure is between 0° and 90°.

2. An obtuse angle is an angle whose measure is between 90° and 180°.

3. A right angle is an angle whose measure is 90°.

4. A right triangle is a triangle with a right angle.

5. Perpendicular lines are two lines that form right angles.

6. acute

7. acute

8. obtuse

9. right

10. right   **11.** acute

12. obtuse   **13.** obtuse

14. (c)   **15.** (c)

16. a. obtuse   b. 93°

17. a. acute   b. 87°

18. Many possible answers. Samples: angle of ceiling with wall, angle at corner of window.

19. a. right   b. 90°

20. a. obtuse   b. 134°

21. a. acute   b. 60°

22. a. acute, 30° ($\frac{1}{12}$ of 360°);

b. obtuse, 120° ($\frac{4}{12}$ of 120°);

c. right, 90° ($\frac{1}{4}$ of 360°);

d. acute, 15° (The minute hand is on the 6 and the hour hand is half-way between the 6 and 7. Find $\frac{1}{24}$ of 360°.)

23. Samples:
a.
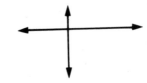

b.
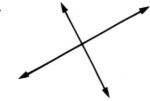

24. $m\angle X = 40°$, $m\angle Y = 124°$, $m\angle Z = 16°$

25. a. .0004 inches;

b. 4×10^{-4} (Write 4. The decimal point must move 4 places to the left to get .0004 so the exponent of 10 is −4.)

26. $1.20 (Boy: 32% of $20 = .32 \times $20 = $6.40; Girl: 26% of $20 = .26 \times $20 = $5.20. Subtract: $6.40 − $5.20 = $1.20)

27. a. $3\frac{1}{2}$ in.   b. $3\frac{1}{4}$ in.

28. a. km (kilometers)

b. L (liter)

c. g (grams)

29. a. > (2 m ≈ 2 × 39.37 in. ≈ 78.7 in.; 1 yd = 36 in.)

b. < (1 kg = 1000 g)

c. < (1 kg ≈ 2.2 lb)

d. < (2 L ≈ 2 × 1.06 qt ≈ 2.1 qt; 1 gal = 4 qt)

e. = (2 in. = 2 × 2.54 cm = 5.08 cm)

f. = (1 m = 1000 mm)

30. a. Acute appendicitis is a sharp, severe case of appendicitis.

b. An acute angle forms a sharp point.

31. a. Obtuse means slow in understanding or dull.
   b. An obtuse angle is dull in that it does not come to a sharp point.

32. Answers will vary.

LESSON 3-7 (pp. 126-129)

1. Area measures the space inside a figure.

2. Square centimeters

3. A square is a four-sided figure with four sides of equal length and four right angles.

4. b and d

5. Many possible answers. Sample: a caution sign on a street

6. A square is a two-dimensional figure.

7. To find area (1) count, (2) cut and rearrange parts of the figure, or (3) use a formula.

8. $(2 \text{ cm})^2 = 2 \text{ cm} \times 2 \text{ cm} = 4 \text{ cm}^2$

9. $(75 \text{ ft})^2 = 75 \text{ ft} \times 75 \text{ ft} = 5625 \text{ ft}^2$

10. $(6 \text{ km})^2 = 6 \text{ km} \times 6 \text{ km} = 36 \text{ km}^2$

11. $(1.5 \text{ in.})^2 = 1.5 \text{ in} \times 1.5 \text{ in.} = 2.25 \text{ in.}^2$

12. squared

13. 6 in.² (count the squares)

14.

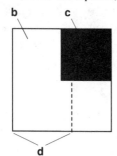

15. a. Sketch 1 square yard split into square feet:

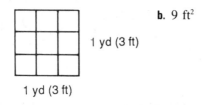

1 yd (3 ft)

1 yd (3 ft)

   b. 9 ft²

16. $(90 \text{ ft})^2 = 90 \text{ ft} \times 90 \text{ ft} = 8100 \text{ ft}^2$

17. a. m² (square meters)
   b. ft² (square feet)

18. $10 \times 43,560 \text{ ft}^2 = 435,600 \text{ ft}^2$

19. $\frac{1}{2} \times 43,560 \text{ ft}^2 = 21,780 \text{ ft}^2$

20. $< (13\frac{4}{13} = .307 \ldots)$

21. 1,074,000,000 (key in 2 $\boxed{y^x}$ 30 $\boxed{=}$. The display, $\boxed{1.0737 \quad 09}$, means 1.0737×10^9, or 1,073,700,000. 1,073,700,000 is between 1,073,000,000 and 1,074,000,000 and is nearer to 1,074,000,000.)

22. $10^0 (10^0 = 1)$

23. a. 10% of 60 = .1 × 60 = 60
   b. 120,240,420 (Multiply 60 by 2, 4, and 7 respectively.)

24. 10.5 cm

25. 322.6 km = 322.6 × 1 km
   $\approx$ 322.6 × 0.62 mi
   $\approx$ 200 mi

26. 60 kg = 60 × 1 kg
   $\approx$ 60 × 2.2 lb
   $\approx$ 132 lb

27. 60 kg = 60 × 1 kg
   = 60 × 1000 g
   = 60,000 g
   60 kg is exactly 60,000 g.

28. 9°

29. acute

30. Many possible answers. Sample: Descartes was one of the inventors of analytic geometry and the use of coordinates in graphs.

31. It squares the number entered (or the number in the display).

LESSON 3-8 (pp. 130-132)

1. Volume measures the space in a 3-dimensional figure.

2. m³ (cubic meters)

3. A cube is a figure with 6 square faces.

4. Many possible answers. Sample: sugar cube

5. A cube is a 3-dimensional figure.

6. Volume can be found by (1) counting cubes, (2) cutting and pasting cubic units together, or (3) using formulas.

7. Volume of a cube = length of an edge cubed

8.

9. $(4 \text{ in.})^3 = 4 \text{ in.} \times 4 \text{ in.} \times 4 \text{ in.} = 64 \text{ in.}^3$

10. $(40 \text{ cm})^3 = 40 \text{ cm} \times 40 \text{ cm} \times 40 \text{ cm} = 64,000 \text{ cm}^3$

11. $(7 \text{ yd})^3 = 7 \text{ yd} \times 7 \text{ yd} \times 7 \text{ yd} = 343 \text{ yd}^3$

12. 10 cm

13. 1000 cm^3

14. 2000

15. a. $(3.25 \text{ ft})^3 = 3.25 \text{ ft} \times 3.25 \text{ ft} \times 3.25 \text{ ft} = 34.328125 \text{ ft}^3$

    b. 34.33 ft^3 (34.328125 is between 34.32 and 34.33 and is nearer to 34.33.)

16. a. $(12 \text{ in.})^2 = 12 \text{ in.} \times 12 \text{ in.} = 144 \text{ in.}$

    b. $(12 \text{ in.})^3 = 12 \text{ in.} \times 12 \text{ in.} \times 12 \text{ in.} = 1728 \text{ in.}^3$

17. $6^3 + 5^2 = (6 \times 6 \times 6) + (5 \times 5) = 216 + 25 = 241$

18. From smallest to largest, the volumes are 89 cm³, volume of a cube with edge 9 cm, 1 liter. (Volume of cube with edge 9 cm = $(9 \text{ cm})^3 = 9 \text{ cm} \times 9 \text{ cm} \times 9 \text{ cm} = 729 \text{ cm}^3$; 1 liter = 1000 cm^3)

19. 1 kg (1 L = 1000 mL; 1000 mL of water weighs 1000×1 gram = 1000 g = 1 kg)

20. a. $(50 \text{ cm})^3 = 50 \text{ cm} \times 50 \text{ cm} \times 50 \text{ cm} = 125,000 \text{ cm}^3 = 125,000 \text{ mL}$

    b. 125,000 g, or 125 kg

    c. $125 \text{ kg} = 125 \times 1 \text{ kg}$
       $\approx 125 \times 2.2 \text{ lb}$
       $\approx 275 \text{ lb}$

21. a. 17,000,000 (16,969,260 is between 16,900,000 and 17,000,000, and is nearer to 17,000,000.)

    b. $2 \times 17,000,000 = 34,000,000$

    c. 3.4×10^7 (Write 3.4. The decimal point must move 7 places to the right to get 34,000,000, so the exponent of 10 is 7.)

22. c, (75 kg $\approx 75 \times 2.2$ lb ≈ 165 lb)

23. a. .00034 (Move the decimal point 4 places to the left.)

    b. $\dfrac{34}{100,000} = \dfrac{17}{50,000}$ (Divide the numerator and denominator of $\dfrac{34}{100,000}$ by 2.)

24. $\dfrac{1}{2}$ is not an integer.

25. $(10 \text{ cm})^2 = 10 \text{ cm} \times 10 \text{ cm} = 100 \text{ cm}^2$

26. $10^3 \text{ m} = 1000 \text{ m} = 1 \text{ km}$

27. Yes. A hectare is a metric measure equal to 10,000 square meters. In the U.S. system, a hectare is about 2.477 acres, so 250 hectares $\approx$ 620 acres. 620 acres = $620 \times 43,560 \text{ ft}^2 \approx 27,000,000 \text{ ft}^2$. 1 mi² = $(5280 \text{ ft})^2 = 5280 \text{ ft} \times 5280 \text{ ft} \approx 27,900,000 \text{ ft}^2$. So 250 hectares is nearly 1 square mile.

CHAPTER 3 PROGRESS SELF-TEST (p. 134)

1. $2\dfrac{5}{8}$ in.

2. _____

3. 2.54 cm = 1 in.   4. kg (kilogram)

5. $\dfrac{3}{4} \text{ mi} = \dfrac{3}{4} \times 1 \text{ mi}$
   $= \dfrac{3}{4} \times 5280 \text{ ft}$
   $= .75 \times 5280 \text{ ft}$
   $= 3960 \text{ ft}$

6. 1 gal = 4 qt   7. 1000 tons

8. 1103 mg = 1103×1 mg
   $= 1103 \times .001$ g
   $= 1.103$ g

9. 5 cm = 5 × 1 cm
    = 5 × .01 m
    = .05 m

10. 3.2 m = 3.2 × 1 m
    ≈ 3.2 × 39.37 in.
    ≈ 125.98 in.

11. 4 km = 4 × 1 km
    ≈ 4 × 0.62 mi
    ≈ 2.48 mi

12. 135°   13. 76°   14. 0°, 90°

15. a right angle

16.

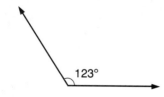

123°

17. (4.5 in.)² = 4.5 in. × 4.5 in = 20.25 in²

18. cm² (square centimeters)   19. 1

20. Angles *B* and *C* are acute; angle *A* is obtuse;
    there are no right angles.

21. (5 cm)³ = 5 cm × 5 cm × 5 cm = 125 cm³

22. 4 yd² (Area of rug: (6 ft)² = 6 ft × 6 ft =
    36 ft²; Area of 1 square yard in feet: 1 yd² =
    (3 ft)² = 3 ft × 3 ft = 9 ft²; Area of rug is
    4 times area of 1 square yd, so area of rug
    is 4 yd².)

23. 1 kg ≈ 2.2 lb

24. 10 quarts is larger. (9L = 9 × 1 L ≈ 9 ×
    1.06 qt ≈ 9.54 qt)

25. England

CHAPTER 3 REVIEW (pp. 135-137)

1. 2 in.   2. 4.9 cm   3. 7 cm

4. $2\frac{5}{8}$ in.   5. 63°   6. 157°

7. 36°

8. ∠*B*, ∠*ADC*

9. obtuse

10. ∠*ADE*

11. (2 cm)² = 2 cm × 2 cm = 4 cm²

12. (6.5 in)² = 6.5 in. × 6.5 in. = 42.25 in²

13. m² (square meters)

14. (4 mm)³ = 4 mm × 4 mm × 4 mm =
    64 mm³

15. (3.75 in.)³ = 3.75 in. × 375 in. × 3.75 in.
    = 52.734375 in.³ ≈ 53 in³

16. 2 pt = 1 qt

17. 16 oz = 1 lb

18. 5280 ft = 1 mi

19. Milli- means .001 or $\frac{1}{1000}$.

20. 1000 cm³ = 1 L

21. 1 kg = 1000 g

22. 2.2 lb ≈ 1 kg

23. 2.54 cm = 1 in.

24. A mile is larger. (1 km ≈ 0.62 mi)

25. A meter is larger. (1 m ≈ 39.37 in.;
    1 yd = 3)

26. If two numbers are nearly equal, then when
    one is substituted for the other in a
    computation, the results of the computations
    will be nearly equal.

27. 1 L ≈ 1.06 qt

28. mi (mile), km (kilometer)

29. cm (centimeter)

30. mg (milligram)

31. gal (gallon)

32. 2.5 yd = 2.5 × 1 yd
    = 2.5 × 3 ft
    = 7.5 ft

    7.5 ft = 7.5 × 1 ft
    = 7.5 × 12 in.
    = 90 in.

33. 7.3 gal = 7.3 × 1 gal
    = 7.3 × 4 qt
    = 29.2 qt

34. 3 short tons = 3 × 1 short ton
   = 3 × 2000 lb
   = 6000 lb

35. 660 yd = 660 × 1 yd
   = 660 × 3 ft
   = 1980 ft

36. 200 cm = 200 × 1 cm
   = 200 × .01 m
   = 2 m

37. 5 km = 5 × 1 km
   = 5 × 1000 m
   = 5000 m

38. 265 mL = 265 × 1 mL
   = 265 × .001 L
   = .265 L

39. 60 mg = 60 × 1 mg
   = 60 × .001 g
   = .06 g

40. 2 ft = 2 × 1 ft
   = 2 × 12 in.
   = 24 in.
   24 in. = 24 × 1 in.
   = 24 × 2.54 cm
   = 60.96 cm

41. 872 km = 872 × 1 km
   ≈ 872 × 0.62 mi
   ≈ 540.64 mi

42. 6.8 L = 6.8 × 1 L
   ≈ 6.8 × 1.06 qt
   ≈ 7.208 qt
   ≈ 7.21 qt

43. 100 kg = 100 × 1 kg
   ≈ 10 × 2.2 lb
   ≈ 220 lb

44. 70°

45. $\angle ABC$, $\angle BEA$, $\angle BCD$, $\angle DEC$

46. No (Area of table = (2.5 ft)^2 = 2.5 ft × 2.5 ft = 6.25 ft^2)

47. (12 cm)^3 = 12 cm × 12 cm × 12 cm = 1728 cm^3

48.

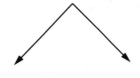

49.

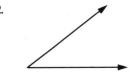

50.

51. Many possible answers. Sample:

52.

53.

54. The metric system originated in France in the 1790s.

55. The length of a yard was first determined as the distance from Henry I nose to his fingertips.

56. Our system for measuring angles is based on measuring done by the Babylonians.

LESSON 4-1 (pp. 140-144)

1. numerical

2. $13.004 - 3.976 = 9.028$

3. Finding the value of an expression is called evaluating the expression.

4. Rules for order of operations are needed to avoid confusion when there is more than one operation to be performed.

5. Division is done before addition.

6. A power is evaluated before performing subtraction.

7. The operation to the left is done first.

8. The operation to the left is done first.

9. 27 (Multiply first.)

10. 6.3 (Multiply first.)

11. 10 (Divide from left to right.)

12. $1 \div 9 + 1 \div 7$
    $= .\overline{1} + .\overline{142857}$
    $= .\overline{253968}$, or $\frac{16}{63}$

13. $1000 - 3 \times 17^2$
    $= 1000 - 3 \times 289$
    $= 1000 - 867$
    $= 133$

14. $4^2 + 8^3$
    $= 16 + 512$
    $= 528$

15. For multiplication, $\times$ is used in arithmetic and on calculators; $\cdot$ is used in albegra; $*$ is used in some computer languages.

16. $3 \div 9$, $3/9$, $\frac{3}{9}$, $3:9$, $3\overline{)9}$

17. The symbol $+$ was invented about 500 years ago; the symbol $\times$ was invented about 350 years ago.

18. sum

19. difference

20. product

21. quotient

22. Mathematicians invent symbols to make things easier to understand.

23. $11 + 4.2 = 15.2$

24. $6 \times 0.3 = 1.8$

25. $2 \div 4 = 0.5$

26. $500 - 0.87 = 499.13$

27. $2 * 3 + 8$
    $= 2 \times 3 + 8$
    $= 6 + 8$
    $= 14$

28. $120 - 3 * 4/4$
    $= 120 - 3 \times 4 \div 4$
    $= 120 - 12 \div 4$
    $= 120 - 3$
    $= 117$

29. $200/2 * 10 - 4$
    $= 200 \div 2 \times 10 - 4$
    $= 100 \times 10 - 4$
    $= 1000 - 4$
    $= 996$

30. $17 + 16 * 3\char`^2$
    $= 17 + 16 \times 3^2$
    $= 17 + 16 \times 9$
    $= 17 + 144$
    $= 161$

31. c, $(.1 + .2 = .3; .1 \times .2 = .02; .1 \div .2 = .5; .1^2 = .01)$

32. Many possible answers. Sample: 2 and 3 $(2 + 3 < 2 \times 3)$

33. The order of operations makes no difference in $87 + 12 - 3$. (For the first expression, if subtraction is done first, $87 - 12 + 3 = 75 + 3 = 78$. But if addition is done first, $87 - 12 + 3 = 87 - 15 = 72$. For the second expression, if addition is done first, $87 + 12 - 3 = 99 - 3 = 96$. The same answer is obtained if subtraction is done first: $87 + 12 - 3 = 87 + 9 = 96$.)

34. obtuse

35. $115°$

36.
___

37. 6.543×10^{-12} (Write 6.543. The decimal point must move 12 places to the left to get 0.00000 00000 06543, so the exponent of 10 is -12.)

38. You will save money after the first year. (Cost of 3 smoke detectors = 3 × $14.99 = $44.97. Amount saved on insurance = 15% of $250 = .15 × 250 = $37.50)

39. $(5 \text{ in.})^3 = 5 \text{ in.} \times 5 \text{ in.} \times 5 \text{ in.} = 125 \text{ in.}^3$

40. Many possible answers. Samples: music symbols, some traffic signs, airport signs

41. Esperanto is a language that was invented about 100 years ago in an attempt to create a worldwide spoken and written language.

42. **a.** Outputs will be 14, 117, 996, 161
b. Yes, computer follows rules for order of operations.

LESSON 4-2 (pp. 145-148)

1. A variable is a symbol that can stand for any one of a set of numbers or other objects.

2. Variables can help describe patterns.

3. Variables look like the instances, and they are shorter.

4. Many possible answers. Sample: $\frac{3}{3} = 1$; $\frac{7.2}{7.2} = 1$; $\frac{5}{5} = 1$

5. Many possible answers. Samples: 5% = 5 × .01; 1.2% = 1.2 × .01; 300% = 300 × .01

6. Many possible answers. Sample: 3 people have 2 · 3 eyes; 5 people have 2 · 5 eyes; 165 people have 2 · 165 eyes

7. Many possible answers. Samples: 3 + 4 = 4 + 3; 1/2 + 3/4 = 3/4 + 1/2; 0.8 + 6 = 6 + 0.8

8. François Viète was the first person to use variables to describe patterns.

9. Elementary algebra studies variables and the operations of arithmetic with them.

10. François Viète is considered the "father of algebra."

11. c

12. Many possible answers.
Sample: 12 + 3 = 5 + 3 + 7;
12 + 0 = 5 + 0 + 7;
12 + 8.8 = 5 + 8.8 + 7

13. Many possible answers.
Sample: 6 · 4 + 13 · 4 = 19 · 4;
6 · 9.7 + 13 · 9.7 = 19 · 9.7;
6 · 100 + 13 · 100 = 19 · 100

14. Many possible answers. Sample:
for 8 days overdue, 20 + 8 · 5 cents;
for 2 days overdue, 20 + 2 · 5 cents;
for 365 days overdue, 20 + 365 · 5 cents

15. $a \cdot 0 = 0$. (Any letter can be used.)

16. $5 \cdot n = 3 \cdot n + 2 \cdot n$

17. In n years we expect $n \cdot 100$ more students and $n \cdot 5$ more teachers.

18. Many possible answers. Sample:
6 · 3 = 3 · 6;
5 · 4.41 = 4.41 · 5;
$7 \cdot \frac{1}{2} = \frac{1}{2} \cdot 7$

19. $\frac{a}{3} = \frac{b}{3} = \frac{a + b}{3}$

20. **a.** $a + .5$ is not an integer.
b. Many possible answers. Sample: 3.5 + .5 is an integer.
c. Even when a pattern describes 3 examples, it may still be possible to find an exception.

21. 25% × 60 + 40
= .25 × 60 + 40
= 15 + 40
= 55

22. $7 \times 2 \times 8 - 7 \times 2$
    $= 14 \times 8 - 7 \times 2$
    $= 112 - 7 \times 2$
    $= 112 - 14$
    $= 98$

23. $60 + 40 \div 4 + 4$
    $= 60 + 10 + 4$
    $= 70 + 4$
    $= 74$

24. $12.5 - 11.5 \div 5$
    $= 12.5 - 2.3$
    $= 10.2$

25. $12 - 3^2$
    $= 12 - 9$
    $= 3$

26. $170 - 5^3$
    $= 170 - 125$
    $= 45$

27. $50/.0001$; $500,000$

28. $500 \cdot .05$; 25

29. 3 meters (300 cm $= 300 \times 1$ cm $= 300 \times .01$ m $= 3$ m)

30. Many possible answers. Sample: $0.1^2 < 0.1$

31. **b.** Add 6 to each number to get the next number.
    c. 36 $(6 + 30 = 36)$

32. **b.** Square the natural numbers to get the numbers in the sequence.
    c. 36 $(6^2 = 36)$

33. **b.** Alternately add 1 and 3 to get the next number.
    c. 17 $(3 + 14 = 17)$

34. **b.** Take the cube of each natural number, then divide by 3.
    c. $\frac{216}{3}$ $\left(\frac{6^3}{3} = \frac{216}{3} \right)$

LESSON 4-3   (pp. 149-153)

1. A numerical expression contains only numbers and operation symbols; an algebraic expression contains a variable or variables as well.

2. $2 \cdot n$

3. $n + 3$ or $3 + n$

4. $n \cdot 4$ or $4 \cdot n$

5. $n - 5$

6. $6 - n$

7. $n - 7$

8. $\frac{n}{8}$ 9. $\frac{n}{9}$

10. $n + 10$ or $10 + n$

11. $11 - n$

12. Ambiguous means having more than one meaning.

13. Many possible answers. Sample: five times a number increased by six (This is ambiguous because you don't know whether to increase by six or multiply by five first.)

14. Several possible answers. Sample: 10 more than a number; a number plus 10; a number increased by 10

15. Many possible answers. Sample: two minus a number; subtract a number from two; two decreased by a number

16. $6 \cdot n - 5$

17. It could mean $14 - 5 + 3$, with either the addition or the subtraction done first. (If the addition is done first, $14 - 5 + 3 = 6$. If the subtraction is done first, $14 - 5 + 3 = 12$.)

18. $\frac{1}{2} \cdot t$

19. $6\% \cdot t$ or $.06 \cdot t$

20. $t \cdot t$; t^2

21. **a.** $C + 50$ or $50 + C$
    b. $C - 12$
    c. $C \cdot 3$ or $3 \cdot C$

22. a. Quintupled means multiplied by 5.

  b. Quadrupled means multiplied by 4.

23. a. $6 < n$ **b.** $n - 6$ **c.** $6 - n$

24. It could mean $\frac{2}{4}$ or $\frac{4}{2}$.

25. $2\frac{1}{2}$ or $2\frac{4}{8}$ inches

26. Many possible answers. Sample:

  $7 \cdot 3 - 6 \cdot 3 = 3$;

  $7 \cdot .05 - 6 \cdot .05 = .05$;

  $7 \cdot 398 - 6 \cdot 398 = 398$

27. $\frac{a}{1} = a$

28. $a + 5 + b - 5 = a + b$

29. $1110 \text{ km} = 1110 \times 1 \text{ km}$

  $\approx 1110 \times 0.62 \text{ mi}$

  $\approx 688.2 \text{ mi}$

30. 29 medals (21% of $138 = .21 \times 138 = 28.98$)

31. Many possible answers. Samples:

  a.

  b.

  c.

32. $(10 \text{ ft})^3 = 10 \text{ ft} \times 10 \text{ ft} \times 10 \text{ ft} = 1000 \text{ ft}^3$

33. a. .00001

  b. .001% (Move the decimal point in .00001 2 places to the right.)

34. b. Add 3 to each number to get the next number;

  c. 17 $(3 + 14 = 17)$

35. b. Add 2, then 3, then 4, and so on.

  c. 28 $(7 + 21 = 28)$

36. b. Add the previous two numbers to get the next.

  c. 21 $(8 + 13 = 21)$

37. b. Add 3, then 6, then 12, doubling what you add each time.

  c. 97 $(48 + 49 = 97)$

LESSON 4-4 (pp. 154-157)

1. c, $(5n = 5 \times 3 = 15)$

In the expression $5 \cdot n$:

2. n is the variable.

3. 3 is the value of the variable when $n = 3$.

4. $5 \cdot n$ is the expression.

5. 15 is the value of the expression when $n = 3$.

6. $5n$

7. yes

8. 25¢ $(20 + 5 \cdot 1 \text{ cents})$

9. 50¢ $(20 + 5 \cdot 6 \text{ cents})$

10. $1.20 $(20 + 5 \cdot 20 \text{ cents})$

11. example 8

12. $d + d = 5 + 5 = 10$

13. $88 - 4d$

  $= 88 - 4 \cdot 5$

  $= 88 - 20$

  $= 68$

14. $2 + 3d$

  $= 2 + 3 \cdot 5$

  $= 2 + 15$

  $= 17$

15. 5%

16. $4m + 7x$

  $= 4 \cdot 5 + 7 \cdot 9$

  $= 20 + 63$

  $= 83$

17. $2mx$

  $= 2 \cdot 5 \cdot 9$

  $= 10 \cdot 9$

  $= 90$

18. $1.6x + m^3$
$$= 1.6 \cdot 9 + 5^3$$
$$= 1.6 \cdot 9 + 125$$
$$= 14.4 + 125$$
$$= 139.4$$

19. πx^2
$$= \pi \cdot 9^2$$
$$= \pi \cdot 81$$
$$= 81\,\pi$$
$$\approx 254.469$$

20. **a.** $17 + 5A$ lb
$$= 17 + 5 \cdot 6 \text{ lb}$$
$$= 17 + 30 \text{ lb}$$
$$= 47 \text{ lb}$$
b. $17 + 5A$ lb
$$= 17 + 5 \cdot 2 \text{ lb}$$
$$= 17 + 10 \text{ lb}$$
$$= 27 \text{ lb}$$
c. 5 lb

21. **a.** $xy - yx$
$$= 100 \cdot 25 - 25 \cdot 100$$
$$= 2500 - 2500$$
$$= 0$$
b. No, because $xy = yx$ for any numbers.

22. **a.** $2 \cdot 1 + 1 = 3; 2 \cdot 2 + 1 = 5; 2 \cdot 3 + 1 = 7; 2 \cdot 4 + 1 = 9; 2 \cdot 5 + 1 = 11;$
b. To get the next number, add 2 to the previous number. (Or list the odd numbers beginning with 3.)

23. **a.** $5n - 8$
b. $5n - 8$
$$= 5 \cdot 10 - 8$$
$$= 50 - 8$$
$$= 42$$

24. **a.** $4n + 9$
b. $4n + 9$
$$= 4 \cdot 10 + 9$$
$$= 40 + 9$$
$$= 49$$

25. **a.** n^3
b. $10^3 = 1000$

26. $a + 0 = a$

27. $1 \times b = b$

28. **a.** 6, 6;
b. $4 \cdot 11, 2 \cdot 11, 11$
c. $4h, 2h, h$

29. a, $(10 + 1 = 11; 10 \times 1 = 10;$
$10 \div 1 = 10; 10^1 = 10)$

30. milli-

31. b and d (Both the natural numbers and the positive integers are 1, 2, 3, 4, ...
The whole numbers are 0, 1, 2, 3, ...
The integers are . . . , -3, -2, -1, 0, 1, 2, 3, ...)

32. $\frac{15}{64}$ (Multiply numerator and denominator of $\frac{2.4}{10.24}$ by 100 to get $\frac{240}{1024}$. Then divide numerator and denominator of $\frac{240}{1024}$ by 16.)

33. $m + A \cdot d$

34. **a.** $30x - 12$
b. 93
c. Change line 30 to V = 25 * x + x^4.
Output: 26, 66, 83946

LESSON 4-5 (pp. 158-162)

1. Parentheses can be used to change the order of operations.

2. False $(5 + 4 \times 3 = 5 + 12 = 17$.
But $(5 + 4) \times 3 = 9 \times 3 = 27$.)

3. True (Both expressions are equal to 17.)

4. True (Both expressions are equal to 15.)

5. False $(2 + (4) = 2 + 4 = 6$. But $8 = 8$.)

6. c

7. $4 + 3 (7 + 9)$
$$= 4 + 3 (16)$$
$$= 4 + 3 \cdot 16$$
$$= 4 + 48$$
$$= 52$$

8. $(12) (3 + 4)$
$$= (12) (7)$$
$$= 12 \cdot 7$$
$$= 84$$

9. $10 + 20 \div (2 + 3 \cdot 6)$
$= 10 + 20 \div (2 + 18)$
$= 10 + 20 \div (20)$
$= 10 + 20 \div 20$
$= 10 + 1$
$= 11$

10. $40 - (30 - 5)$
$= 40 - (25)$
$= 40 - 24$
$= 15$

11. $(6 + 6)(6 - 6)$
$= (12)(0)$
$= 12 \cdot 0$
$= 0$

12. Multiplication occurs between 2 and $(5 + 4n)$ and between 4 and n.

13. $2 \boxed{\times} \boxed{(} 5 \boxed{+} 4 \boxed{\times} 8 \boxed{)} \boxed{=}$

14. $0.30 (c - b)$
$= 0.30 (5 - 3)$
$= 0.30 (2)$
$= 0.30 \cdot 2$
$= 0.6$

15. $(a + b)(7a + 2b)$
$= (2 + 3)(7 \cdot 2 + 2 \cdot 3)$
$= (5)(14 + 6)$
$= (5)(20)$
$= 5 \cdot 20$
$= 100$

16. $(a + 100\,b) - (7a - 2b)$
$= (2 + 100 \cdot 3) - (7 \cdot 2 - 2 \cdot 3)$
$= (2 + 300) - (14 - 6)$
$= (302) - (8)$
$= 302 - 8$
$= 294$

17. $20a + 5 (c - 3)$
$= 20 \cdot 2 + 5 (5 - 3)$
$= 40 + 5 (2)$
$= 40 + 5 \cdot 2$
$= 40 + 10$
$= 50$

18. Nested parentheses are parentheses inside parentheses

19. **a.** Do $10 - 1$ first
b. $1000 - (100 - (10 - 1))$
$= 1000 - (100 - (9))$
$= 1000 - (91)$
$= 1000 - 91$
$= 909$

20. $2(x + 12) - 3$
$= 2(8 + 12) - 3$
$= 2(20) - 3$
$= 2 \cdot 20 - 3$
$= 40 - 3$
$= 37$

21. $3 + x(2 + x(1 + x))$
$= 3 + 5(2 + 5(1 + 5))$
$= 3 + 5(2 + 5(6))$
$= 3 + 5(2 + 5 \cdot 6)$
$= 3 + 5(2 + 30)$
$= 3 + 5(32)$
$= 3 + 5 \cdot 32$
$= 3 + 160$
$= 163$

22. $4 (n + 2)$ $\qquad$ $4n + 8$
$= 4 (3 + 2)$ $\qquad$ $= 4 \cdot 3 + 8$
$= 4 (5)$ $\qquad$ $= 12 + 8$
$= 4 \cdot 5$ $\qquad$ $= 20$
$= 20$
Yes, same value

23. $33 - 7n$ $\qquad$ $(33 - 7)n$
$= 33 - 7 \cdot 3$ $\qquad$ $= (33 - 7)3$
$= 33 - 21$ $\qquad$ $= (26)3$
$= 12$ $\qquad$ $= 26 \cdot 3$
$\qquad\qquad\qquad$ $= 78$

No, different values

24. $b - (a - 2)$
$= 31 - (10 - 2)$
$= 31 - (8)$
$= 23$
$b - a - 2$
$= 31 - 10 - 2$
$= 21 - 2$
$= 19$
The first expression has the larger value.

25. $a + 4 (b + 3)$
$= 10 + 4 (31 + 3)$
$= 10 + 4 (34)$
$= 10 + 4 \cdot 34$
$= 10 + 136$
$= 146$
$(a + 4) b + 3$
$= (10 + 4) 31 + 3$
$= (14) 31 + 3$
$= 14 \cdot 31 + 3$
$= 434 + 3$
$= 437$
The second expression has the larger value.

26. b

27. d

28. $a (b + c) = ab + ac$

29. $2 (3 + n (n + 1) + 5)$
$= 2 (3 + 14 (14 + 1) + 5)$
$= 2 (3 + 14 (15) + 5)$
$= 2 (3 + 14 \cdot 15 + 5)$
$= 2 (3 + 210 + 5)$
$= 2 (213 + 5)$
$= 2 (218)$
$= 2 \cdot 218$
$= 436$

30. $16 - (15 - 9) = 10$
Verify by evaluating:
$16 - (15 - 9)$
$= 16 - (6)$
$= 10$

31. $16 - (8 - 4 - 2) = 14$
Verify by evaluating
$16 - (8 - 4 - 2)$
$= 16 - (4 - 2)$
$= 16 - (2)$
$= 14$

32. $(6 \text{ mi})^2 = 6 \text{ mi} \times 6 \text{ mi} = 36 \text{ mi}^2$

33. $6T + E + 3F + 2S$
$= 6 \cdot 3 + 2 + 3 \cdot 1 + 2 \cdot 0$
$= 18 + 2 + 3 + 0$
$= 20 + 3 + 0$
$= 23 + 0$
$= 23$

34. **a.** T = number of touchdowns
E = number of extra points
F = number of field goals
S = number of safeties
b. The total score

35. $n^4 = n \cdot n \cdot n \cdot n$

36. 5.7 seconds $-$ .1 second = 5.6 seconds

37. Answers will vary. 4 or 5 parentheses are typical.

38. **a.** The value 23 is given.
b. Sample output:
GIVE VALUE OF YOUR VARIABLE
? 10
VALUE OF EXPRESSION IS 29
c. Add 19 to the value inputted. (Notice that the value of the expression is always 19 more than the value of the variable.)

39. Change line 20 to INPUT Y; change line 30 to
$V = (Y + 15)*(11 - 2*Y)$

LESSON 4-6 (pp. 163-166)

1. area, length, width

2. The variables are the first letters of the words they represent.

3. $A = \ell w$
$= 43 \text{ cm} \times 0.1 \text{ cm}$
$= 4.3 \text{ cm}^2$

4. a. Either solution is correct. In Solution 1, 4 ft is converted to 48 in. In Solution 2, 3 in. is converted to .25 ft.

Solution 1
$$A = \ell w$$
$$= 3 \text{ in.} \times 48 \text{ in.}$$
$$= 144 \text{ in.}^2$$

Solution 2
$$A = \ell w$$
$$= .25 \text{ ft} \times 4 \text{ ft}$$
$$= 1 \text{ ft}^2$$

b. The units must be the same.

5. No

6. S stands for the length of a side of the big square; s stands for the length of a side of the small square.

7. $A = S^2 - s^2$
$$= (1.6 \text{ cm})^2 - (0.6 \text{ cm})^2$$
$$= 2.56 \text{ cm}^2 - .36 \text{ cm}^2$$
$$= 2.2 \text{ cm}^2$$

8. Capital letters often stand for different things than small letters do.

9. a. Sample:

ABCDEFGHIJKLMNOPQRSTUVWXYZ

b. Sample:

abcdefghijklmnopqrstuvwxyz

10. cost, selling price

11. They are the first letters of the quantities they represent.

12. $p = s - c$
$$= \$25 - \$15$$
$$= \$10$$

13. $p = s - c$
$$= \$3 - \$.02$$
$$= \$2.98$$

14. $N = 7LH$
$$= 7 \cdot 30 \cdot 10$$
$$= 210 \cdot 10$$
$$= 2100$$
2100 bricks

15. $N = 7LH$
$$= 7 \cdot 20 \cdot 8\frac{1}{2}$$
$$= 140 \cdot 8.5$$
$$= 1190$$
No, 1190 are needed.

16. $A = S^2 - s^2$
$$= (7 \text{ m})^2 - (5 \text{ m})^2$$
$$= 49 \text{ m}^2 - 25 \text{ m}^2$$
$$= 24 \text{ m}^2$$

17. inside parentheses, then powers, then multiplications or divisions from left to right, then additions and subtractions from left to right

18. $9 + 5 (3 + 2 \cdot 7)$
$$= 9 + 5 (3 + 14)$$
$$= 9 + 5 (17)$$
$$= 9 + 85$$
$$= 94$$

19. $3 + 4 \cdot 5^2$
$$= 3 + 4 \cdot 25$$
$$= 3 + 100$$
$$= 103$$

20. $12 - 4x$
$$= 12 - 4 \cdot .5$$
$$= 12 - 2$$
$$= 10$$

21. $8/(8/(2 + 6)$
$$= 8/(8/8)$$
$$= 8/1$$
$$= 8$$

22. $6 \text{ kg} = 6 \times 1 \text{ kg}$
$$= 6 \times 1000 \text{ g}$$
$$= 6000 \text{ g}$$

23. 1000 cubic centimeters

24. $-5 > -5.1$ (-5 is to the right of -5.1.)

25. $4.09 < 4\frac{1}{11}$ $(4\frac{1}{11} = 4.0909\ldots)$

26. $x + 14 > x - 14$ when $x = 20$ $(x + 14 = 20 + 14 = 34; x - 14 = 20 - 14 = 6)$

27. $a^3 < a^2$ when $a = 0.7$ $(a^3 = (0.7)^3 = .343; a^2 = (0.7)^2 = .49$

28. $\frac{8}{4} = 2, \frac{9}{4} = 2.25, \frac{10}{4} = 2.5, \frac{11}{4} = 2.75,$

$\frac{12}{4} = 3$

29. a. 7 bricks (The formula implies that the number of bricks is 7 times the square footage of the wall.)

b. The formula for the area of a rectangle is related to the bricklayer's formula. *LH* gives the area of the wall in square feet.

LESSON 4-7 (pp. 167-171)

1. [ ] are brackets.

2. True, brackets and parentheses mean the same thing.

3. Brackets are usually used when there are nested parentheses.

4. Parentheses, brackets, and fraction bars are grouping symbols.

5. Work with the innermost grouping symbols first.

6. $3\,[2 + 4\,(5 - 2)]$

$= 3\,[2 + 4 \cdot 3]$

$= 3\,[2 + 12]$

$= 3 \cdot 14$

$= 42$

7. $39 - [20 \div 4 + 2\,(3 + 6)]$

$= 39 - [20 \div 4 + 2 \cdot 9]$

$= 39 - [5 + 18]$

$= 39 - 23$

$= 16$

8. $[(3 - 1)^3 + (5 - 1)^4]^2$

$= [2^3 + 4^4]^2$

$= [8 + 256]^2$

$= 264^2$

$= 69{,}696$

9. $3\;\boxed{\times}\;\boxed{(}\;\boxed{(}\;2\;\boxed{+}\;4\;\boxed{\times}\;\boxed{(}\;5\;\boxed{-}\;2\;\boxed{)}\;\boxed{)}\;\boxed{=}$

10. d, (Fraction bars are grouping symbols.)

11. $\dfrac{50 + 40}{50 - 40}$

$= \dfrac{90}{10}$

$= 9$

12. $\dfrac{560}{7\,(6 + 3 \cdot 4.5)}$

$= \dfrac{560}{7\,(6 + 13.5)}$

$= \dfrac{560}{7 \cdot 19.5}$

$= \dfrac{560}{136.5}$

$= 4.102564$

13. $560\;\boxed{\div}\;\boxed{(}\;7\;\boxed{\times}\;\boxed{(}\;6\;\boxed{+}\;3\;\boxed{\times}\;4.5\;\boxed{)}\;\boxed{(}\;\boxed{=}$

14. $\dfrac{a + 3x}{a + x}$

$= \dfrac{5 + 3 \cdot 4}{5 + 4}$

$= \dfrac{5 + 12}{9}$

$= \dfrac{17}{9}$ or $1.\overline{8}$

15. $\dfrac{5x - 2}{(x - 1)(x - 2)}$

$= \dfrac{5 \cdot 4 - 2}{(4 - 1)(4 - 2)}$

$= \dfrac{20 - 2}{3 \cdot 2}$

$= \dfrac{18}{2}$

$= 3$

16. $\dfrac{a + b + c}{3}$

17. $\dfrac{x + y + z}{3}$

$= \dfrac{236 + 141 + 318}{3}$

$= \dfrac{377 + 318}{3}$

$= \dfrac{695}{3}$

$= 231.\overline{6}$

18. $\dfrac{x + y + z}{3}$

$= \dfrac{83 + 91 + 89}{3}$

$= \dfrac{174 + 89}{3}$

$= \dfrac{263}{3}$

$= 87.\overline{6}$

19. a. The third score is 0:

$\dfrac{x + y + z}{3}$

$= \dfrac{85 + 90 + 0}{3}$

$= \dfrac{175 + 0}{3}$

$= \dfrac{175}{3}$

$= 58.\overline{3}$

b. The third score is 100:

$\dfrac{x + y + z}{3}$

$= \dfrac{85 + 90 + 199}{3}$

$= \dfrac{175 + 100}{3}$

$= \dfrac{275}{3}$

$= 91.\overline{6}$

20. $\dfrac{W}{W + L}$

$= \dfrac{11}{11 + 4}$

$= \dfrac{11}{15}$

$\approx .733$

21. $\dfrac{W}{W + L}$

$= \dfrac{6}{6 + 0}$

$= \dfrac{6}{6}$

$= 1.000$

22. $\dfrac{W}{W + L}$

$= \dfrac{7}{7 + 7}$

$= \dfrac{7}{14}$

$= .500$

23. $\dfrac{W}{W + L}$

$= \dfrac{3}{3 + 12}$

$= \dfrac{3}{15}$

$= .200$

24. $T \approx t - \dfrac{2f}{1000}$

$\approx 75 - \dfrac{2 \cdot 1000}{1000}$

$\approx 75 - \dfrac{2000}{1000}$

$\approx 75 - 2$

$\approx 73^0$

25. $T \approx t - \dfrac{2f}{1000}$

$\approx 75 - \dfrac{2 \cdot 3000}{1000}$

$\approx 75 - \dfrac{6000}{1000}$

$\approx 75 - 6$

$\approx 69^0$

26. b

27. $7\frac{2}{3} > 7.65 > 7\frac{3}{5}$ $(7\frac{2}{3} = 7.666 \ldots ; 7\frac{3}{5} = 7.6)$

28. a. 220,698,000,000; **b.** 221,000,000,000 (220,698,000,000 is between 220,000,000,000 and 221,000,000,000 and is nearer to 221,000,000,000.); **c.** 2.20698×10^{11} (Write 2.20698. The decimal point must move 11 places to the right to get 220,698,000,000, so the exponent of 10 is 11.)
1992 Edition: **a.** 161,501,000,000;
b. 162,000,000,000 (161,501,000,000 is between 161,000,000,000 and 162,000,000,000 and is nearer to 162,000,000,000.); **c.** 1.61501×10^{11} (Write 1.61501. The decimal point must move 11 places to the right to get 161,501,000,000, so the exponent of 10 is 11.)

29. Answers will vary, depending on the table.

30. a. $30 + 20$ or $20 + 30$
b. $3 + n$ or $n + 3$ **c.** $n - .1$

31. Many possible answers. Samples: $2 = \frac{4}{4} + \frac{4}{4}$;

$3 = \dfrac{4 + 4 + 4}{4}$; $4 = (4 - 4) \times 4 + 4$;

$5 = \dfrac{4 + 4 \times 4}{4}$; $6 = \dfrac{4 + 4}{4} + 4$;

$7 = 4 + 4 - \left(\dfrac{4}{4}\right)$; $8 = 4 + 4 + 4 - 4$;

$9 = 4 + 4 + \left(\dfrac{4}{4}\right)$; $10 = \dfrac{44 - 4}{4}$

32. **a.** W (W + L)

    b. Output: .733333333

    c. Many possible answers. Sample: If W = 5 and L = 4, then the computer will print:

```
WINS
? 5
LOSSES
? 4
PCT = .555555556
```

LESSON 4-8 (pp. 172-175)

1. An equation is a sentence with an equal sign.

2. Many possible answers. Sample: 1 + 1 = 3

3. An open sentence is a sentence with variables.

4. Many possible answers. Sample: $x + 7 = 50$

5. A solution to an open sentence is a value of the variable that makes the sentence true.

6. Solving an open sentence is finding values of the unknown that make the sentence true.

7. (a) (4 · 2.25 + 3 = 9 + 3 = 12, so 2.25 is a solution; 4 · 0 + 3 = 0 + 3 = 3, so 0 does not work; 4 · 2.5 + 3 = 10 + 3 = 13, so 2.5 does not work; 4 · 1 + 3 = 4 + 3 = 7, so 1 does not work.)

8. 1 (18 + 1 = 19)   **9.** 5 (2 · 5 = 10)

10. 4.9 (5 − .1 = 4.9)   **11.** .5 (3.5 + .5 = 4)

12. 1000 = ℓ · 40 (Use $A = \ell w$. Substitute 1000 for A and 40 for w.)

13. 25 m (25 · 40 = 1000)

14. In 1989, George Bush

15. Many possible answers. Samples: Los Angeles, London, Mexico City, Chicago

16. three   **17.** eight   **18.** 1000

19. Many possible answers. Sample: −9

20. 100   **21.** 6

22. c, (.20 + .05 · 20 = .20 + 1 = 1.20, so 20 does not work; .20 + .05 · 15 = .20 + .75 = .95, so 15 does not work; .20 + .05 · 16 = .20 + .8 = 1.00, so 16 is a solution; .20 + .05 · 25 = .20 + 1.25 = 1.45, so 25 is not a solution.)

23. 11 (2 · 4 + 3 = 8 + 3 = 11)

24. 8 (8 + 8 = 16)   **25.** 4 (4 · 4 = 16)

26. 103 (103 − 4 = 99)

27. 1 (1 · 25 = 25)

28. **a.** 5,030,000,000 (5,026,000,000 is between 5,020,000,000 and 5,030,000,000 and is nearer to 5,030,000,000.)

    b. 5.03×10^9 (Write 5.03. The decimal point must move 9 places to the right to get 5,030,000,000, so the exponent of 10 is 9.)

    1992 Edition: **a.** 5,240,000,000 (5,239,000,000 is between 5,230,000,000 and 5,240,000,000 and is nearer to 5,240,000,000.); **b.** 5.24×10^9 (Write 5.24. The decimal point must move 9 places to the right to get 5,240,000,000, so the exponent of 10 is 9.)

29. 50,000 mm < 500 m < 5 km or 5 km > 500 m > 50,000 mm (500 m = 500 × 1000 mm = 500,000 mm; 5 km = 5 × 1000 m = 5000 m = 5000 × 1000 mm = 5,000,000 mm)

30. 5280 ft < 2000 yd < 2 mi or 2 mi > 2000 yd > 5280 ft (2000 yd = 2000 × 3 ft = 6000 ft; 2 mi = 2 × 5280 ft = 10,560 ft)

31. **a.** $\dfrac{n(n+1)}{2}$

$$= \dfrac{5(5+1)}{2}$$

$$= \dfrac{5 \cdot 6}{2}$$

$$= 15$$

    b. 1 + 2 + 3 + 4 + 5 = 15

    c. $\dfrac{n(n+1)}{2}$

$$= \dfrac{100(100+1)}{2}$$

$$= \dfrac{100 \cdot 101}{2}$$

$$= \dfrac{10,100}{2}$$

$$= 5050$$

---

*These are solutions to questions changed in or added to the *1992 Edition.*

32. $2x - (y + 3(y + 2))$

$= 2 \cdot 5.5 - (0.5 + 3(0.5 + 2))$

$= 2 \cdot 5.5 - (0.5 + 3 \cdot 2.5)$

$= 2 \cdot 5.5 - (0.5 + 7.5)$

$= 2 \cdot 5.5 - 8$

$= 11 - 8$

$= 3$

33. $\dfrac{[6(2 + 4^3)^2 - 3^2]}{40 - 13 \cdot 3}$

$= \dfrac{[6(2 + 64)^2 = 3^2]}{40 - 39}$

$= \dfrac{[6 \cdot 66^2 - 3^2]}{1}$

$= \dfrac{[6 \cdot 4356 - 9]}{1}$

$= \dfrac{[26,136 - 9]}{1}$

$= \dfrac{26,127}{1}$

$= 26,127$

34. a. 9×10^{-3} (Write 9. The decimal point must move 3 places to the left to get 0.009, so the exponent of 10 is -3.);

b. $\dfrac{9}{1000}$

35. a. between 8 and 9 (8 is too low: $(8 + 1)$ $(8 + 2) = 9 \cdot 10 = 90$; 9 is too high: $(9 + 1)(9 + 2) = 10 \cdot 11 = 110$)

b. between 8.5 and 8.6 (8.5 is too low: $(8.5 + 1)(8.5 + 2) = 9.5 \cdot 10.5 = 99.75$; 8.6 is too high: $(8.6 + 1)(8.6 + 2) = 9.6 \cdot 10.6 = 101.76$)

c. between 8.51 and 8.52 (8.51 is too low: $(8.51 + 1)(8.51 + 2) = 9.51 \cdot 10.51 = 99.9501$; 8.52 is too high: $(8.52 + 1)(8.52 + 2) = 9.52 \cdot 10.52 = 100.1504$)

36. a. ? $(83 + 91 + 89)/3$

b. Sample output: 87.6666667

LESSON 4-9 (pp. 176-179)

1. An inequality is a sentence with one of the symbols $<$, $>$, $\le$, $\ge$, or $\ne$. (Some inequalities use more than one such symbol.)

2. is greater than

3. is greater than or equal to

4. is less than

5. is less than or equal to

6. $5 < y$

7. yes

8. no

9. true (-2 is to the left of 1.)

10. true ($\frac{6}{2} = 3$, so the two quantities are equal.)

11. false (-5 is to the left of 5, so $-5 < 5$.)

12. false ($5 + 1 = 6$, so the two quantities are equal.)

13. Many possible answers. Sample: 5001

14. Many possible answers. Sample: -13

15. Many possible answers. Sample: $6\frac{3}{4}$

16. Many possible answers. Sample: 47

17. (c) (Numbers to the right of 8 are greater than 8. The filled-in circle at 8 indicates that 8 is included in the solutions.)

18. c   **19.** b   **20.** d

21. a

22. $55 \ge s \ge 45$ or $45 \le s \le 55$

23. d

24.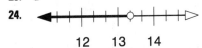

25.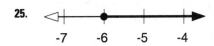

26.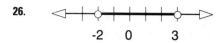

27. **a.** $f > 55$

    b. Many possible answers. Samples: 60, 57, 61

    c.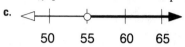

28. **a.** $0 \leq d < 25{,}000$

    b. Many possible answers. Samples: 5132, 4.32, 24,999

    c.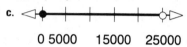

29. **a.** $400 < A \leq 500$

    b. Many possible answers. Samples: 490, 421, 439.36

    c.

30. $c = .30 + .18 (m - 1)$
$= .30 + .18 (6 - 1)$
$= .30 + .18 \cdot 5$
$= .30 + .90$
$= \$1.20$

31. $c = .30 + .18 (m - 1)$
$= .30 + .18 (10 - 1)$
$= .30 + .18 \cdot 9$
$= .30 + 1.62$
$= \$1.92$

32. d, $(.30 + .18 (7 - 1) = .30 + .18 \cdot 6 = .30 + 1.08 = 1.38$, so 7 does not work. $.30 + .18 (9 - 1) = .30 + .18 \cdot 8 = .30 + 1.44 = 1.74$, so 9 does not work. 10 does not work, as shown in the solution to Question 31. $.30 + .18 (11 - 1) = .30 + .18 \cdot 10 = .30 + 1.8 = 2.10$, so 11 is a solution.)

33. Many possible answers. Sample: there are $6 \cdot 3$ legs on 3 insects; there are $6 \cdot 108$ legs on 108 insects; there are 6 million legs on 1 million insects

34. $\dfrac{a}{b} \cdot \dfrac{b}{a} = 1$

35. $3 (c + 10b - a^2)$
$= 3 (7 + 10 \cdot 5 - 3^2)$
$= 3 (7 + 10 \cdot 5 - 9)$
$= 3 (7 + 50 - 9)$
$= 3 (57 - 9)$
$= 3 \cdot 48$
$= 144$

36. $a [a + b (b + c)]$
$= 3 [3 + 5 (5 + 7)]$
$= 3 [3 + 5 \cdot 12]$
$= 3 [3 + 60]$
$= 3 \cdot 63$
$= 189$

37. Answers will vary depending on calculator.

    a. First 3.1415927, then (after multiplying by 100,000), 314159.27, then (after subtracting 314,159) 0.2654. The digits 654 were not originally displayed (and follow the 2 in the decimal representation of π).

    b. First, 0.0588235 (shown for $1 \div 17$), then (after multiplying by 100,000) 5882.3529, then (after subtracting 5882) 0.3529. The digits 29 were not originally displayed (and follow 35).

    c. First, 0.0769231 (shown for $1 \div 13$), then (after multiplying by 100,000) 7692.3077, then (after aubtracting 7692) 0.3076. The digits 076 were not originally displayed (and follow 23).

    d. 076923 (The work in part **c** revealed that the next 3 digits are 076. Hence, the digits repeat after the 3.)

38. **a.** is greater than or equal to ($\geq$)

    b. is less than or equal to ($\leq$)

    c. is not equal to ($\neq$)

1. $6 + 8 \cdot 7 + 9$
   $= 6 + 56 + 9$
   $= 62 + 9$
   $= 71$

2. $(40 - 5) + (60 - 10)$
   $= 35 + 50$
   $= 85$

3. $75 - 50 - 3 - 1$
   $= 25 - 3 - 1$
   $= 22 - 1$
   $= 21$

4. $5 + 3 \cdot 4^2$
   $= 5 + 3 \cdot 16$
   $= 5 + 48$
   $= 53$

5. $\dfrac{100 + 2 \cdot 5}{10 + 5}$
   $= \dfrac{100 + 10}{15}$
   $= \dfrac{110}{15}$
   $= 7.\overline{3}$
   ≈ 7

6. $x + 3y$
   $= 10 + 3 \cdot 100$
   $= 10 + 300$
   $= 310$

7. $(a + b)(b - a)$
   $= (3 + 4)(4 - 3)$
   $= 7 \cdot 1$
   $= 7$

8. $y + 5[y + 4(y + 3)]$
   $= 100 + 5[100 + 4(100 + 3)]$
   $= 100 + 5[100 + 4 \cdot 103]$
   $= 100 + 5[100 + 412]$
   $= 100 + 5 \cdot 512$
   $= 100 + 2560$
   $= 2660$

9. a, $((4 \cdot 2)^2 = 8^2 = 64$, so 2 is a solution.
   $(4 \cdot 4)^2 = 16^2 = 256$, so 4 is not a solution.
   $(4 \cdot 8)^2 = 32^2 = 1024$, so 8 is not a solution.
   $(4 \cdot 16)^2 = 64^2 = 4096$, so 16 is not a
   solution.)

10. $10 \cdot a = 6 \cdot a + 4 \cdot a$

11. $a + b = b + a$

12. In p years, we expect the town to grow by
    $p \cdot 200$ people.

13. $c = 20n + 5$
    $= 20 \cdot 5 + 5$
    $= 100 + 5$
    $= 105¢$

14. $c = 20n + 5$
    $= 20 \cdot 9 + 5$
    $= 180 + 5$
    $= 185¢$
    $= \$1.85$

15. 12×16 (or 16×12)

16. $47 + 40$ (or $40 + 47$)

17. $n < 0$

18. $9/a$ 19. p, s, and c

20. $p = s - c$
    $= \$45 - \$22.37$
    $= \$22.63$

21. b, $\left(\dfrac{W}{W + L} = \dfrac{W}{(W + L)} = W/(W + L) \right)$

22. c, (See table on page 139.)

23. b

24. $6 \cdot 7 = 42$, so $x = 7$

25. Many possible answers. Sample: -4.2, -4.9,
    $-4\frac{1}{2}$ (Any number between -5 and -4 is a
    solution.)

26. Many possible answers. Sample: If width is
    3 inches and length is 4 feet, the area is not
    12 of either unit, even though $A = LW$.

27. $x = 7 \cdot 3 = 21$

28.

29. $4.5 \le y < 6$ (all numbers between 4.5 and 6,
    including 4.5 but not including 6)

30. Many possible answers. Samples: If you are 10 years old, your sister is $10 - 5$, or 5, years old. If you are 14 years old, your sister is $14 - 5$, or 9, years old.

31. $30 \cdot 2/5 = 6 \cdot 2.$ $30 \cdot 8/5 = 6 \cdot 8.$

CHAPTER 4 REVIEW (pp. 183-185)

1. $234 - 5 \times 4$
$= 235 - 20$
$= 215$

2. $32 \div 16 \div 8 \times 12$
$= 2 \div 8 \times 12$
$= .25 \times 12$
$= 3$

3. $2 + 3^4$
$= 2 + 81$
$= 83$

4. $4 \times 2^3 + \dfrac{28}{56}$
$= 4 \times 8 + \dfrac{28}{56}$
$= 32 + .5$
$= 32.5$

5. $5 + 8 \times 3 + 2$
$= 5 + 24 + 2$
$= 29 + 2$
$= 31$

6. $100 - \dfrac{80}{5} - 1$
$= 100 - 16 - 1$
$= 84 - 1$
$= 83$

7. $6 + 8 (12 + 7)$
$= 6 + 8 \cdot 19$
$= 6 + 152$
$= 158$

8. $40 - 30/(20 - 10/2)$
$= 40 - 30/(20 - 5)$
$= 40 - 30/15$
$= 40 - 2$
$= 38$

9. $1984 - (1947 - 1929)$
$= 1984 - 18$
$= 1966$

10. $(6 + 3) (6 - 4)$
$= 9 \cdot 2$
$= 18$

11. $3 + [2 + 4 (6 - 3 \cdot 2)]$
$= 3 + [2 + 4 (6 - 6)]$
$= 3 + [2 + 4 \cdot 0]$
$= 3 + [2 + 0]$
$= 3 + 2$
$= 5$

12. $4 [7 - 2 (2 + 1)]$
$= 4 [7 - 2 \cdot 3]$
$= 4 [7 - 6]$
$= 4 \cdot 1$
$= 4$

13. $\dfrac{4 + 5 \cdot 2}{13 \cdot 5}$
$= \dfrac{4 + 10}{65}$
$= \dfrac{14}{65}$
$= .215 \ldots$

14. $\dfrac{3^3}{3^2}$
$= \dfrac{27}{9}$
$= 3$

15. $6x = 6 \cdot 4 = 24$

16. $3m + (m + 2)$
$= 3 \cdot 7 + (7 + 2)$
$= 3 \cdot 7 + 9$
$= 21 + 9$
$= 30$

17. $2 + a + 11$
$= 2 + 5 + 11$
$= 7 + 11$
$= 18$

18. $3x^2$
$= 3 \cdot 10^2$
$= 3 \cdot 100$
$= 300$

19. $2 (a + b - c)$
$= 2 (11 + 10 - 9)$
$= 2 (21 - 9)$
$= 2 (12)$
$= 24$

20. $x^3 + 2^y$
$= 5^3 + 2^5$
$= 125 + 32$
$= 157$

21. $(3m + 5)(2m - 4)$
$= (3 \cdot 6 + 5)(2 \cdot 6 - 4)$
$= (18 + 5)(12 - 4)$
$= 23 \cdot 8$
$= 184$

22. $(3m + 5) - (2m + 4)$
$= (3 \cdot 6 + 5) - (2 \cdot 6 + 4)$
$= (18 + 5) - (12 + 4)$
$= 23 - 16$
$= 17$

23. $\dfrac{3a + 2b}{2a + 4b}$

$= \dfrac{3 \cdot 1 + 2 \cdot 2.5}{2 \cdot 1 + 4 \cdot 2.5}$

$= \dfrac{3 + 5}{2 + 10}$

$= \dfrac{8}{12}$

$= .\overline{6}$

24. $x + [1 + x(2 + x)]$
$= 7 + [1 + 7(2 + 7)]$
$= 7 + [1 + 7 \cdot 9]$
$= 7 + [1 + 63]$
$= 7 + 64$
$= 71$

25. b, $(3 \cdot 15 + 11 = 45 + 11 = 56$, so 15 is not a solution. $3 \cdot 5 + 11 = 15 + 11 = 26$, so 5 is a solution. $3 \cdot 45 + 11 = 135 + 11 = 146$, so 45 is not a solution. $3 \cdot 37 + 11 = 111 + 11 = 122$, so 37 is not a solution.)

26. a, (-4 is to the right of -5. The other numbers are to the left, so they are less than -5.)

27. $x = 4$ $(3 \cdot 4 = 12)$

28. $t = 1$ $(100 - 1 = 99)$

29. $y = 2$ $(2 + 8 = 10)$

30. $m = 5$ $(5 \cdot 4 = 20)$

31. Powering is done before multiplication.

32. False; inside parentheses are worked first.

33. d, $\left(\dfrac{30 + 5}{30 - 5} = \dfrac{(30 + 5)}{(30 - 5)} = (30 + 5)/ \right.$

$\left. (30 - 5) \right)$

34. b, $(10 - (7 - 2) = 10 - 5 = 5$, but $10 - 7 - 2 = 3 - 2 = 1$. $(4 \cdot 87 \cdot 0) + 5 = (348 \cdot 0) + 5 = 0 + 5 = 5$, and $4 \cdot 87 \cdot 0 + 5 = 348 \cdot 0 + 5 = 0 + 5 = 5$.
$10/(5 - 2^2)/2 = 10/(5 - 4)/2 = 10/1/2 = 10/2 = 5$, but $10/5 - 2^2/2 = 10/5 - 4/2 = 2 - 2 = 0$. $(9 \cdot 3)^2 = 27^2 = 729$, but $9 \cdot 3^2 = 9 \cdot 9 = 81$)

35. $5 \cdot x + 9 \cdot x = 14 \cdot x$

36. $a + b - c = a - c + b$

37. $\dfrac{a}{9} + \dfrac{b}{9} + \dfrac{a + b}{9}$

38. Many possible answers. Samples:
$5(3 + 4) = 5 \cdot 3 + 5 \cdot 4$;
$5(.5 + 1) = 5 \cdot .5 + 5 \cdot 1$

39. Many possible answers. Samples:
$2 + 6 = 1 + 6 + 1$;
$2 + \dfrac{3}{4} = 1 + \dfrac{3}{4} + 1$

40. Many possible answers. Samples:
$2 \cdot 4 - 3 = 4 \cdot 2 - 3$;
$100 \cdot 6 - 9 = 6 \cdot 100 - 9$

41. If the weight is w ounces, the postage is $s + 20 \cdot w$ cents.

42. p people have $p \cdot 10$ fingers.

43. $18 + 27$ (or $27 + 18$)

44. $100,000 - 15$

45. $4 \times 20 - 1$ (or $20 \times 4 - 1$)

46. $7 - 6$

47. $2x + 7$

48. $\dfrac{n}{6} - 3$

49. $x < 5$

50. $39n$

51. $I = 100 \, m/c$
$= 100 \cdot 7/5.5$
$= 700/5.5$
$= 127.\overline{27}$
≈ 127

52. $F = 1.8c + 32$
$= 1.8 \cdot 10 + 32$
$= 18 + 32$
$= 50$

53. $A = bh$
$= 12 \text{ in.} \cdot 6 \text{ in.}$
$= 72 \text{ in.}^2$
or
$A = bh$
$= 1 \text{ ft} \cdot .5 \text{ ft}$
$= .5 \text{ ft}^2$

54. $C = 0.6n + 4$
$= 0.6 \cdot 25 + 4$
$= 15 + 14$
$= 19°$

In 55-62, remember that an open circle on the graph indicates that the number is *not* a solution, while a filled-in circle means that the number *is* a solution.

55.
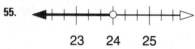
23   24   25

56.
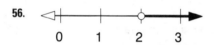
0   1   2   3

57.

-4   -2   0   2

58.
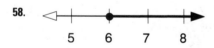
5   6   7   8

59. $y \geq 2$
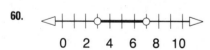
0   1   2   3   4

60.
0   2   4   6   8   10

61.
-3   -2   -1   0   1   2

62. $0 < x \leq 3$

63. **, ↑ (These are used in powering.)

64. c, (François Viète is considered "the father of algebra.")

Chapter 5   Patterns Leading to Addition

LESSON 5-1   (pp. 186-187)

1. A model for an operation is a general pattern including many uses of the operation.

2. An addend is a number to be added.

3. When a count or measure x is put together with a count or measure y with the same units and no overlap, the result is a count or measure $x + y$.

4. Many possible answers. Sample: If two letters weigh 15 g and 32 g, then the total weight is 47 g.

5. Many possible answers. Sample: If you bike 1/4 mile and 1/2 mile, then altogether you have biked (1/4 + 1/2) miles.

6. $M + 60 = 108$ (or $60 + M = 108$)

7. Both are. If you change the units to pieces of fruit, then Carla is right. If you do not change the units, Peter is right.

8. 3.04 m (Change 4 cm to .04 m.), or 304 cm (Change 3 m to 300 cm.)

9. (1) 13 pieces ($8 + 5 = 13$)
(2) 49,050,525 people ($11,847,186 + 37,203,339 = 47,050,525$)
(3) $3.13 ($2.95 + $0.18)
(4) 27% ($20\% + 7\% = 27\%$)
(5) 5.25 lb $\left(2\frac{1}{2} + 2\frac{3}{4} = 2.5 + 2.75 = 5.25\right)$

10. Not enough information is given. (The amount of money Diane has is an overlap, so addition does not answer the question.)

11. $15 + r = 43$ (or $r + 15 = 43$)

12. $23\frac{1}{2} + 45 = T$ (or $45 + 23\frac{1}{2} = T$)

13. $M + 112 \leq 250$ (or $112 + M \leq 250$)

14. 40 (change 3 ft to 36 in. $36 + 4 = 40$)

15. 109 (change 6 lb to 96 oz. $96 + 13 = 109$)

16. 4351 (change 4 m to 4000 mm $4000 + 351 = 4351$)

17. 2100 (change 2 kg to 2000 g. $100 + 2000 = 2100$)

18. 4 (Addition alone does not give the answer. The brothers are an overlap. Altogether, the children are: Jane, Joan, and *just* 2 boys.)

19. $b + s + 1$ (1 is added to account for Michelle.)

20. **a.** Yes

b. Some students may be in more than one activity.

21. No, rain (or snow) and sun could appear on the same day.

22. 12 (There are 10 numbers in the "Total" column, 3 in the "Total" row. But one of these numbers is in both. Don't count it twice.)

23. Mountain region

24. 3 (The total of South Atlantic urban and rural populations; the total of all urban populations; and the total of all regions, urban and rural)

25. a, b, d, f (35.2 is between 0 and 50. 0 is a solution because $0 \leq x$ means 0 is included. -4 is not between 0 and 50. $\frac{1}{100}$ is between 0 and 50. 50 is not a solution because $x < 50$ means 50 is not included. $60\% = .6$, and .6 is between 0 and 50.)

26. $99.3\% = .993 \approx 1$

27. 3 ($4 + 3 = 7$)

28. **a.** A right angle has 90°.

b. A half circle has $\frac{360°}{2} = 180°$.

c. An acute angle has less than 90° (and more than 0°).

29. True (-10 is to the left of -8 on a horizontal number line.)

30. **a.** -6

b. 0

31. $\frac{3}{10}$ is larger. $\left(\frac{3}{10} = .3; \frac{29}{97} = .298 \ldots\right)$

32. Every answer in the "Total" column is wrong except for the South Atlantic entry. From top to bottom, the correct totals in this column are: 11,841,663; 37,199,040; 40,252,476; 16,319,187; 30,671,337 (already correct); 12,803,470; 19,320,560; 8,281,562; 26,522,631; 203,211,926.

33. There is overlap in the volumes of the sugar and water when they are combined.

34.

16	3	2	13
5	10	11	8
9	6	7	12
4	15	14	1

LESSON 5-2 (pp. 193-197)

1. $\frac{16}{4}$ km or 4 km $\left(\frac{7}{4} + \frac{9}{4} = \frac{7+9}{4} = \frac{16}{4} = 4\right)$

2. $\frac{8}{2}$ cups or 4 cups $\left(\frac{5}{2} + \frac{3}{2} = \frac{5+3}{2} = \frac{8}{2} = 4\right)$

3. **a.** $1/3 + 1/4$

b. Many possible answers. Sample: 2/6, 3/9, 4/12, 5/15, 6/18

c. MPA. Sample. 2/8, 3/12, 4/16, 5/20, 6/24

d. $\frac{7}{12}$ $\left(\frac{1}{3} + \frac{1}{4} = \frac{4}{12} + \frac{3}{12} = \frac{4+3}{12} = \frac{7}{12}\right)$

4. **a.** Many possible answers. Sample: 35 ($7 \times 5 = 35$)

b. $\frac{2}{7} + \frac{3}{5}$

$= \frac{10}{35} + \frac{21}{35}$

$= \frac{31}{35}$

5. **a.** $\frac{4}{5} + \frac{3}{10}$

$= \frac{8}{10} + \frac{3}{10}$

$= \frac{11}{10}$

b. $.8 + .3 = 1.1 = \frac{11}{10}$

$\left(\frac{4}{5} = .8, \text{ and } \frac{3}{10} = .3\right)$

6. $\frac{50}{11} + \frac{5}{11} = \frac{55}{11}$, or 5

7. $\frac{13}{x} + \frac{4}{x} = \frac{17}{x}$

8. $\frac{8}{9} + \frac{1}{15}$

$= \frac{40}{45} + \frac{3}{45}$

$= \frac{43}{45}$

9. $\frac{5}{8} + \frac{2}{5}$

$= \frac{25}{40} + \frac{16}{40}$

$= \frac{41}{40}$

10. $\frac{11}{7} + \frac{6}{7} + \frac{15}{7} = \frac{32}{7}$

11. $\frac{2}{3} + \frac{5}{3} + \frac{5}{6}$

$= \frac{4}{6} + \frac{10}{6} + \frac{5}{6}$

$= \frac{19}{6}$

12. a. $\frac{22}{5}$ (Multiply 5 by 4, and then add 2.)

b. $4\frac{2}{5}$

13. $\frac{5}{2}$ km $\left(2 + \frac{1}{2} = \frac{2}{1} + \frac{1}{2} = \frac{4}{2} + \frac{1}{2} = \frac{5}{2}\right)$,

or $2\frac{1}{2}$ km $\left(2 + \frac{1}{2} = 2\frac{1}{2}\right)$

14. $4\frac{3}{8} + 2\frac{1}{5}$

$= \frac{35}{8} + \frac{11}{5}$

$= \frac{175}{40} + \frac{88}{40}$

$= \frac{263}{40}$

15. $4\frac{3}{8} + 2\frac{2}{3}$

$= \frac{35}{8} + \frac{8}{3}$

$= \frac{105}{24} + \frac{64}{24}$

$= \frac{169}{24}$

16. $\frac{6}{7} + 3\frac{7}{12}$

$= \frac{6}{7} + \frac{43}{12}$

$= \frac{72}{84} + \frac{301}{84}$

$= \frac{373}{84}$

17. $9.75 + \frac{100}{11} + 3$

$= 9\frac{3}{4} + \frac{100}{11} + \frac{3}{1}$

$= \frac{39}{4} + \frac{100}{11} + \frac{3}{1}$

$= \frac{429}{44} + \frac{400}{44} + \frac{132}{44}$

$= \frac{961}{44}$

18. a. $1\frac{1}{2} + 2\frac{1}{4}$

$= \frac{3}{2} + \frac{9}{4}$

$= \frac{6}{4} + \frac{9}{4}$

$= \frac{15}{4}$ in., (or 3.75 in. or $3\frac{3}{4}$ in.)

b. 9 ft $3\frac{3}{4}$ in., or $111\frac{3}{4}''$ (9 ft + $3\frac{3}{4}$ in. =

108 in. + $3\frac{3}{4}$ in. = $111\frac{3}{4}$ in.)

19. 20 pieces (6 + 12 + 2 = 20)

20. 8 children (Minnie, Dennis, 4 other boys and 2 other girls)

21. 6×10^4 (Write 6. The decimal point must move 4 places to the right to get 60,000, so the exponent of 10 is 4.)

22. 166°

23. a. Many possible answers. Samples: −3, 0, 1/2

b.

24. a. Many possible answers: −1, .01, 5

b.

25. a. $\frac{1}{8} + \frac{1}{8} = \frac{2}{8} = \frac{1}{4}$

b. $\frac{1}{16} + \frac{1}{16} = \frac{2}{16} = \frac{1}{8}$

1992 Edition only: **a.** 28: 1, 2, 4, 7, 14, 28; 49: 1, 7, 49; 196: 1, 2, 4, 7, 14, 28, 49, 98, 196; **b.** 30: 1, 2, 3, 5, 6, 10, 15, 30; 40: 1, 2, 4, 5, 8, 10, 20, 40; 120: 1, 2, 3, 4, 5, 6, 8, 10, 12, 15, 20, 24, 30, 40, 60, 120; **c.** Divide the l.c.m. by each factor of each of the two numbers. The factors of the l.c.m. are all of these divisors and quotients.

LESSON 5-3 (pp. 198-201)
1. If slide x is followed by slide y, the result is slide $x + y$.
2. a slide to the right or up
3. a slide to the left or down
4. followed by
5. the net result
6. the same length but pointed left:

7. twice the length, pointed right:

8. twice the length pointed left:

9. 6/5 of the length, a little longer than what is drawn, pointed right:

10. **a.**

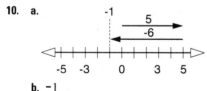
   b. $^-1$

11. **a.**
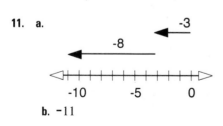
   b. $^-11$

12. 24 $\boxed{+}$ 5 $\boxed{\pm}$ $\boxed{=}$
13. 1 $\boxed{\pm}$ $\boxed{+}$ 8 $\boxed{\pm}$ $\boxed{=}$
14. **a.** $^-5 + {}^-3$ **b.** $^-8$
15. **a.** $250 + {}^-150$ **b.** 100
16. **a.** $15 + {}^-17$ **b.** $^-2$
17. **a.** $^-50 + {}^-40.27$
    b. $^-90.27$
18. **a.** $2.3 + {}^-2.3$ **b.** 0
19. Many possible answers. Sample: Joe loses seven yards in football and then loses five more; the result is a loss of twelve yards, $^-12$.
20. Many possible answers. Sample: A stock went up $\frac{3}{8}$, then down $\frac{2}{8}$; the result is a gain of $\frac{1}{8}$.
21. It goes 20 km in the opposite direction.
22. You wind up 250 ft north.
23. The temperature is $^-7°$.
24. b   **25.** a   **26.** c
27. **a.** 18% (26% + 25% + 12% + 7% + 6% + 6% = 82%; 100% − 82% = 18%)
    b. 128,000 people (12% of 1,070,000 = .12 × 1,070,000 = 128,400 ≈ 128,000)
28. **a.** $p = 100 (1 - n/g)$
         $= 100 (1 - 1/2)$
         $= 100 (1 - .5)$
         $= 100 \cdot .5$
         $= 50$
       50% discount
    b. $p = 100 (1 - n/g)$
         $= 100 (1.95/2.95)$
         $\approx 100 (1 - .661)$
         $\approx 100 (.339)$
         ≈ 33.9
       33.9% discount
29. $[40 - (4a - 10)]/4x$
     $= [40 - (4 \cdot 3.2 - 10)]/4 \cdot 1.5$
     $= [40 - (12.8 - 10)]/6$
     $= [40 - 2.8]/6$
     $= 37.2/6$
     $= 6.2$

30. $\frac{11}{6} + \frac{2}{3}$

$= \frac{11}{6} + \frac{4}{6}$

$= \frac{15}{6}$, or $\frac{5}{2}$

31. Many possible answers. Sample: 0 or 1/2

32. $h + 4 + 1 = c$ (h brothers + 4 sisters + Steve = c children)

33. **a.** 6 mi + 1000 ft = 6 · 5280 ft + 1000 ft = 31,680 ft + 1000 ft = 32,680 ft

b. 6 mi + 1000 ft = 6 mi + $\frac{1000}{5280}$ mi = $6\frac{1000}{5280}$ mi = $6\frac{25}{132}$ mi ≈ 6.189 mi

34.

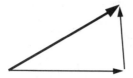

The arrows would be placed end to end. The sum is the thicker arrow.

LESSON 5-4 (pp. 202-205)

1. Adding zero to a number keeps the identity of that number.

2. 7

3. -7

4. opposite

5. -70   **6.** 13

7. 1/2

8. x

9. For any number n, $n + -n = 0$.

10. Many possible answers. Sample: 7 people came to a party, then 7 people left. The net result is that there is no change in the number at the party.

11. For any number n, $-(-n) = n$.

12. Property of Opposites

13. Additive Identity Property of Zero

14. Op-op Property

15. Property of Opposites

16. $-51 + 51 + 2 = 0 + 2 = 2$

17. $x + 0 + -x = x + -x = 0$

18. a (Apply the Property of Opposites and the Additive Identity Property of Zero.)

19. $\frac{14}{11}$ (Apply the Property of Opposites and the Additive Identity Property of Zero.)

20. **a.** -25 to = -25

b. Additive Identity Property of Zero

21. **a.** $40 + -40 = 0$

b. Property of Opposites

22. $-(-(-5)) = -(5) = -5$

23. $-(-(-(-6))) = -(-(6)) = -(6) = 6$

24. $-(-(-x)) = -(x) = -x$

25. $-(-(-7 + 1)) = -(-(-6)) = -(6) = -6$

26. 5 (Press $\boxed{\pm}$ once, and the display is -5. Press it twice, and it is 5. Press it an even number of times, and the display is 5.)

27. 3 ($-x = -(-3) = 3$)

28. 9 $-(a + b) = -(-4 + -5) = -(-9) = 9$

29. **a.** The temperature is -9°

b. $-11 + 2 = -9$

30. **a.** You are $250 in debt.

b. $-150 + -100 = -250$

31. $t + -35 = -60$

32. $y + 14.50 > 50$

33. From smallest to largest, the numbers are 9.7×10^{-5}; 3.2×10^4; 5.1×10^7 ($3.2 \times 10^4 = 32,000$; $9.7 \times 10^{-5} = .000097$; $5.1 \times 10^7 = 51,000,000$)

34. **a.** $a + \frac{c}{3} + b$

$= \frac{20}{3} + -\frac{11}{3} + \frac{17}{6}$

$= \frac{40}{6} + -\frac{22}{6} + \frac{17}{6}$

$= \frac{18}{6} + \frac{17}{6}$

$= \frac{35}{6}$

b. $\frac{35}{6}$ (already in lowest terms)

35. a. $w = 5000d\,(d + 1)$
$$= 5000 \cdot 1\,(1 + 1)$$
$$= 5000 \cdot 1 \cdot 2$$
$$= 5000 \cdot 2$$
$$= 10{,}000 \text{ lb}$$

b. $w = 5000d\,(d + 1)$
$$= 5000 \cdot \frac{1}{2}\left(\frac{1}{2} + 1\right)$$
$$= 5000 \cdot .5\,(.5 + 1)$$
$$= 5000 \cdot .5\,(1.5)$$
$$= 2500 \cdot 1.5$$
$$= 3750 \text{ lb}$$

c. $w = 5000d\,(d + 1)$
$$= 5000 \cdot \frac{9}{16}\left(\frac{9}{16} + 1\right)$$
$$= 5000 \cdot .5625\,(.5625 + 1)$$
$$= 5000 \cdot .5625\,(1.5625)$$
$$= 2812.5\,(1.5625)$$
$$\approx 4394.5 \text{ lb}$$

No, it cannot lift 5000 lb.

36. dove and hawk (war politics); bear and bull (stock market); moose and shrimp (size); tiger and mouse (aggression)

LESSON 5-5 (pp. 206-210)
1. d
2. 58   3. 4.01
4. 0   5. 11
6. $|12| = 12$ 7. $|-20| = 20$
8. $|0.0032| = 0.0032$
9. $|0| = 0$
10. **a.** positive (41 has the larger absolute value.);
    b. 1 ($41 - 40 = 1$ and the sum is positive: 1)
11. **a.** positive (7.0 has the larger absolute value.);
    b. 6.2 ($7.0 - 0.8 = 6.2$ and the sum is positive: 6.2)

12. **a.** negative
    b. $-\frac{8}{9}$ (Add the absolute values: $\frac{4}{9} + \frac{4}{9} = \frac{8}{9}$ Take the opposite: $-\frac{8}{9}$)
13. **a.** positive
    b. 13 (Simply add $6 + 7 = 13$)
14. true   **15.** true   **16.** true
17. false (If the positive number has the larger absolute value, the sum is positive.)
18. true
19. true (Absolute value is always positive.)
20. -3 (Subtract the absolute values: $6 - 3 = 3$. -6 has the larger absolute value, so the sum is negative: -3)
21. -14 (Add the absolute values: $10 + 4 = 14$. Take the opposite: -14)
22. $-.85$ (Subtract the absolute values: $1.7 - .85 = .85$. -1.7 has the larger absolute value, so the sum is negative: $-.85$)
23. $\quad -3 + 8 + -6$
$$= 5 + -6$$
$$= -1$$
24. $\quad \frac{2}{5} + -5 + \frac{3}{5}$
$$= -4\frac{3}{5} + \frac{3}{5}$$
$$= -4$$
25. $\quad -\frac{112}{3} + \frac{1}{10}$
$$= -\frac{1120}{30} + \frac{3}{30}$$
$$= -\frac{1117}{30}$$
26. $-|-2| = -(2) = -2$
27. $-\left|\frac{15}{2}\right| = -\left(\frac{15}{2}\right) = -\frac{15}{2}$
28. $|-0.74| = 0.74$
29. $|3| - |-3| = 3 + 3 = 6$
30. $|3| - |-3| = 3 - 3 = 0$

31. $\quad -|2.5| + |-6.8|$
$= -(2.5) + 6.8$
$= -2.5 + 6.8$
$= 4.3$

32. $|x + y| = |-5 + 4| = |-1| = 1$

33. true

34. false (For example, $|-4| = 4$)

35. true

36. **a.** $^-150 + 50$
b. $^-100$; You are \$100 in debt.

37. $\quad ^-c + 13$
$= ^-13 + 13$
$= 0$

38. $\quad ^-c + 13$
$= ^-(-2) + 13$
$= 2 + 13$
$= 15$

39. $\quad ^-c + 13$
$= -\left(-\dfrac{51}{6}\right) + 13$
$= \dfrac{51}{6} + \dfrac{78}{6}$
$= \dfrac{129}{6}$, or 21.5

40. $\quad ^-c + 13$
$= ^-0 + 13$
$= 0 + 13$
$= 13$

41. $n + ^-n = 0$

42. $147°$

43. $2\dfrac{1}{4}$ in. or $2\dfrac{2}{8}$ in.

44. $\quad \dfrac{(24 + 1)}{11} + \dfrac{4}{(3 + 5)}$
$= \dfrac{25}{11} + \dfrac{4}{8}$
$= \dfrac{200}{88} + \dfrac{44}{88}$
$= \dfrac{244}{88}$
$= \dfrac{61}{22}$

45. Nine 2 by 2 squares, four 3 by 3, and one 4 by 4, a total of 14

46. with horizontal and vertical sides: sixteen 1 by 1 squares, nine 2 × 2 squares, four 3 by 3 squares, and one 4 by 4 square; with "diagonal" sides: four smaller squares and one larger square; total: $16 + 9 + 4 + 1 + 4 + 1 = 35$

LESSON 5-6 (pp. 211-215)

1. $360°$

2. $360°$

3. $\dfrac{360°}{2} = 180°$

4. $\dfrac{360°}{4} = 90°$

5. counterclockwise

6. Counterclockwise turns have positive magnitudes.

7. Clockwise turns have negative magnitudes.

8. $60° + 60° = 120°$

9. $60° + 60° + 60° = 180°$

10. $^-60°$ (All small angles at 0 have same measure. Clockwise turns have negative magnitude.)

11. $^-60° + ^-60° + ^-60° + ^-60° + ^-60° = ^-300°$

12. $280°$ (Turn $360° - 80°$ in the positive direction.)

13. $90° + 35° = 125°$

14. $90° + ^-35° = 55°$

15. $^-5° + ^-6° = ^-11°$

16. $\dfrac{1°}{4} + \dfrac{1°}{2} = \dfrac{1°}{4} + \dfrac{2°}{4} = \dfrac{3°}{4}$

17. If a turn of magnitude x is followed by a turn of magnitude y, the result is a turn of magnitude $x + y$.

18. $^-27°$ (Measure $\angle BAC$.)

19. $\dfrac{360°}{3} = 120°$

20. $\dfrac{360°}{5} = 72°$

21. **a.** $2 \cdot 30° = 60°$ (or $^-300°$) (The spokes form 30-degree angles.)
b. D (2 positions counterclockwise)

22. **a.** $8 \cdot 30° = 240° \cdot$ (or $-120°$)

 b. $120°$ (or $-240°$)($240° + 120° = 360°$, a full revolution)

23. I (Each seat moves 4 positions counterclockwise, or 8 positions clockwise.)

24. **a.** $-360°$

 b. $-60°$ $\left(\dfrac{360°}{6}\text{ in clockwise, or negative,}\right.$

 $\left.\text{direction: } -60°\right)$

25. **a.** $-30°$ $\left(\dfrac{360°}{12}\text{ in clockwise direction: } -30°\right)$

 b. $-5°$ $\left(\dfrac{30°}{6}\text{ in clockwise direction: } -5°\right)$

26. $2160°$ ($6 \cdot 360°$)

27. $45 + m = 180$ (in minutes), or $m + 3/4 = 3$ (in hours)

28. -64.2 (Subtract the absolute values: $74 - 9.8 = 64.2$. -74 has the larger absolute value, so the sum is negative: -64.2)

29. $\left(-\dfrac{2}{5} + \dfrac{2}{5}\right) + \left(-\dfrac{6}{7} + \dfrac{6}{7}\right) = 0 + 0 = 0$

30. $-(-(2 + -4))$
 $= -(-(-2))$
 $= -(2)$
 $= -2$

31. $|7| + |-4|) \cdot 5$
 $= (7 + 4) \cdot 5$
 $= 11 \cdot 5$
 $= 55$

32. $3 + 4 \cdot 2 + -2$
 $= 3 + 8 + -2$
 $= 11 + -2$
 $= 9$

33. $6\text{ km} = 6 \times 1000\text{ m} = 6000\text{ m}$

34. **a.** $63,200,000$

 b. 6.32×10^7 (Write 6.32. The decimal point must move 7 places to the right to get $63,200,000$, so the exponent of 10 is 7.)

35. $x + y + x = y + (x + x)$

36. $Y - 2$

37. **a.** revolutions per minute

 b. Many possible answers. Samples: car engine speeds, blender speeds, propeller speeds

LESSON 5-7 (pp. 216-220)

1. Many possible answers. Sample: $3 + 2.4 = 2.4 + 3$

2. Many possible answers. Sample: $(12 + 95) + 5 = 12 + (95 + 5)$

3. Associative Property of Addition

4. a, (Only the order of the numbers is changed.)

5. b, (Only the order of the operations is changed.)

6. a, (Only the order of the numbers is changed.)

7. c, (The order of the numbers is changed. The order of the operations also is changed because in the expression on the left, $1 + 2$ is done first, but in the expression on the right $3 + 2$ is done first.)

8. 19th century

9. Many possible answers. Sample: gaining and losing weight

10. **a.** $400 + 102 + -35 + -75 + 40 + -200$

 b. \$232 (($400 + 102 + 40$) + ($-35 + -75 + -200$) $= 542 + -310 = 232$)

11. 12 (Group -1 and -4 together.)

12. -6 (Rearrange and regroup: $(0 + 4 + 1) + (-3 + -2 + -6)$)

13. 0 (Rearrange and regroup: $(99 + -99) + (-46 + 46) + (12 + -12)$)

14. $-\dfrac{3}{8} + -\dfrac{3}{8} + \dfrac{40}{3} + -\dfrac{3}{8} + -\dfrac{3}{8} + \dfrac{40}{3}$

 $= \left(\dfrac{40}{3} + \dfrac{40}{3}\right) + \left(-\dfrac{3}{8} + -\dfrac{3}{8} + -\dfrac{3}{8} + -\dfrac{3}{8}\right)$

 $= \dfrac{80}{3} + -\dfrac{12}{8}$

 $= \dfrac{640}{24} + -\dfrac{36}{24}$

 $= \dfrac{604}{24}$

 $= \dfrac{151}{6}$, or $25.1\overline{6}$

15. They are $10.25 over budget. ((12.50 + 21) + (-6.30 + -7.05 + -9.90))

16. 9° ((50 + 120 + 17) + (-75 + -103))

17. $\dfrac{a + b + c + d}{4}$

$= \dfrac{-1 + 6 + 3 + -4}{4}$

$= \dfrac{(6 + 3) + (-1 + -4)}{4}$

$= \dfrac{9 + -5}{4}$

$= \dfrac{4}{4}$

$= 1°$

18. **a.** Many possible answers. Sample:
    $5 - 3 \neq 3 - 5$
    b. Subtraction is not commutative.

19. **a.** Many possible answers. Sample:
    $(9 - 6) - 2 \neq 9 - (6 - 2)$
    b. Subtraction is not associative.

20. a, (Order of addends is changed.)

21. b, (Order of operations is changed.)

22. **a.** $\dfrac{360°}{4} = 90°$ **b.** right

23. **a.** $\dfrac{360°}{6} = 60°$ **b.** acute

24. $\dfrac{360°}{2} = 180°$

25. -60° ($\dfrac{360°}{6}$ in clockwise, or negative, direction: -60°)

26. *H* (Each seat moves 5 positions counterclockwise, or 7 positions clockwise.)

27. 8453 g (8000 g + 453 g), or 8.453 kg (8 kg + .453 kg)

28. 3 pt (2 pt + 1 pt), or 1.5 qt (1 qt + .5 qt)

29. $t - 3$ degrees

30. There is not enough information. Lori's tickets are an overlap.

31. For any number a, $a + -a = 0$.

32. opposite

33. 6 (6 + 45 = 51)

34. $-5 + 6 (3.7 + 1.3/2) - 4$
    $= -5 + 6 (3.7 + .65) - 4$
    $= -5 + 6 \cdot 4.35 - 4$
    $= -5 + 26.1 - 4$
    $= 21.1 - 4$
    $= 17.1$

35. **a.** 378804 (Key in 203275 $\boxed{+}$ 89635 $\boxed{\pm}$ $\boxed{+}$ 265164 $\boxed{=}$.)
    b. hOBBLE
    c. Many possible answers. (Sample: -999 + -2 + 4046 (ShOE, turned 180°, is 3045. The sum of the three numbers chosen must be 3045.)

LESSON 5-8 (pp. 221-225)

1. 5

2. a variable (letter)

3. **a.** yes (6 was added to both sides of the equation.)
   b. yes (-1 was added to both sides of the equation.)
   c. yes (17.43 was added to both sides of the equation.)
   d. Addition Property of Equality

4. **a.** Addition Property of Equality
   b. Property of Opposites
   c. Additive Identity Property of Zero
   d. arithmetic computation

5. **a.** -86
   b. $x + 86 = 230$
   $x + 86 + -86 = 230 + -86$
   $x + 0 = 230 + -86$
   $x = 144$
   c. 144 + 86 = 230

6. **a.** 12
   b. $-12 + y = 7$
   $12 + -12 + y = 12 + 7$
   $0 + y = 12 + 7$
   $y = 19$
   c. $-12 + 19 = 7$

7. **a.** $-\frac{22}{3}$

b.
$$60 = z + \frac{22}{3}$$
$$60 + -\frac{22}{3} = z + \frac{22}{3} + -\frac{22}{3}$$
$$\frac{180}{3} + -\frac{22}{3} = z + 0$$
$$\frac{158}{3} = z$$

c. $60 = \frac{158}{3} + \frac{22}{3} \left(\frac{180}{3} = 60 \right)$

8. **a.** 3.2

b.
$$-5.9 = A + -3.2$$
$$-5.9 + 3.2 = A + -3.2 + 3.2$$
$$-5.9 + 3.2 = A + 0$$
$$-2.7 = A$$

c. $-5.9 = -2.7 + -3.2$

9. b, (In a, c, and d, the equations mean, "the sum of 13 and x is -6." In b, the equation means, "the sum of -6 and x is 13."

10. **a.** $-15 + c = -20$

b.
$$-15 + c = -20$$
$$15 + -15 + c = 15 + -20$$
$$0 + c = 15 + -20$$
$$c = -5$$

c. $-15 + -5 = -20$

11. $5°$ $(-2 + 5 = 3)$

12. Commutative Property of Addition

13.
$$A + 43 + -5 = 120$$
$$A + 38 = 120$$
$$A + 38 + -38 = 120 + -38$$
$$A + 0 = 120 + -38$$
$$A = 82$$

14.
$$-35 = 16 + d + 5$$
$$-35 = 21 + d$$
$$-21 + -35 = -21 + 21 + d$$
$$-21 + -35 = 0 + d$$
$$-56 = d, \text{ or } d = -56$$

15.
$$I = F + M + C$$
$$40{,}325 = 18{,}800 + 20{,}500 + C$$
$$40{,}325 = 39{,}300 + C$$
$$-39{,}300 + 40{,}325 = -39{,}300 + 39{,}300 + C$$
$$-39{,}300 + 40{,}325 = 0 + C$$
$$1025 = C, \text{ or } C = 1025$$
The children earned $1025.

16. Let i represent the amount of interest.
$$103.52 + 35 + -12.50 + i = 130.05$$
$$126.02 + i = 130.05$$
$$-126.02 + 126.02 + i = -126.02 + 130.05$$
$$0 + i = -126.02 + 130.05$$
$$i = 4.03$$
$4.03 interest was paid.

17. **a.** $G + 10$

b. $W + 10$

c. $G = W$

d. If $G = W$, then $G + 10 = W + 10$

e. Addition Property of Equality

18.
$$a + b = c$$
$$-a + a + b = -a + c$$
$$0 + b = -a + c$$
$$b = -a + c (\text{or } b = c + -a)$$

19. Step 1: Associative Property of Addition;
Step 2: Commutative Property of Addition;
Step 3: Associative Property of Addition;
Step 4: Property of Opposites;
Step 5: Additive Identity Property of Zero

20. $(4 \cdot 3 - 2 \cdot 1)(4 \cdot 3 + 2 \cdot 1)$
$$= (12 - 2)(12 + 2)$$
$$= 10 \cdot 14$$
$$= 140$$

21. **a.** Many possible answers. Sample: -4

b. Many possible answers. Sample: 2

22.

23. 30

24. $\frac{\pi}{16}$ = .4375 ≈ .44 (.4375 is between .43 and .44 and is nearer to .44.)

25.

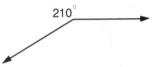

210°

26. a 360 $\frac{5}{8}$° turn, or a $\frac{5}{8}$° turn ($210\frac{1}{2}$° + $150\frac{1}{8}$° = $210\frac{4}{8}$° + $150\frac{1}{8}$° = $360\frac{5}{8}$°. The resulting position is only a $\frac{5}{8}$° turn from the original position.)

27.

_____

28. $3n$

29. $t - 5$

30. $\frac{B}{2C}$ or $B/(2C)$

31. the ray with endpoint A containing B

32. The measure of angle LNP is thirty-five degrees.

33.   347
       619
     _612_
      1578

34. **a.** It subtracts B from A.

b. yes

c. yes

d. Change line 30 to X = (A + B)/2

LESSON 5-9 (pp. 226-229)

1. $\overleftrightarrow{AB}$

2. All points on line CD between C and D and including C and D

3. $\overline{FE}$ or $\overline{EF}$

4. **a.** Several possible answers. Samples: *GAME* or *AGEM*

b. $\overline{GA}$ (or $\overline{AG}$), $\overline{AM}$ (or $\overline{MA}$), $\overline{ME}$ (or $\overline{EM}$), $\overline{EG}$ (or $\overline{GE}$)

c. *G, A, M, E*

d. ∠*G*, ∠*A*, ∠*M*, ∠*E*

e. quadrilateral

5. pentagon   **6.** hexagon   **7.** heptagon

8. octagon   **9.** nonagon   **10.** decagon

11. 11-gon   **12.** *n*-gon   **13.** triangle

14. quadrilateral   **15.** 26-gon

16. 4302-gon   **17.** 12   **18.** 10, 10, 10

19. **a.** Many possible answers. Sample: *POLYGN, LOPNGY, GNPOLY*

b. hexagon

20. quadrilateral

21. nonagon

22. The Pentagon

23. **a.**   **b.** 5

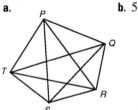

$\overline{PR}, \overline{PS}, \overline{QT}, \overline{QS}, \overline{TR}$

24. **a**   **b.** 9

25. c

26. d, (In a, b, and c, the equations mean, "the sum of 60 and y is 23." But in d, the equation means, "the sum of 23 and y is 60.")

27.
$$x + 12 = -10$$
$$x + 12 + -12 = -10 + -12$$
$$x + 0 = -10 + -12$$
$$x = -22$$

$$-22 + 12 = -10$$

28.
$$300 = 172 + (45 + w)$$
$$300 = (172 + 45) + w$$
$$300 = 217 + w$$
$$-217 + 300 = 0 + w$$
$$83 = w$$

$$300 = 172 + (45 + 83)$$

29. Step 1: Addition Property of Equality
Step 2: Property of Opposites
Step 3: Additive Identity Property of Zero

30. **a.** 8 ft = 96 in., so an equation is $s + 3 = 96$.
b.
$$s + 3 = 96$$
$$s + 3 + -3 = 96 + -3$$
$$s + 0 = 96 + -3$$
$$s = 93$$

31. **a.** 8 (For each vertex, there are 2 names that have that vertex listed first. $2 \times 4 = 8$
b. 10 (For each vertex, there are 2 names that have that vertex listed first. $2 \times 5 = 10$)

LESSON 5-10 (pp. 230-234)
1. 436 miles ($241 + 195 = 436$)
2. the Putting-together Model
3. **a.** a line through P and Q
b.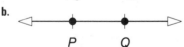
4. **a.** ray from P through Q
b.

5. **a.** line segment from P to Q
b.

![P Q segment]
P Q

6. **a.** length of segment PQ
b. picture not possible
7. $8(5 + 3)$ **8.** $x + y$
9. $x + 3$
10. $14.3 + t = v$
11. The perimeter of a polygon is the sum of the lengths of its sides.
12. 11 mm + 20 mm + 20 mm + 29 mm + 21 mm = 101 mm
13. x ft + 243 ft + 300 ft = $(x + 543)$ft
14. **a.** $x + 543 = 689$
b.
$$x + 543 = 689$$
$$x + 543 + -543 = 689 + -543$$
$$x = 146$$
146 feet
15. **a.** $9 + 9 + 5 + 5 + x = 30$
b. $9 + 9 + 5 + 5 + x = 30$
$$28 + x = 30$$
$$-28 + 28 + x = -28 + 30$$
$$x = 2$$
16. **a.** $2800 + 650 + x = 10{,}000$
b.
$$2800 + 650 + x = 10{,}000$$
$$3450 + x = 10{,}000$$
$$-3450 + 3450 + x = -3450 + 10{,}000$$
$$x = 6550$$
6550 meters
17. 40 and 20; 30 and 30 (If two sides have length 40, then the third side has length 20: $40 + 40 + 20 = 100$. If only one side has length 40, two sides have length 30: $40 + 30 + 30 = 100$.)
18. b, ($\overrightarrow{AB}$ has endpoint A. $\overrightarrow{BA}$ has endpoint B.)
19. **a.** yes
b. 20 (All 4 sides have equal length. $4 \cdot 5 = 20$)

20. 11 in. (11 in. + 1 in. = 12 in. = 1 ft)

21.

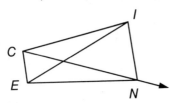

22. **a.** $E + {}^-4$ **b.** $A + {}^-4$

     c. If $E = A$, then $E + {}^-4 = A + {}^-4$.

     d. Addition Property of Equality

23. **a.** ${}^-22 + t = 10$

     b.
$$\begin{aligned} {}^-22 + t &= 10 \\ 22 + {}^-22 + t &= 22 + 10 \\ t &= 32 \end{aligned}$$

     c. ${}^-22 + 32 = 10$

24.
$$\frac{1}{50} + n = 1$$
$$-\frac{1}{50} + \frac{1}{50} + n = -\frac{1}{50} + 1$$
$$n = -\frac{1}{50} + 1$$
$$n = -\frac{1}{50} + \frac{50}{50}$$
$$n = \frac{49}{50}$$

25. **a.** ${}^-6 + {}^-(-6) = {}^-6 + 6 = 0$

     b. ${}^-(-x) + {}^-(-y) = x + y$

26. $TS = 38$ mm; $UT = 7$ mm; $UV = 47$ mm;

     $VS = 30$ mm

27. All the angles of *HIJKLM* are obtuse.

28. $\angle Q$ is acute.

29. 93°

30.

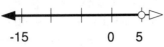

31.

32.
$$\begin{aligned} {}^-0.3 + A &= 6.3 \\ 0.3 + {}^-0.3 + A &= 0.3 + 6.3 \\ A &= 6.6 \end{aligned}$$

33. Look for 3 different numbers whose sum is 40 all of which are ≥ 10.

     10, 11, 19   11, 12, 17   12, 13, 15

     10, 12, 18   11, 13, 16

     10, 13, 17   11, 14, 15

     10, 14, 16

CHAPTER 5 PROGRESS SELF-TEST (p. 235)

1. ${}^-7$ (Subtract the absolute values: $10 - 3 = 7$. ${}^-7$ has the larger absolute value, so the sum is negative: ${}^-7$)

2. ${}^-710$ (Add the absolute values: $460 + 250 = 710$. Take the opposite: ${}^-710$)

3. ${}^-9.8 + {}^-(-1) = {}^-9.8 + 1 = {}^-8.8$

4. $x + y + {}^-x + 4 = x + {}^-x + y + 4 = 0 + y + 4 = y + 4$

5. 8

6. $2 + 1 + 0 = 3$

7. $(42 + 16) + (-6 + {}^-11 + {}^-12) = 58 + {}^-29 = 29$

8.
$$\begin{aligned} |{}^-A + 8| &= |{}^-(-3) + 8| \\ &= |3 + 8| \\ &= |11| \\ &= 11 \end{aligned}$$

9.
$$\begin{aligned} x + 43 &= 31 \\ x + 43 + {}^-43 &= 31 + {}^-43 \\ x &= {}^-12 \end{aligned}$$

10.
$$\begin{aligned} {}^-25 + y &= 12 \\ 25 + {}^-25 + y &= 25 + 12 \\ y &= 37 \end{aligned}$$

11.
$$\begin{aligned} 8 &= {}^-2 + z + {}^-5 \\ 8 &= {}^-7 + z \\ 7 + 8 &= 7 + {}^-7 + z \\ 15 &= z, \text{ or } z = 15 \end{aligned}$$

12. $\dfrac{53}{12} + \dfrac{11}{12} = \dfrac{53 + 11}{12} = \dfrac{64}{12} = \dfrac{16}{3}$

13. $\frac{5}{x} + \frac{10}{x} = \frac{5 + 10}{x} = \frac{15}{x}$

14. 9 is the common denominator.

    So $\frac{8}{3} = \frac{24}{9}$ and $\frac{17}{9} + \frac{24}{9} = \frac{41}{9}$.

15. Notice that $\frac{2}{16} = \frac{1}{8}$.

    So 8 is a common denominator.

    $\frac{2}{8} + \frac{3}{8} + \frac{1}{8} = \frac{6}{8} = \frac{3}{4}$

16. 20

17. Addition Property of Equality

18. Associative Property of Addition (Order of operations is changed.)

19. Many possible answers. Sample: $3 + 0 = 3$

20. hexagon

21. $3 \text{ cm} + 3 \text{ cm} + 4 \text{ cm} + 4 \text{ cm} + 4 \text{ cm} = 18 \text{ cm}$

22. a, (b is a segment, c is a ray, and d is a line)

23. $m + n = 50$

24. $-20 + c = 150$

25. $\qquad -20 + c = 150$
    $20 + -20 + c = 20 + 150$
    $\qquad\qquad c = 170$

26. $MP = MA + AP = 16 + 8 = 24$

27. $MA + PA = MP$, so $2.3 + PA = 3$.
    $\qquad 2.3 + PA = 3$
    $-2.3 + 2.3 + PA = -2.3 + 3$
    $\qquad\qquad PA = .7$

28.

29. $5 \text{ m} + 3 \text{ cm} = 5 \text{ m} + .03 \text{ m} = 5.03 \text{ m}$

30. Positive, since the absolute value of the second addend is larger than the absolute value of the first addend.

31. $\frac{360°}{5} = 72°$

32. Clockwise turn of $72° + 72°$ has a magnitude of $-144°$.

33. $-50° + 250° = 200°$ ($200°$ counterclockwise turn)

34. b, $\overline{WY}$ ($\overline{WY}$ is a diagonal.)

CHAPTER 5 REVIEW (pp. 237-239)

1. -12 (Subtract the absolute values: $16 - 4 = 12$. -16 has the larger absolute value, so the sum is negative: -12)

2. -24 (Add the absolute values: $7 + 8 + 9 = 24$. Take the opposite: -24)

3. $7 + -2.4 + 5 = 7 + 5 + -2.4 = 12 + -2.4 = 9.6$ (Subtract the absolute values: $12 - 2.4 = 9.6$. 12 has the larger absolute value, so the sum is positive: 9.6)

4. 1 (Subtract the absolute values: $32 - 31 = 1$. 32 has the larger absolute value, so the sum is positive: 1)

5. $\frac{6}{11} + \frac{5}{11} = \frac{11}{11} = 1$

6. 0

7. $6 + -\frac{8}{9} = \frac{54}{9} + -\frac{8}{9} = \frac{46}{9}$ (Write 6 as $\frac{6}{1}$. Then multiply numerator and denominator by 9 to change it to $\frac{54}{9}$.)

8. $\frac{2}{3} + \frac{6}{7} = \frac{14}{21} + \frac{18}{21} = \frac{32}{21}$ (Use 21 for the common denominator. Multiply the numerator and denominator of $\frac{2}{3}$ by 7; multiply the numerator and denominator of $\frac{6}{7}$ by 3.)

9. $\frac{1}{2} + \frac{1}{3} + \frac{1}{4} = \frac{6}{12} + \frac{4}{12} + \frac{3}{12} = \frac{13}{12}$ (Use 12 for the common denominator. Multiply the numerator and denominator of $\frac{1}{2}$ by 6; multiply the numerator and denominator of $\frac{1}{3}$ by 4; multiply the numerator and denominator of $\frac{1}{4}$ by 3.)

10. $\frac{40}{c} + \frac{-10}{c} = \frac{40 + -10}{c} = \frac{30}{c}$

11. 12 **12.** 4

13. $0 + 3 + 5 = 8$ **14.** $-7 + 4 = -3$

15. $-(-(-17)) = -(17) = -17$

16. $-(-4) + 3 = 4 + 3 = 7$

17. -40

18. $(86 + {}^-14) + (-86 + 14) = (86 + {}^-86) +$
$(-14 + 14) = 0 + 0 = 0$

19. $-\left(-\left(0 + \frac{2}{7}\right)\right) = -\left(-\left(\frac{2}{7}\right)\right) = -\left(-\frac{2}{7}\right) = \frac{2}{7}$

20. $\frac{11}{4} + y + {}^-\frac{11}{4} = \frac{11}{4} + {}^-\frac{11}{4} + y =$
$0 + y = y$

21. $-a + 6 = -(-42) + 6 = 42 + 6 = 48$

22. $b + {}^-b = 2 + {}^-2 = 0$

23. $\quad x + {}^-32 = {}^-12$
$x + {}^-32 + 32 = {}^-12 + 32$
$\quad\quad\quad x = 20$

24. $\quad\quad 6.3 = t + 2.9$
$6.3 + {}^-2.9 = t + 2.9 + {}^-2.9$
$\quad\quad 3.4 = t, \text{ or } t = 3.4$

25. $\quad\quad \frac{10}{3} + y = \frac{1}{3}$
$-\frac{10}{3} + \frac{10}{3} + y = -\frac{10}{3} + \frac{1}{3}$
$\quad\quad\quad y = -\frac{9}{3}$
$\quad\quad\quad y = {}^-3$

26. $0 + a = 4 + 1$
$\quad\quad a = 5$

27. $3 + c + {}^-5 = 36$
$\quad {}^-2 + c = 36$
$2 + {}^-2 + c = 2 + 36$
$\quad\quad\quad c = 38$

28. $\quad\quad {}^-8 = 14 + (d + {}^-6)$
$\quad\quad {}^-8 = 14 + {}^-6 + d$
$\quad\quad {}^-8 = 8 + d$
$\quad {}^-8 + {}^-8 = {}^-8 + 8 + d$
$\quad\quad {}^-16 = d, \text{ or } d = {}^-16$

29. $\quad\quad x + y = 180$
$x + y + {}^-y = 180 + {}^-y$
$\quad\quad\quad x = 180 + {}^-y$

30. $\quad\quad a + b + c = p$
$a + b + c + {}^-a + {}^-b = p + {}^-a + {}^-b$
$a + {}^-a + b + {}^-b + c = p + {}^-a + {}^-b$
$\quad 0 + 0 + c = p + {}^-a + {}^-b$
$\quad\quad\quad c = p + {}^-a + {}^-b$

31. $3 \cdot 4 = 12$

32. $12 + 18 + 20 + 7 + 23 = 80$

33. $6.4 \text{ cm} + 1 \text{ cm} + 6.4 \text{ cm} + 1 \text{ cm} =$
$14.8 \text{ cm} \approx 15 \text{ cm}$

34. Not enough information (An octagon has 8 sides. The lengths of only 7 sides were given.)

35. $12 + 18 + 20 + 7 + x = 82$

36. Commutative Property of Addition (The order of the addends is changed.)

37. Addition Property of Equality ($\frac{1}{2}$ was added to both sides of the original equation.)

38. Property of Opposites

39. Commutative Property of Addition (The order of the addends inside the parentheses is changed.)

40. quadrilateral, not convex (A diagonal lies outside the polygon.)

41. pentagon, convex

42. 12-gon, not convex (Some diagonals lie outside the polygon.)

43. $LEAK$ (The vertices must be named in order.)

44. $\overline{LK}$ (or $\overline{KL}$) and $\overline{EA}$ (or $\overline{AE}$)

45. 4, 4

46. any of $\overline{AB}$ (or $\overline{BA}$), $\overline{BC}$ (or $\overline{CB}$), $\overline{CD}$ (or $\overline{DC}$), $\overline{DE}$ (or $\overline{ED}$), $\overline{EA}$ (or $\overline{AE}$)

47. $1\frac{1}{2} + \frac{3}{5} = M$

48. $x + y = 16$

49. $T = D + M + C$

50. $AB + BC = AC$

51. $x + 3$

52. **a.** $AB + 7.8 = 10.4$

  b. $\quad\quad AB + 7.8 = 10.4$
  $AB + 7.8 + {}^-7.8 = 10.4 + {}^-7.8$
  $\quad\quad\quad AB = 2.6$

53. a. $\frac{3}{8} + -\frac{1}{4}$

b. $\frac{1}{8}$ point increase $\left(\frac{3}{8} + -\frac{1}{4} = \frac{3}{8} + -\frac{2}{8} = \frac{1}{8}\right)$

54. a. $5 + -7 + -3$

b. -5 lb $(5 + -7 + -3 = 5 + (-7 + -3) = 5 + -10 = -5)$

55. a. $-250 + 75$

b. 175 feet below the surface
$(-250 + 75 = -175)$

56. $\quad -3 + c = -10$
$3 + -3 + c = 3 + -10$
$\qquad\qquad c = -7$

57. $135°$ (or $-225°$) (The measure of each small angle is $\frac{360°}{8} = 45°$)

58. $-90°$ (or $270°$)

59. *A*

60. a $50°$ counterclockwise turn
$(90° + -40° = 50°)$

61.

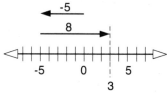

62.

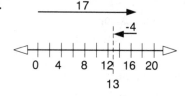

63.

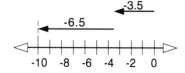

CHAPTER 6   PROBLEM-SOLVING STRATEGIES

LESSON 6-1   (pp. 242-246)

1. An algorithm is a sequence of steps that lead to a desired result.

2. Many possible answers. Sample: long division

3. A problem is a question you do not know how to answer.

4. An exercise is a question you know how to answer.

5. What is 34.2×5.67?

6. $34.2 \;\boxed{\times}\; 5.67 \;\boxed{=}$

7. Take your time.

8. Be flexible.

9. Don't give up.

10. George Polya was a mathematician famous for writing about solving problems.

11. *How to Solve It*

12. He should have tried another way.

13. She gave up instead of trying.

14. They read the problem carefully, devise a plan, carry it out, and check their work.

15. Many possible answers. Sample: Draw a picture, arrange information in tables, or think of similar problems.

16. He did not check his work and he did not take his time.

17.

AA	EA	IA	OA	UA
AE	EE	IE	OE	UE
AI	EI	II	OI	UI
AO	EO	IO	OO	UO
AU	EU	IU	OU	UU

There are 25 monograms.

18. **a.** 1

b. 0 (You can list the integers from 1 to 100 and tally how often each digit is used. Or you could reason that from 1 to 99, the digits 1-9 appear with equal frequency in the ones columns and the tens column. By including 100, the digit 1 appears one more time. While there are 2 more zeros to be tallied in 100, 0 does not appear in the tens place in any of the numbers 1-99. Yet each of the other digits appears 10 times in the tens place.)

19. 13 trains (There are 12 hours from 7 A.M. to 7 P.M., but 13 times that are *on* the hour such as 7:00 A.M., 8:00 A.M., and so on.)

20. 25 trains   21. 12 edges

22. $(5 \text{ cm})^3 = 5 \text{ cm} \cdot 5 \text{ cm} \cdot 5 \text{ cm} = 125 \text{ cm}^3$

23. $\frac{2}{3} + \frac{5}{7} - \frac{1}{14}$

$= \frac{28}{42} + \frac{30}{42} - \frac{3}{42}$

$= \frac{58}{42} - \frac{3}{42}$

$= \frac{55}{42}$

24. $5 \cdot 5280 \text{ ft} = 26,400 \text{ ft}$

25. $3 + 4a$

$= 3 + 4 \cdot 2.5$

$= 3 + 10$

$= 13$

26. **a.** $\frac{1}{10}$ **b.** $\frac{1}{4}$ **c.** $\frac{3}{4}$ **d.** $\frac{2}{3}$

27. $16.\overline{6}$ or $16\frac{2}{3}$ $(\frac{1}{6} = .1\overline{6})$

28. **a.** Los Angeles and Houston
    b. −1,233,967
    1992 Edition: **a.** Chicago, Philadelphia, and Detroit; **b.** 1,096,860

29. 51 million $(5,100,000,000 \cdot .01 = 51,000,000 = 51$ million
    1992 Edition: 53 million $(5,300,000,000 \cdot .01 = 53,000,000 = 53$ million)

30. Several possible answers. Sample:

```
      3
    782
     45
   9610
 10,440
```

LESSON 6-2 (pp. 247-250)

1. Know the meaning of all the words in the problem, sort out unneeded information, and see if there is enough information to solve the problem.

2. Yes

3. Many possible answers. Sample: the dash −

4. 7 (Its only factors are 1 and 7.)

5. 15 (Its factors are 1, 3, 5, 15.)

6. 2, 3, 5, 7, 11, 13, 17, 19, 23, 29

7. 7 $(91 \div 7 = 13)$

8. 13 $(91 \div 13 = 7)$

9. 36 $(20 + 16)$

10. "these" children

11. Not enough information is given.

12. dictionary, glossary in back of book, encyclopedia

13. (c) (The set of whole numbers includes 0; the set of integers includes 0 and the negative integers.)

14. 8, 9

15. 39 (1, 2, 3, . . . , 39)

16. 1, 2, 3, 4, 6, 9, 12, 18, 36

17. 35

18. 2 (Its only factors are 1 and 2. Besides itself and 1, each of the other numbers has at least one other factor. For example, 3 is a factor of 57, 8 is a factor of 8^6, 5 is a factor of 5×10^4.)

19. The sides must have the same length; the angles must have the same measure.

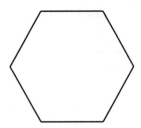

*These are solutions to questions changed in or added to the *1992 Edition.*

20. A perfect number is a number that is the sum of all its divisors other than itself. Samples: 6 (1 + 2 + 3 = 6) or 28 (1 + 2 + 4 + 7 + 14)

21. Twin primes are two consecutive odd numbers that are both primes. Sample: 29 and 31

22. 76 students (23 + 25 + 28)

23. last year (This year there are 27 + 26 + 22, or 75 students.)

24. $b + e + h$

25. Not enough information given. It depends on which is larger, $b + e + h$ or $c + f + g$.

26. Read the problem carefully, devise a plan, carry out the plan, check the work.

27. 0 is the total difference
(12 + 65 + 47 + -30 + -3 + -91 = 0)

28. $-(-(-(-y))) = -(-(y)) = -(-y) = y$

29. $5 + -(-(-3 + 4 \cdot 2))$
$= 5 + -(-(-3 + 8))$
$= 5 + -(-(5))$
$= 5 + -(-5)$
$= 5 + 5$
$= 10$

30. $x + 3 + y = y + 8$
$x + 3 + y + -y = y + 8 + -y$
$x + 3 = 8$
$x + 3 + -3 = 8 + -3$
$x = 5$

31. $\overline{BC}$ and $\overline{CD}$

32. 2 (Every other even number has at least one factor other than itself and 1. That factor is 2.)

LESSON 6-3 (pp. 251-254)

1. 14 diagonals   **2.** 21 games

3. 2 diagonals

4. 6 games (Let the vertices of a quadrilateral represent the teams. There are 6 segments that join them: 2 diagonals and 4 sides.)

5. 56 games (Let the vertices of an octagon represent the teams. There are 28 segments that join them: 20 diagonals and 8 sides. The teams play each other twice, so there will be 2 × 28, or 56 games.)

6. 20 posts

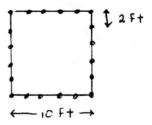

7. Wanda (Use the first sentence to arrange B, W, and J from youngest (on the left) to oldest: W B J. Add the information that J is younger than (to the left of) P: W B J P. Add the information that C is older than (to the right of) B and younger than (to the left of) J: W B C J P)

8. 228 miles (Draw $\overline{CJ}$ to represent the trip from Collinsville to Joliet. L and A represent Litchfield and Atlanta. It is given that $AJ = 114$. Also, $AJ = 3 \cdot (CL)$, so $CL = 38$. And since $CL = \frac{1}{2} \cdot (LA)$, we know that $LA = 76$. 38 + 76 + 114 = 228)

9. a. 110 ft (25 + 30 + 25 + 30)
b. 146 ft (34 + 39 + 34 + 39)

10. $6x^4 = 6 \cdot 3^4 = 6 \cdot 81 = 486$

11. 1, 2, 4, 5, 8, 10, 20, 40

12. glossary, dictionary, encyclopedia

13. 16,009 (This key sequence calculates $20^3 \cdot 2 + (5 + 4)$.)

14. 5, 6, 7, 8   15. 41, 43, 47

16. Sarah and Dana have the same amount of money.

17. If Sarah and Dana have the same amount of money, then they will still have the same amount if each receives $2 more.

18. $-(a + b) = -(-3 + 6) = -(3) = -3$

19. 30

20. 800 mm (45 cm = .45 m; 800 m = .8 m)

21. 56.83 (56.831 is between 56.83 and 56.84 and is nearer to 56.83.)

22. 3.5×10^{-8} (Write 3.5. The decimal point must move to the left 8 places to get .00000 0035, so the exponent of 10 is -8.)

23. 22 pounds (10 kg $\approx$ 10 $\cdot$ 2.2 lb $\approx$ 22 lb)

24. Many possible answers. Samples:

    $4 + 4 + 4 = 3 \cdot 4; \frac{1}{2} + \frac{1}{2} + \frac{1}{2} = 3 \times \frac{1}{2};$

    $-2 + -2 + -2 = 3 \cdot -2$

25. 12 cubes (The middle cube on each edge of the larger cube is painted on exactly 2 sides. Since there are 12 edges, there are 12 such smaller cubes.)

26. 30 games (Connect each of the 5 dots on the left to each of the 6 dots on the right.)

LESSON 6-4 (pp. 255-258)

1. Try an answer. If it doesn't work, try another one.

2. Trial and error is useful when a question has only a few possible answers.

3. 5 (When $x = 4$, $(x + 3)(x - 2) = 7 \cdot 2 = 14$, so 4 is not a solution. When $x = 5$, $(x + 3)(x - 2) = 8 \cdot 3 = 24$, so 5 is a solution. When $x = 6$, $(x + 3)(x - 2) = 9 \cdot 4 = 36$, so 6 is not a solution.)

4. 4 (Refer to trials in Question 3.)

5. 3 (When $x = 1$, $(x + 7)(x + 2)(x + 3) = 8 \cdot 3 \cdot 4 = 96$.
   When $x = 2$, $(x + 7)(x + 2)(x + 3) = 9 \cdot 4 \cdot 5 = 180$.
   When $x = 3$, $(x + 7)(x + 2)(x + 3) = 10 \cdot 5 \cdot 6 = 300$.
   When $x = 4$, $(x + 7)(x + 2)(x + 3) = 11 \cdot 6 \cdot 7 = 462$.
   When $x = 5$, $(x + 7)(x + 2)(x + 3) = 12 \cdot 7 \cdot 8 = 672$. Only 3 works.)

6. 4 (When $y = 1$, $3y - 2 + 5y = 3 \cdot 1 - 2 + 5 \cdot 1 = 6$.
   When $y = 2$, $3y - 2 + 5y = 3 \cdot 2 - 2 + 5 \cdot 2 = 14$.
   When $y = 3$, $3y - 2 + 5y = 3 \cdot 3 - 2 + 5 \cdot 3 = 22$.
   When $y - 4$, $3y - 2 + 5y = 3 \cdot 4 - 2 + 5 \cdot 4 = 30$.
   When $y = 5$, $3y - 2 + 5y = 3 \cdot 5 - 2 + 5 \cdot 5 = 38$. Only 4 works.)

7. 3 (When $A = 1$, $1 + A/3 = 1 + 1/3 = 1.\overline{3}$. When $A = 2$, $1 + A/3 = 1 + 2/3 = 1.\overline{6}$. When $A = 3$, $1 + A/3 = 1 + 3/3 = 2$. When $A = 4$, $1 + A/3 = 1 + 4/3 = 2.\overline{3}$. When $A = 5$, $1 + A/3 = 1 + 5/3 = 2.\overline{6}$. Only 3 works.)

8. 2 (When $x = 1$, $11 - x = 11 - 1 = 10$, and $7 + x = 7 + 1 = 8$.

When $x = 2$, $11 - x = 11 - 2 = 9$, and $7 + x = 7 + 2 = 9$.

When $x = 3$, $11 - x = 11 - 3 = 8$, and $7 + x = 7 + 3 = 10$.

When $x = 4$, $11 - x = 11 - 4 = 7$, and $7 + x = 7 + 4 = 11$.

When $x = 5$, $11 - x = 11 - 5 = 6$, and $7 + x = 7 + 5 = 12$. Only 2 works.)

9. Pentagon (See diagram on page 256.)

10. 7 (A hexagon has 9 diagonals. Try a heptagon. It has 14 diagonals.)

11. No (The more sides a polygon has, the more diagonals. To have 10 diagonals, a polygon must have more than 6 sides and less than 7 sides. This is impossible.)

12. Yes

13. 147, 118, 35

14. 1976 (13 is a factor of 1989. $1989 - 13 = 1976$)

15. 13 and 1

16. $-4, 0, 4$; $-4, 1, 3$; $-3, -1, 4$; $-3, 0, 3$; $-3, 1, 2$; $-2, -1, 3$; $-2, 0, 2$; $-1, 0, 1$

17. Several possible answers. Samples: 91 and 37, 82 and 28, or 73 and 19

18. 12

19. Ali (Start with the second sentence and arrange C, A, and B from youngest (on the left) to oldest: $B\ C\ A$. Add the fact that K is older than (to the right of) A and B: $B\ C\ A\ K$. Add the fact that D is older than (to the right of) C and A, and younger than (to the left of) K: $B\ C\ A\ D\ K$)

20. 12, 14, 15, 16, 18, 20, 21, 22

21. Work inside parentheses, then do powers, then multiplications or divisions from left to right, then additions or subtractions from left to right.

22. $2xy + x/z = 2 \cdot 3 \cdot 4 + 3/1.5 = 6 \cdot 4 + 2 = 24 + 2 = 26$

23.

24. $\dfrac{1}{10} + \dfrac{-2}{7} + \dfrac{7}{18}$

$= \dfrac{63}{630} + \dfrac{-180}{630} + \dfrac{245}{630}$

$= \dfrac{63 + {}^-180 + 245}{630}$

$= \dfrac{128}{630} = \dfrac{64}{315}$

25. Many possible answers. Sample: $(2 + 3) + 7 = 2 + (3 + 7)$

26. Many possible answers. Sample: $30\% \cdot 20 = .3 \cdot 20$

27. 32 inches (2.7 ft $\approx 2.7 \cdot 12$ in. ≈ 32.4 in.)

28. **a.** 0.05843 (Move the decimal point 2 places to the left.)

b. 0.058 (0.05843 is between 0.058 and 0.059 and is nearer to 0.058.)

c. 0 and 1

29. **a.** $1.4\overline{142857}$ ($99 \div 70 = 1.4\overline{142857}$)

b. 1.414 ($1.4\overline{142857}$ is between 1.414 and 1.415 and is nearer to 1.414.)

c. 1 and 2

30. Many possible answers. Sample: $97531 + 86420$ (The digits in each decimal place may be switched without affecting the sum, 183,951.)

31. **a.** The computer finds integer solutions from 1 to 100 to $(n + 3)(n - 2) = 696$.

b. Change lines 10 and 20 as follows:
```
10 FOR X = 1 TO 50
20 IF X * (X + 40) = 329 THEN PRINT X
```

c. Change lines 10 and 20 as follows:
```
10 FOR N = -100 TO 100
20 IF N * (N + 18) = 25 * (3 * N + 28)/N THEN
PRINT N
```

LESSON 6-5 (pp. 259-263)

1. 35   2. 44

3. 65 diagonals
   (12 sides: 44 + 10 = 54 diagonals;
   13 sides: 54 + 11 = 65 diagonals)

4. 97¢ (.25 + (m − 1) · .18 =
   .25 + (5 − 1) · .18 = .97)

5. $5.47 (.25 + (m − 1) · .18 =
   .25 + 29 · .18 = 5.47)

6. .25 + (m − 1) · .18 dollars

7. $21.67 (.25 + (m − 1) · .18 =
   .25 + (120 − 1) · .18 = 21.67)

8. A generalization is a statement that is true
   about many instances.

9. The cost of an m-minute call for Francie is
   .25 + (m − 1) · .18.

10.
number of sides	number of triangles
3	1
4	2
5	3
6	4
•	•
•	•
•	•
n	n − 2

If there are 50 sides, 48 triangles are
formed.

11. **a.**
number of minutes	cost
1	$1.46
2	$1.46 + .82
3	$1.46 + 2 · .82
4	$1.46 + 3 · .82
5	$1.46 + 4 · .82

   b. $1.46 + 24 · .82 = $21.14
   c. 1.42 + (m − 1) · .82 dollars

12. **a.** 25¢ + 3 · 20¢ = 85¢
   b. 25¢ + 9 · 20¢ = 205¢ = $2.05
   c. .25 + (w − 1) · .20 dollars

13. 43

14. 11 (Look up undecagon in the dictionary.)

15. $x = 7$ and $y = 3$

16. 1, 2, 3, 6, 9, 18, 27, 54

17. $5 + c = -3$
   $-5 + 5 + c = -5 + -3$
   $c = -8$
   The change is −8 lb.

18. **a.** 91.44 cm (1 yd = 3 ft = 3 × 12 in. = 36
   in. = 36 · 2.54 cm = 91.44 cm)
   b. 91 cm (91.44 is between 91 and 92 and is
   nearer to 91.)

19. **a.** The difference between consecutive squares
   increases by 2. So add 41 to 400 to get 21^2.
   b. 9 (7 · 7 = 49)
   c. Many possible answers. Sample: The square
   of an even number is even and the square of
   an odd number is odd.

20. **a.** Change line 20 to FOR M = 1 TO 10
Output:	MINUTES	COST
	1	.25
	2	.43
	3	.61
	4	.79
	5	.97
	6	1.15
	7	1.33
	8	1.51
	9	1.69
	10	1.87

   b. 10 PRINT "INTEGER", "SQUARE"
   20 FOR N = 1 TO 10
   30 S = N * N
   40 PRINT N,S
   50 NEXT N
   60 END

*21. *1992 Edition only:*

   a.
8	9	10
65,536	262,144	1,048,576

   b. the sum of the two exponents.

   c.
1	2	3	4
5	25	125	625

5	6	7
3,125	15,625	78,125

; yes

   d. $x^a · x^b = x^{(a + b)}$

LESSON 6-6 (pp. 264-268)

1. A special case of a pattern is an instance of the pattern used for some definite purpose.

2. Many possible answers.
   Sample: $-(4 + 3) = -4 + -3$

3. yes $(-(-5 + -11) = -(-16) = 16,$
   and $-(-5) + -(-11) = 5 + 11 = 16)$

4. yes $(-(4.8 + 3.25) = -(8.05) = -8.05,$ and
   $-4.8 + -3.25 = -8.05)$

5. false (Example 4 verifies this.)

6. true

7. **a.** quadrilateral
   b. yes

8. **a.** heptagon
   b. yes (Verify with a diagram that there are 4 diagonals from 1 vertex.)

9. **a.** 6
   b. yes (Verify with a diagram that there are 3 diagonals from 1 vertex.)

10. **a.** 3
    b. yes (A triangle has no diagonals)

11. An octagon has 8 sides. There should be $8 - 3$, or 5 diagonals from each vertex.

12. Move the decimal point 3 places to the left.
    (Example: $5000 \div 1000 = 5$)

13. Move the decimal point 3 places to the right
    (Example: $8 \div .001 = 8000$)

14. **a.** Many possible answers. Samples: $5^2 \geq 5,$
    $1^2 \geq 1$
    b. Many possible answers. Sample: $.2^2 = .04,$
    which is less than .2.
    c. Although many special cases are true, the general pattern may be false.

15. **a.** yes $(0 \cdot 0 - 0 = 0)$
    b. yes $(1 \cdot 1 - 1 = 0)$
    c. no $(2 \cdot 2 - 2 = 2)$
    d. no

16. (b) (Example: choose $a = 4$ and $b = 5.$
    Then $2a + 3b = 2 \cdot 4 + 3 \cdot 5 = 23.$
    But $6ab = 6 \cdot 4 \cdot 5 = 120.$)

17. **a.** Many possible answers. Sample: if $m = 2,$
    $-(-2 + 9) = -7,$ and $2 + -9 = -7.$ This case is true.
    b. Many possible answers. Sample: if
    $m = -4, -(-(-4) + 9) = -(4 + 9) = -13,$
    and $-4 + -9 = -13.$ This case is true.
    c. possibly true

18. (c) (For example, try $n = 5.$
    $1 + 2 + 3 + 4 + 5 = 15,$ and
    $n(n + 1)/2 = 5 \cdot 6/2 = 15$)

19. (b) (Draw several quadrilaterals and measure the angles.)

20. 935

21. 10 games (The games are represented by the diagonals and sides of a pentagon.)

22. 12 stakes

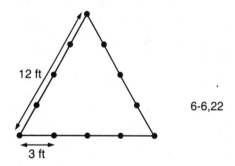

6-6,22

23. **a.** \$4.50 $(1.00 + 7 \cdot .50 = 1.00 + 3.50 = 4.50)$
    b. $1.00 + (h - 1) .50$ dollars

24. An algorithm is a sequence of steps that lead to a desired result.

25. $0.\overline{3}, 33\frac{1}{3}\%$

26.
$$14 + x = 14 + {}^-438$$
$${}^-14 + 14 + x = {}^-14 + 14 + {}^-438$$
$$x = {}^-438$$

27. perimeter

28. positive
$(|382,471.966642| > |{}^-382,471.966638|)$

29. 60, 72, 84, 90, and 96 (Each has 12 divisors.)

LESSON 6-7 (pp. 269-273)

1. $10 (2 · $5 = $10)

2. $11.72 (2.61 · $4.49 = $11.7189)

3. The same operation is used; only the numbers differ.

4. **a.** Many possible answers. Sample: If turkey is $2.00 per half pound, what is the cost for 3 pounds?

b. $12

c. The cost per half pound was multiplied by 2 (to give the cost per pound), then the result was multiplied by the number of pounds.

d. $8.57 (2 · $2.29 · 1.87 = $8.5646)

5. If you cannot do a problem with complicated numbers, try simpler numbers.

6. **a.** Many possible answers. Sample: Buzz can bike 1 mile in 10 minutes. At this rate, how far can he bike in 60 minutes?

b. 6 miles

c. The number of minutes in an hour, 60, was divided by 10, the number of minutes it takes Buzz to bike 1 mile.

d. 8.6 miles (60 ÷ 7 = 8.57 . . .)

7. $30/M$ miles

8. false

9. **a.** $2.45 (2.5 · .98 = 2.45)

b. $98k$ cents

c. ck cents

10. **a.** about 22.3 miles per gallon
(250 ÷ 11.2 = 22.32 . . .)

b. $\frac{m}{11.2}$ miles per gallon

c. $\frac{m}{g}$ miles per gallon

11. $(R - Z)$ sheets (Suppose the roll originally had 100 sheets, and 25 were used. Then $100 - 25$, or 75 sheets remain.)

12. 56 (Suppose there are 3 boys and 2 girls. Then each of the 3 boys is paired with the first girl and then each is paired with the second girl. The total number of pictures is $3 · 2$, or 6.)

13. $(G - 49.95)$ dollars (Suppose you give the clerk $50.00. Then you receive $50.00 - $49.95, or $.05 change.)

14. Many possible answers.
Sample: Let $a = 2$, $b = {}^-3$, $c = 4$.
Then $a + {}^-b + {}^-c = 2 + {}^-({}^-3) + {}^-4 = 2 + 3 + {}^-4 = 1$, and ${}^-(b + {}^-a + c) = {}^-({}^-3 + {}^-2 + 4) = {}^-({}^-1) = 1$.
Other special cases show the pattern to be probably true always.

15. 4 places to the left

16. 14 (a quadrilateral has 2 diagonals, a pentagon has 5, a hexagon has 9 and so on. Each time the number of diagonals increases by 1 more than the previous time.)

17. ${}^-2$ (Try ${}^-1$, ${}^-2$, ${}^-3$, . . . until you find a value that satisfies all the facts.)

18. A problem is a question you do not know how to answer; an exercise is a question you do know how to answer.

19. 3.5×10^{11} (Write 3.5. The decimal point must move 11 places to the right to get 350,000,000,000, so the exponent of 10 is 11.)

20. 9×10^{-1} (Write 9. The decimal point must move 1 place to the left to get 0.9, so the exponent of 10 is ${}^-1$.)

21. 4 kg + 25g + 43 mg
= 4000 g + 25 g + .043 g
= 4025.043 g

22. 70 kg (70 kg ≈ 70 · 2.2 lb ≈ 154 lb)

23. a^{b+c}

    $= 5^{2+4}$

    $= 5^6$

    $= 15,625$

24. 98765 − 10234 (Make the minuend as large as possible and the subtrahend as small as possible.)

CHAPTER 6 PROGRESS SELF-TEST (p. 275)

1. Look it up in any two of dictionary, glossary in a math book, or encyclopedia.

2. Below is an octagon with its diagonals. There are 20 diagonals.

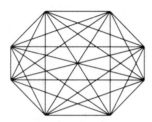

3. Name the teams *A, B, C, D, E* and *F*. Draw all the segments connecting these points. The figure created is a hexagon (see below). The number of games is equal to the number of diagonals plus the number of sides in the hexagon. That is 9 + 6 = 15 games.

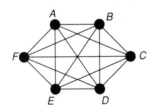

4. Use trial and error.

The sums of each pair of factors of 24 are:

1 + 24 = 25; 2 + 12 = 14; 3 + 8 = 11; and 4 + 6 = 10. So 4 and 6 give the smallest sums.

5. False (If you know an algorithm for an operation, you know how to answer the question. So multiplying fractions is only an exercise, not a problem.)

6. 53, 59

7. If one value is positive and one is negative, the pattern will be false. For instance, |−5| + |3| = 5 + 3 = 8, but |−5 + 3| = |−2| = 2.

8. 2 pounds at $3 per pound cost $6, so multiplication gives the answer. $1.49 per pound · 1.62 pounds = $2.4138, which rounds up to $2.42.

9. True

10. If $x = 5$, $(x − 3) + (x − 4) =$ $(5 − 3) + (5 − 4) = 3$, so 5 does not work. If $x = 6$, $(x − 3) + (x − 4) =$ $(6 − 3) + (6 − 4) = 5$, so 6 does not work. Continue to test 7, 8, 9, and 10. 8 works: $(x − 3) + (x − 4) =$ $(8 − 3) + (8 − 4) = 9$. 8 is a solution.

11. Read carefully and draw a picture. There are 6 disks between 3 and 10 (4, 5, 6, 7, 8, and 9). So there must be 6 disks placed between 3 and 10 going in the other direction. This gives a total of 6 + 6 + 2, or 14 disks.

12. Use trial and error. A 3-gon has 0 diagonals, a 4-gon has 2 diagonals, a 5-gon has 5 diagonals, a 6-gon has 9 diagonals.

13. Use a special case. .05/.01 = 5, which means that the decimal point is moved two places to the right.

14.

Weeks	amount left
1	1000 − 25
2	1000 − 2 · 25
3	1000 − 3 · 25
4	1000 − 4 · 25

15. After 31 weeks, Phyllis will have 1000 − 31 · 25 dollars left. $1000 − 31 · $25 = $225.

16. After you find an answer, you should check your work.

CHAPTER 6 REVIEW   (pp. 276-277)

1. (b) A good problem solver is flexible by trying different ways to solve a problem.

2. exercise

3. Several possible answers. Sample: She could multiply 309×1487 on her calculator, or divide by 309 to see if she gets 1487.

4. 17 (Try the various values for x. Only 17 works: $3x + 15 = 3 \cdot 17 + 15 = 66$)

5. (b) (If $n = 0.5$, $n^2 = 0.5^2 = 0.25$)

6. 84, 69, 102

7. 1036

8. composite; 7 is a factor besides 1 and 49

9. prime; only 1 and 47 are factors.

10. 21, 22, 24, 25, 26, 27, 28

11. 31, 37

12. A tetrahedron is a three-dimensional figure with four triangular faces.

13. A perfect number is a number that equals the sum of all its divisors except itself.

14. **a.** $\$10 + 12 \cdot \$5 = \$70$
    b. $10 + 5w$ dollars

15. 64, 128, and 256 are the next rows in the table below, so 256 has nine factors.

power of 2	factors
2	1, 2
4	1, 2, 4
8	1, 2, 4, 8
16	1, 2, 4, 8, 16
32	1, 2, 4, 8, 16, 32

16. No (A 5-gon has 5 diagonals, a 6-gon has 9, and thereafter the number of diagonals increases greatly.)

17. 6, left

18. There is more evidence that the property is true. (If $a = 5$ and $b = -4$, $2a + b = 2 \cdot 5 + -4 = 6$, and $a + (b + a) = 5 + (-4 + 5) = 6$. Try several more special cases.)

19. Many possible answers. Sample: If $x = 2$ and $y = 3$, then $5x + 5y = 5 \cdot 2 + 5 \cdot 3 = 25$, but $10xy = 10 \cdot 2 \cdot 3 = 60$.

20. 172 mph (Simpler numbers indicate division: $430 \div 2.5 = 172$)

21. $\$8.69$ (Simpler numbers indicate multiplication. $7.3 \cdot 1.19 = 8.687$)

22. 36 games (Draw a nonagon and its diagonals. There are 9 sides and 27 diagonals. $9 + 27 = 36$)

23. 20 games (Draw a pentagon and its diagonals. There are 5 sides and 5 diagonals. $5 + 5 = 10$. Since they play each other twice, multiply 10 by 2.)

24. Barbara is second oldest. (Arrange people from youngest on the left to oldest. Bob is older than Barbara and Barbara is older than Bill: BILL BARBARA BOB. Add the fact that Bill is older than Becky: BECKY BILL BARBARA BOB)

25. A diagram will help. Begin with the facts that Cheyenne is north of Denver and is 101 mi from Denver. Since Colorado Springs is more than 101 miles from Cheyenne, but only 70 miles from Denver, Colorado Springs must be south of Denver. And since Pueblo is more than 70 miles from Denver, but only 42 miles from Colorado Springs, Pueblo must be south of Colorado Springs.

    • Cheyenne
       101 mi
    • Denver
       70 mi
    • Colorado Springs
       42 mi
    • Pueblo

    Pueblo is the farthest south.

26. 9 (Draw a hexagon and its diagonals.)

27. The decagon below has 35 diagonals.

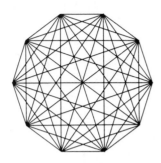

28. 11 regions are formed by the diagonals of a pentagon.

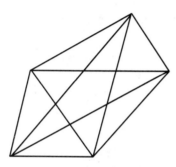

29. 7 triangles are formed by the diagonals from A.

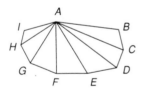

Chapter 7

Patterns Leading to Subtraction

LESSON 7-1 (pp. 280-284)

1. 1 dozen rolls − 8 rolls =
12 rolls − 8 rolls = 4 rolls

2. $12 - A$

3. 320 passengers − 4 passengers =
316 passengers

4. $S - V$

5. the Take-Away Model

6. $100° - 84° = 16°$

7. $103° - 22° = 81°$

8. m∠DBA

9. m∠DBC

10. If a quantity y is taken away from a quantity x
with the same units, the quantity left is $x - y$.

11. $b^2 - a^2$

12. $10^2 - 8^2 = 100 - 64 = 36$ square units

13. $6.7^2 - 4.5^2 = 44.89 - 20.25 =$
24.64 square units

14. **a.** CD
b. 10 km − 6 km = 4 km

15. $AB = 260$ miles − 147 miles = 113 miles

16. **a.** AC **b.** BC

17. $100\% - 20\% - 25\% = 55\%$

18. **a.** $100,000 - 57,044 = 42,956$
b. 74 to 80 years ($1981 - 1906 = 75$. Some
of the people were 74 years old during that
part of 1981 before their birthday.
$1981 - 1901 = 80$)
1992 Edition:
a. 54,161
b. 79 to 85 years ($1987-1907 = 80$. Some of
the people were 79 years old during that part
of 1987 before their birthday.)

19. **a.** $\$510.75 - \$40 = \$470.75$
b. $\$510.75 - W$

20. **a.** 60 ($8 \cdot 8 = 64$; $64 - 4 = 60$)
b. $n \cdot n - C$

21. $60\% = .6 = \dfrac{6}{10} = \dfrac{3}{5}$

22. **a.** −5   **b.** $3 \cdot 4$ **c.** 0

23. $3p + q^4$
$= 3 \cdot 4 + 5^4$
$= 3 \cdot 4 + 625$
$= 12 + 625$
$= 637$

24. false $\left(\frac{5}{4} + \frac{5}{4} = \frac{10}{4} \right)$

25. 1 milligram $= .001$ gram (or 1000 mg $= 1$ g)

26. Since 1 kg $= 1000$ g and 1 kg ≈ 2.2 lb,
1000 g ≈ 2.2 lb

27. Many possible answers. Sample: let $a = 5$,
$b = -2$. Then $-(a + b) = -(5 + -2) = -3$
and $-b + -a = -(-2) + -5 = -3$. It is true
in this instance.

28. $\qquad -5 + x = -5$
$5 + -5 + x = 5 + -5$
$\qquad\qquad x = 0$

29. Many possible answers. Samples: 3.001,
3.004, 3.009 (Write 3 as 3.000 and 3.01 as
3.010. 3.001, 3.004, and 3.009 are between
3.000 and 3.010.)

30. $\frac{22}{7}$ $(\pi = 3.1415926 \ldots ;$

$\frac{22}{7} = 3.1428571 \ldots)$

31. **a.** Add 3.   **b.** Add 4.   **c.** Add 11.

139	4909	1128
-100	-2000	-1000
39	2909	128

LESSON 7-2 (pp. 285-289)

1. 3, 4, left

2. If a quantity a is decreased by an amount b,
the result is a quantity $a - b$.

3. **a.** $74 - 20$ **b.** $74 + -20$
c. $54°$ F

4. **a.** $-4 - 10$ **b.** $-4 + -10$
c. $-14°$C

5. **a.** $72 - 3$ **b.** $72 + -3$
c. 69 kg

6. **a.** For any numbers a and b, $a - b = a + -b$
b. Subtracting b is the same as adding the
opposite of b.

7. 8 (The opposite of -8 is 8.)

8. y (The opposite of $-y$ is y.)

9. $-8 - 45 = -8 + -45 = -53$

10. $83 - 100 = 83 + -100 = -17$

11. $1 - 5 = 1 + -5 = -4$

12. $-22 - 8 = -22 + -8 = -30$

13. $3 - -7 = 3 + 7 = 10$

14. $0 - -41 = 0 + 41 = 41$

15. $-9 - -6 = -9 + 6 = -3$

16. $m - -2 = m + 2$

17. You already know how to add positive and
negative numbers; addition has the
Commutative and Associative properties.

18. **a.** center   **b.** right   **c.** left

19. the opposite of A minus negative four

20. $40 - 50 - 20$
$= 40 + -50 + -20$
$= -50 + -20 + 40$
$= -50 + -20 + 40$
$= -70 + 40$
$= -30$

21. **a.** $5 - 2 = 3$ **b.** $5 - 3 = 2$
c. $5 - 4 = 1$ **d.** $5 - 5 = 0$
e. $5 - 6 = 5 + -6 = -1$
f. $5 - 7 = 5 + -7 = -2$

22. **a.** $p = s - c$
$= \$49.95 - \$30.27$
$= \$19.68$
b. $p = s - c$
$= \$49.95 - \$56.25$
$= \$49.95 + -\$56.25$
$= -\$6.30$
c. loss

23. $a - b + c - d$
$= \text{-}1 - \text{-}2 + \text{-}3 - \text{-}4$
$= \text{-}1 + 2 + \text{-}3 + 4$
$= \text{-}1 + \text{-}3 + 2 + 4$
$= \text{-}4 + 6 = 2$

24. a. 3 $\boxed{-}$ 4 $\boxed{\pm}$ $\boxed{=}$
b. 5 $\boxed{\pm}$ $\boxed{-}$ 77 $\boxed{\pm}$ $\boxed{=}$

25. (c) (If $x = 2$, $7 - x = 7 - 2 = 5$, so 2 does not work. If $x = 16$, $7 - x = 7 - 16$ $= 7 + \text{-}16 = \text{-}9$, so 16 does not work. If $x = \text{-}2$, $7 - x = 7 - \text{-}2 = 7 + 2 = 9$, so $\text{-}2$ is a solution. If $x = \text{-}16$, $7 - x = 7 - \text{-}16 = 7 + 16 = 23$, so $\text{-}16$ does not work.)

26. (b) (For example, if a person loses 8 lb, the resulting weight is $165 - 8$.)

27. a. true (For example, if $x = 3$, $x - x = 3 - 3 = 0$.)
b. true (For example, if $x = \text{-}2$, $x - x = \text{-}2 - \text{-}2 = \text{-}2 + 2 = 0$.)

28. a. no (For example, if $x = 5$, $y = 2$, and $z = \text{-}1$, then $(x - y) - z = (5 - 2) - \text{-}1 = 3 + 1 = 4$, but $x - (y - z) = 5 - (2 - \text{-}1) = 5 - (2 + 1) = 2$)
b. no (This is illustrated in 28a.)

29. a. $a - b = b - a$ for all numbers a and b
b. no (For example, $6 - 4 = 2$, but $4 - 6 = 4 + \text{-}6 = \text{-}2$.)

30. $38 - t$ minutes   **31.** $n - 4$

32. $\dfrac{360°}{60} = 6°$

33. Addition Property of Equality

34. 7 (When the 8 teams are paired up, 4 games are played. When the 4 winning teams are paired up, 2 more games are played. When the 2 winning teams are paired up, 1 more game is played. $4 + 2 + 1 = 7$)

35. a. $m = 2$, $n = 11$
$(2^{11} - 11^2 = 2028 - 121 = 1927)$

b. For the year 1989, $m = 1990$, $n = 1$.
$(1990^1 - 1^{1990} = 1990 - 1 = 1989)$
For the year k, $m = k + 1$, $n = 1$
$((k + 1)^1 - 1^{k + 1} = (k + 1) - 1 =$
$(k + 1) + \text{-}1 = k + (1 + \text{-}1) = k)$

LESSON 7-3 (pp. 290-294)

1. 4 is the difference.   **2.** 12 is the minuend.
3. 8 is the subtrahend.
4. $x - y$ is how much more x is than y.
5. $150 \text{ lb} - 144 \text{ lb} = 6 \text{ lb}$
6. $\$395 - \$240 = \$155$
7. $535 - \text{-}5 = 535 + 5 = 540 \text{ ft}$
8. $13° - 27° = 13° + \text{-}27° = \text{-}14°$
9. $\text{-}8° - \text{-}9° = \text{-}8° + 9° = 1°$
10. $13 - 20 = 13 + \text{-}20 = \text{-}7$ points (His guess was 7 points too low.)
11. $13 - \text{-}4 = 13 + 4 = 17$ points (His guess was 17 points too high.)
12. $y - x$ **13.** $\text{-}368$ **14.** $\text{-}40$
15. positive (The minuend is larger.)
16. negative (The subtrahend is larger.)
17. positive (The minuend is larger.)
18. positive (The minuend is larger.)
19. negative (The subtrahend is larger.)
20. negative (The subtrahend is larger.)
21. $x - y = 205,000$
*1992 Edition: $x - y = 1,034,000$
22. $E - D$ dollars
23. a. from 1950 to 1960,
$373,676 - 373,628 = 48$
from 1960 to 1970,
$379,967 - 373,676 = 6291$
from 1970 to 1980,
$366,383 - 379,967 =$
$366,383 + \text{-}379,967 = \text{-}13,584$
b. $48 + 6291 + \text{-}13,584 = \text{-}7245$
c. The population decreased by 7245 from 1950 to 1980.
*See p. 82 for 1992 edition answers.

*23 *1992 Edition:* **a.** from 1960 to 1970, 379,967 − 373,676 = 6291; from 1970 to 1980, 366,383 − 379,967 = -13,584; from 1980 to 1990, 420,920 − 366,383 = 54,547; **b.** 6291 + -13,584 + 54,547 = 47,244 **c.** The population increased by 47,244 from 1960 to 1990.

24. Step 1: Add-Opp Property
Step 2: Associative Property of Addition
Step 3: Property of Opposites
Step 4: Additive Identity Property of Zero
Step 5: Property of Opposites

25. 66 or 67 (1934 − 1867 = 67. She was 66 if she died during that part of 1934 before her birthday.)

26. 74 or 75 (17 − -59 = 17 + 59 = 76. Since there was no year 0, subtract 1: 76 − 1 = 75. If he died during that part of the year before his birthday, he was 74.)

27. **a.** 899 (Using simpler numbers, between 10 and 20 there are 9 integers, or 20 − 10 − 1. So between 100 and 1000, there are 1000 − 100 − 1, or 899 integers.
b. $J − I − 1$

28. 1 ⊞ ⊟ 2 ⊞ ⊟ 8 ⊞ ⊟

29. **a.** 100,000 − 98,590 = 1410 people
b. from 4 to 10 years old (1981 − 1976 = 5. Some of the people were 4 years old in that part of 1981 before their birthday.)
*1992 Edition:
a. 100,000 − 98,536 = 1464 people
b. from 14 to 20 years old

30. $-a + y = b$
$a + -a + y = a + b$
$y = a + b$

31. 2.5 in. + 3.5 in. + 2.5 in. + 3.5 in. = 12 in.

32. $\frac{2}{5} = 2 \div 5 = .4 = 40\%$

33. In each case, the error is calculated by subtracting the number of heads tossed from the number guessed.

34. **a.** X
?5
Y
?3

Y − X	X − Y
-2	2

b. X
?98.7
Y
?-3.456

Y − X	X − Y
-102.156	102.156

c. Answers will vary. The last two numbers printed should be opposites of each other.

LESSON 7-4 (pp. 295-298)

1. Add-Opp Property of Subtraction

2. The subtraction is to be converted to addition.

3. **a.** $x + -14 = -2$
b. $x + -14 = -2$
$x + -14 + 14 = -2 + 14$
$x = 12$

4. **a.** $73 = y + -28$
b. $73 = y + -28$
$73 + 28 = y + -28 + 28$
$101 = y$

5. **a.** $a + -6 = 9$
b. $a + -6 = 9$
$a + -6 + 6 = 9 + 6$
$a = 15$

6. **a.** $c + -12.5 = 3$
b. $c + -12.5 = 3$
$c + -12.5 + 12.5 = 3 + 12.5$
$c = 15.5$

7. no (-42 − 13 = -42 + -13 = -55)

8. yes (-1 − -7 = -1 + 7 = 6)

9. (c) (Rewrite as addition: $x + -a = b$. Then add a to both sides.)

10. $B − -5 = 6$
$B + 5 = 6$
$B + 5 + -5 = 6 + -5$
$B = 1$
Check: $1 − -5 = 6$

11.
$$3.01 = e - 9.2$$
$$3.01 = e + {}^-9.2$$
$$3.01 + 9.2 = e + {}^-9.2 + 9.2$$
$$12.21 = e$$
Check: $3.01 = 12.21 - 9.2$

12. a. Let E be the original elevation;
$$E - 75 = 12,450$$
b.
$$E - 75 = 12,450$$
$$E + {}^-75 = 12,450$$
$$E + {}^-75 + 75 = 12,450 + 75$$
$$E = 12,525$$
c. The original elevation was 12,525 feet.

13. a. Let s be the original score; $s - 3 = {}^-2$
b.
$$s - 3 = {}^-2$$
$$s + {}^-3 = {}^-2$$
$$s + {}^-3 + 3 = {}^-2 + 3$$
$$s = 1$$
c. The team was ahead by one point.

14.
$$p = s - c$$
$$p = s + {}^-c$$
$$p + c = s + {}^-c + c$$
$$p + c = s, \text{ or } s = p + c$$

15.
$$d + 4 - 12 = {}^-15$$
$$d + 4 + {}^-12 = {}^-15$$
$$d + {}^-8 = {}^-15$$
$$d + {}^-8 + 8 = {}^-15 + 8$$
$$d = {}^-7$$
The initial depth was 7 feet below the surface.

16.
$$s - \frac{1}{8} = \frac{1}{2}$$
$$s + {}^-\frac{1}{8} = \frac{1}{2}$$
$$s + {}^-\frac{1}{8} + \frac{1}{8} = \frac{1}{2} + \frac{1}{8}$$
$$s = \frac{1}{2} + \frac{1}{8}$$
$$s = \frac{4}{8} + \frac{1}{8}$$
$$s = \frac{5}{8}, \text{ or } .625$$

17. $2 - 3 - 10 = 2 + {}^-3 + {}^-10 =$
$2 + {}^-13 = {}^-11$

18. $^-8 - 9 = {}^-8 + {}^-9 = {}^-17$

19. a. 58 years (From Jan. 23, 1914 to Jan. 23, 1971, is $1971 - 1914$, or 57 years. From July 10, 1913 to Jan. 23, 1914 is greater than half a year, so round up to 58.)
b. $134° - {}^-80° = 134° + 80° = 214°$

20. $D - B$ or $D - B - 1$ (If the person died during that part of the year before his or her birthday, the person's age was $D - B - 1$.)

21. $G < 21$ or $G > 31$

22. He was overdrawn by \$88. ($312 - 400 = 312 + {}^-400 = {}^-88$)

23. two thousand three hundred five and 00/100

24. $^-17$ (^-x means "the opposite of x.")

25. 70 cm ($1 \text{ m} - 30 \text{ cm} = 100 \text{ cm} - 30 \text{ cm} = 70 \text{ cm}$) or 0.7 m ($1\text{m} - 30 \text{ cm} = 1 \text{ m} - .3 \text{ cm} = .7 \text{ m}$)

26. 0.75 ($3 \div 4 = 0.75$)

27. 1.5 (Move the decimal point 2 places to the left.)

28. $0.\overline{54}$ ($6 \div 11 = 0.545454 \ldots$)

29. 6,340,000 (Move the decimal point in 6.34 6 places to the right.)

30. 5,000,000,000,000

31. .000064   **32.** 10°

33. a. Many possible answers. Sample:
$$462 - 231 = 231$$
b. 16 ($412 - 206 = 206$; $432 - 216 = 216$; $462 - 231 = 231$; $472 - 236 = 236$; $542 - 271 = 271$; $562 - 281 = 281$; $572 - 286 = 286$; $582 - 291 = 291$; $814 - 407 = 407$; $834 - 417 = 417$; $854 - 427 = 427$; $864 - 432 = 432$; $904 - 452 = 452$; $914 - 457 = 457$; $934 - 467 = 467$; $964 - 482 = 482$)

LESSON 7-5 (pp. 299-302)

1. Two sentences are equivalent if they have exactly the same solutions.

2. Find a sentence of the form $x = $ _____ that is equivalent to the original equation.

3. **a.** III

   b. -2 (Simply read the solution in sentence III: $x = -2$.)

4. $x = 5$ (The solution to the second sentence is $x = -5$.)

5. $4 + 1 = y$ (In the first and third sentences, $y = 3$. In the second sentence, $y = 5$.)

6. $a - b = \frac{2}{3}$ (In the first and third sentences, $a = b + -\frac{2}{3}$. In the second sentence, $a = b + \frac{2}{3}$.)

7. **a.** $-15 = y$

   b. between lines 2 and 3 ($-6 + 9 = 3$, not -15)

8. **a.** $A - 10 - 5 = .2$;

   b. between lines 1 and 2 ($A - 10 - 5 = A + -10 + -5 = A + -15 = A - 15$, not $A - 5$)

9. Formulas are equivalent when the same numbers work in both (or all) of them.

10. $p = c - s$ (Solve for p in the first formula: $p = s - c$.)

11.
$$x + 40 = 35$$
$$x + 40 + -40 = 35 + -40$$
$$x = -5$$

12.
$$\frac{6}{5} = \frac{2}{3} + A$$
$$-\frac{2}{3} + \frac{6}{5} = -\frac{2}{3} + \frac{2}{3} + A$$
$$-\frac{2}{3} + \frac{6}{5} = A$$
$$-\frac{10}{15} + \frac{18}{15} = A$$
$$\frac{8}{15} = A, \text{ or } .5\overline{3} = A$$

13.
$$y - 1.8 = 8.7$$
$$y + -1.8 = 8.7$$
$$y + -1.8 + 1.8 = 8.7 + 1.8$$
$$y = 10.5$$

14. Solve.

15. $80 = 94 - 14$ or $94 - 80 = 14$

16. $9 = \frac{711}{9}$ or $79 = \frac{711}{9}$

17. $-1 - -5 = 4$ or $-5 = -1 - 4$

18. $.3 = \frac{.15}{.5}$ or $.5 = \frac{.15}{.3}$

19. $10 = -13 + 23$

20. $\left(\frac{5}{6}\right)\left(\frac{4}{5}\right) = \frac{2}{3}$

21. (c) (Suppose $\ell = 6$ and $w = 4$. Then $A = \ell w = 6 \cdot 4 = 24$. These numbers also work in c: $24/6 = 4$)

22.
$$x - 11 = -11$$
$$x + -11 = -11$$
$$x + -11 + 11 = -11 + 11$$
$$x = 0$$

23.
$$8 = y - 40$$
$$8 = y + -40$$
$$8 + 40 = y + -40 + 40$$
$$48 = y$$

24.
$$c + d = 30$$
$$-c + c + d = 30 + -c$$
$$d = 30 + -c, \text{ or } d = 30 - c$$

25. 58 or 59 years old ($1915 - 1856 = 59$. If he died during that part of 1915 before his birthday, he was 58.)

26. $-6°\,C - -15°\,C = -6°\,C + 15°\,C = 9°\,C$

27. **a.** $3 - x$
$$= 3 - 17$$
$$= 3 + -17$$
$$= -14$$

   b. $3 - x$
$$= 3 - -85$$
$$= 3 + 85$$
$$= 88$$

28. (a), (c), (d) (The angle may be named by just its vertex, O, or by the three points W, O, and C with O, the vertex, in the middle.)

29. $\frac{360°}{2} = 180°$

30. 357.913 (Increase the 2 in the thousandths place.)

31. $2n - 3$

32. Many possible answers. Samples: 810, 729, 648, 243, 108, 117, 126, 135, 144, 999; the sum of the digits is always divisible by 9.

LESSON 7-6 (pp. 303-306)

1. $3 + -x = 20$

2. -14

3. t

4.
$$-5 = 14 - t$$
$$-5 = 14 + -t$$
$$-14 + -5 = -14 + 14 + -t$$
$$-19 = -t$$
$$19 = -(-t)$$
$$19 = t$$

or

$$-5 = 14 - t$$
$$-5 = 14 + -t$$
$$-5 + t = 14 + -t + t$$
$$-5 + t = 14$$
$$5 + -5 + t = 5 + 14$$
$$t = 19$$

5.
$$300 - x = -2$$
$$300 + -x = -2$$
$$-300 + 300 + -x = -300 + -2$$
$$-x = -302$$
$$x = 302$$
Check $300 - 302 = -2$

6.
$$61 = 180 - y$$
$$61 = 180 + -y$$
$$-180 + 61 = -180 + 180 + -y$$
$$-119 = -y$$
$$119 = y$$
Check: $61 = 180 - 119$

7.
$$-45 = 45 - z$$
$$-45 = 45 + -z$$
$$-45 + -45 = -45 + 45 + -z$$
$$-90 = -z$$
$$90 = z$$
Check: $-45 = 45 - 90$

8.
$$m - 3.3 = 1$$
$$m + -3.3 = 1$$
$$m + -3.3 + 3.3 = 1 + 3.3$$
$$m = 4.3$$
Check: $4.3 - 3.3 = 1$

9.
$$A - 57 = -110$$
$$A + -57 = -110$$
$$A + -57 + 57 = -110 + 57$$
$$A = -53$$
Check: $-53 - 57 = -110$

10.
$$\frac{2}{3} - B = \frac{88}{9}$$
$$\frac{2}{3} + -B = \frac{88}{9}$$
$$-\frac{2}{3} + \frac{2}{3} + -B = -\frac{2}{3} + \frac{88}{9}$$
$$-B = -\frac{2}{3} + \frac{88}{9}$$
$$-B = -\frac{6}{9} + \frac{88}{9}$$
$$-B = \frac{82}{9}$$
$$B = -\frac{82}{9}$$
Check: $\frac{2}{3} - -\frac{82}{9} = \frac{88}{9}$

11. a.
$$3500 - S = 212$$
$$3500 + -S = 212$$
$$-3500 + 3500 + -S = -3500 + 212$$
$$-S = -3288$$
$$S = 3288$$

b. 3288 tickets have been sold.

12. a. $14 - d = -3$

b.
$$14 - d = -3$$
$$14 + \,^-d = -3$$
$$^-14 + 14 + \,^-d = -14 + -3$$
$$^-d = -17$$
$$d = 17$$

c. The temperature has decreased 17°.

13. a. $22{,}500 - d = 20{,}250$

b.
$$22{,}500 - d = 20{,}250$$
$$22{,}500 + \,^-d = 20{,}250$$
$$^-22{,}500 + 22{,}500 + \,^-d = -22{,}500 + 20{,}250$$
$$^-d = -2250$$
$$d = 2250$$

c. They came down 2,250 feet.

14.
$$40 - x + 20 = 180$$
$$40 + \,^-x + 20 = 180$$
$$60 + \,^-x = 180$$
$$^-60 + 60 + \,^-x = -60 + 180$$
$$^-x = 120$$
$$x = -120$$

15.
$$^-6 = -1 - y - 5$$
$$^-6 = -1 + \,^-y + -5$$
$$^-6 = -6 + \,^-y$$
$$6 + \,^-6 = 6 + -6 + -y$$
$$0 = \,^-y$$
$$0 = y$$

16.
$$12 - \,^-B = 6$$
$$12 + B = 6$$
$$^-12 + 12 + B = -12 + 6$$
$$B = \,^-6$$

17.
$$13 - 5 \cdot 2 = 9 - K - \,^-7$$
$$13 - 10 = 9 - K - \,^-7$$
$$13 + \,^-10 = 9 + \,^-K + 7$$
$$3 = 16 + \,^-K$$
$$^-16 + 3 = -16 + 16 + \,^-K$$
$$^-13 = \,^-K$$
$$13 = K$$

18.
$$x = 90 - y$$
$$x = 90 + \,^-y$$
$$x + y = 90 + \,^-y + y$$
$$x + y = 90$$
$$^-x + x + y = -x + 90$$
$$y = \,^-x + 90, \text{ or } y = 90 - x$$

19. 1 Add-Opp Property
2 Addition Property of Equality
3 Assoc. Property of Addition
4 Prop. of Opposites
5 Additive Identity Property of Zero
6 Addition Property of Equality
7 Assoc. Property of Addition
8 Property of Opposites
9 Additive Identity Property of Zero

20. (c) (For example, if $a = 3$ and $b = -4$, then $^-b + a = -(-4) + 3 = 7$, but $b + \,^-a = -4 + -3 = -7$.)

21.
$$40 = A + 12$$
$$40 + \,^-12 = A + 12 + -12$$
$$28 = A$$

22. 50%

23.

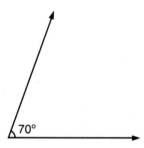

24.

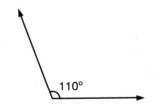

25. a.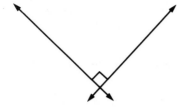

    b. right angles

26. a. $h - 125 = 630$

    b.
$$h - 125 = 630$$
$$h + {}^-125 = 630$$
$$h + {}^-125 + 125 = 630 + 125$$
$$h = 755$$

    It had flown 755 ft high.

27. a. $s - 1.14 = 637.47$

    b.
$$s - 1.14 = 637.47$$
$$s + {}^-1.14 = 637.47$$
$$s + {}^-1.14 + 1.14 = 637.47 + 1.14$$
$$s = 638.61$$

    Louganis's score was 638.61.

28. a. Queen Victoria ($1189 - 1154 = 35$; $1547 - 1509 = 38$; $1603 - 1558 = 45$; $1901 - 1837 = 64$)

    b. $1952 + 65 = 2017$

29. $180°$ (This is a half turn; $\frac{360°}{2} = 180°$)

30. There are seven possible values: $^-5, ^-3, ^-1, 1,$ 3, 5, and 7 (Organize your work and keep track of all the various positions of the grouping symbols.)

LESSON 7-7 (pp. 307-312)

1. straight
2. opposite
3. linear pair
4. $180°$
5. $180° - 88° = 92°$
6. perpendicular
7. supplementary

8. angles 1 and 3, 2 and 4
9. angles 1 and 4, 2 and 3, 3 and 4, 2 and 1
10. angles 1 and 4, 2 and 3, 3 and 4, 2 and 1
11. $m\angle 2 = 55°$, $m\angle 3 = 125°$, $m\angle 4 = 55°$ ($m\angle 1 = m\angle 3 = 125°$; $m\angle 2 = m\angle 4 = 180° - 125°$)
12. $m\angle 1 = m\angle 3 \approx 135°$; $m\angle 2 = m\angle 4 \approx 45°$
13. $180° - 45° = 135°$
14. $180° - 164° = 16°$
15. $d = f = 180° - 89.5° = 90.5°$, $e = 89.5°$
16. a. $180 - x$ **b.** x
    c. $180 - x$
17. true
18. true
19. 6 (Drexel and South Chicago, Drexel and 71st, Ellis and South Chicago, Ellis and 72nd, Ellis and 71st, South Chicago and 71st)
20. Ellis and 72nd
21. 71st and South Chicago
22. If ramp is perpendicular to expressway, the driver has to accelerate into fast-moving traffic while making a $90°$ turn. If ramp and expressway form a very small angle, the car's direction changes very little and acceleration is much easier.
23. angles *DCA* and *ACB*
24. angles *NOM* and *POM*
25. true (If the measure of one angle is less than $90°$, the measure of the other must be greater than $90°$ because the sum of the measures is $180°$.)
26. false (Vertical angles have the same measure.)
27. true (If their measures are less than $90°$, the sum of their measures will be less than $180°$.)
28. false (The 2 angles could be right angles.)
29. $180° - 58° = 122°$
30. $x = y$
31. $x + y = 180°$
32. $180° - 40° = 140°$

33.
$$180 - x = 23$$
$$180 + \text{-}x = 23$$
$$\text{-}180 + 180 + \text{-}x = \text{-}180 + 23$$
$$\text{-}x = \text{-}157$$
$$x = 157$$

34.
$$90 - y = 31$$
$$90 + \text{-}y = 31$$
$$\text{-}90 + 90 + \text{-}y = \text{-}90 + 31$$
$$\text{-}y = \text{-}59$$
$$y = 59$$

35.
$$17 - (2 - 6) + A = 5 - 2(5 + 6)$$
$$17 + \text{-}(2 + \text{-}6) + A = 5 - 2 \cdot 11$$
$$17 + \text{-}(\text{-}4) + A = 5 - 22$$
$$17 + 4 + A = 5 + \text{-}22$$
$$21 + A = \text{-}17$$
$$\text{-}21 + 21 + A = \text{-}21 + \text{-}17$$
$$A = \text{-}38$$

36. 3 ($4 \cdot 3 = 12$, so $c = 3$)

37. $2.60 (98% of $129.95 = .98 \cdot $129.95 ≈ $127.35; $129.95 − $127.35 = $2.60)

38. Complementary angles are two angles whose measures add to 90°.

LESSON 7-8 (pp. 313-317)

1. $180° - 62° = 118°$ (∠1 and the 62° angle form a linear pair.)

2. 118° (Vertical angles have the same measure. ∠1 and ∠2 are vertical angles.)

3. 62° (Corresponding angles have equal measures. ∠3 and the 62° angle are corresponding angles.)

4. $180° - 62° = 118°$ (∠3 and ∠4 form a linear pair.)

5. 118° (Vertical angles have the same measure. ∠4 and ∠5 are vertical angles.)

6. 62° (Vertical angles have the same measure. ∠3 and ∠6 are vertical angles.)

7. p

8. Two lines in a plane are parallel when they have no points in common.

9. angles 1 and 6, 4 and 5, 2 and 8, 3 and 7

10. angles 1, 4, 7, and 8

11. angles 2, 3, 5, and 6

12. angles 3 and 5, 2 and 6

13. yes   **14.** yes

15. m∠2 = m∠1 = m∠6 = m∠8 = 84° (∠1 and ∠2 are vertical angles, ∠1 and ∠6 are corresponding angles, and ∠6 and ∠8 are vertical angles.); m∠3 = m∠4 = m∠5 = m∠7 = 96° (∠2 and ∠3 form a linear pair, so m∠3 = 180° − 84°. ∠3 and ∠4 are vertical angles, ∠4 and ∠5 are corresponding angles, and ∠5 and ∠7 are vertical angles.)

16. m∠1 = m∠2 = m∠6 = m∠8 = 180 − x; m∠3 = m∠4 = m∠5 = m∠7 = x

17. all of the angles 1 through 8

18. angles 1, 2, 6, and 8

19.

20. ⊥   **21.** //   **22.** 90°   **23.** 90°

24.

25. m∠1 = 90°; m∠2 = m∠4 = 40° (m∠4 = 180° − (90° + 50°)); m∠3 = 140° (∠3 and ∠4 form a linear pair)

88

26. m∠1 = 105° (∠1 and the 75° angle form a linear pair.); m∠3 = 110° (∠3 and the 70° angle form a linear pair.); m∠4 = 75° (∠4 and the 75° angle are alternate interior angles.); m∠6 = 70° (∠6 and the 70° angle are alternate interior angles.); m∠5 = 35° (m∠4 + m∠5 + m∠6 = 180°)

27. 360° (Use vertical angles, alternate interior angles or corresponding angles, linear pairs, and right angles to determine angle measures.)

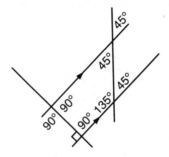

28. angles 1 and 2

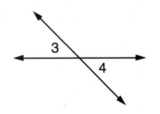

29. angles 3 and 4

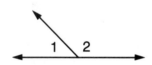

30. Many possible answers. Sample:

45°   135°

31. $a \cdot 1 = a$

32.
$$m - \frac{8}{3} = -3$$
$$m + -\frac{8}{3} = -3$$
$$m + -\frac{8}{3} + \frac{8}{3} = -3 + \frac{8}{3}$$
$$m = -\frac{9}{3} + \frac{8}{3}$$
$$m = -\frac{1}{3}$$

33.
$$a + b + c = 180$$
$$a + b + c + -a + -b = 180 + -a + -b$$
$$c = 180 - a - b$$

34.
$$C - 100 + 30.45$$
$$= C + -100 + 30.45$$
$$= C + -69.55$$
$$= C - 69.55 \text{ dollars}$$

35. $C - W + D$

36. **a.** Answers will vary.
　　b. Answers will vary.

37. Many possible answers. Samples: windows, streets, parking lot stripes, guitar strings and the bridge

LESSON 7-9 (pp. 318-321)

1. 8 (See diagram on page 318.)

2. **a.** 16 (See diagram on page 318.)
　　b. x, $180 - x$
　　c. 30°, 150° (180° − 30°)

3. **a.** $TU = TS = SV = UV = 15$ mm
　　b. m∠U = m∠S ≈ 100°, m∠T = m∠V ≈ 80°

4. **a.** $OP = RO = QR = PQ = 18$ mm
　　b. All angles are right angles.

5. $\overline{MN}$ and $\overline{QP}$, or $\overline{MQ}$ and $\overline{NP}$

6. ∠M and ∠P, or ∠N and ∠Q

7. ∠Q

8. $\overline{MN}$

9. 110° (180° − 70°)

10. 5

11. all sides equal in length

12. *A, C, D*

13. *A, D, E, G*

14. *A, D*

15. *A, B, C, D, E, G, H*

16. rhombuses and squares

17. rectangles and squares

18.-19. parallelograms, rhombuses, rectangles, and squares

20. $10 \cdot 4 = 40$

21. not enough information

22. a.

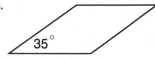

b. 35° or 145°

23. a. 147° ($\angle BAG$ and $\angle ABC$ are alternate interior angles.)

b. 57° ($m\angle GAE = m\angle BAG - m\angle BAE = 147° - 90°$)

c. 123° ($180° - 57°$)

d. 33° ($m\angle CDH = 180° - m\angle CDA = 180° - 147°$)

24.
$$x + y = 180$$
$$-x + x + y = -x + 180$$
$$y = -x + 180$$
$$y = 180 + -x$$
$$y = 180 - x$$

25. *ABG*

26. *CBF*

27. $m\angle DBA = 30°$ (vertical angles); $m\angle CBD = m\angle FBA = 150°$ (linear pair: $180° - 30° = 150°$)

28. a. $m\angle GBC$; **b.** $m\angle GBC = 54°$ (linear pair: $180° - 126° = 54°$)

29. ⊥ (is perpendicular to)

30. a.
$$y - 4 = 20$$
$$y + -4 = 20$$
$$y + -4 + 4 = 20 + 4$$
$$y = 24$$

b.
$$4 - x = 20$$
$$4 + -x = 20$$
$$-4 + 4 + -x = -4 + 20$$
$$-x = 16$$
$$x = -16$$

31. a. from 1950 to 1960, 103,932
from 1960 to 1970, -23,952
from 1970 to 1980, -81,160

b. -1,180

c. From 1950 to 1980 the population decreased by 1180 people.

1992 Edition:

a. From 1950 to 1960, 103,932
from 1960 to 1970, -23,952
from 1970 to 1980, -81,160
from 1980 to 1990, -36,832

b. -38,012

c. From 1950 to 1990 the population decreased by 38,012 people.

32. Many possible answers. Samples:

a. floor tiles, some street signs

b. spaces in expanding "baby gate"

c. diamond symbol in a deck of cards

LESSON 7-10 (pp. 322-327)

1. (b) In all triangles the sum of the measures of the angles is 180°.

2. The Triangle-Sum Property ensures that the sum of the measures of the 3 angles is 180°. So together, these angles make a 180° angle, which is a straight angle.

3. In any triangle, the sum of the measures of the angles is 180.

4.
$$30° + 60° + x = 180°$$
$$90° + x = 180°$$
$$-90° + 90° + x = -90° + 180°$$
$$x = 90°$$

5.
$$117° + 62° + x = 180°$$
$$179° + x = 180°$$
$$-179° + 179° + x = -179° + 180°$$
$$x = 1°$$

6.
$$1° + 2° + x = 180°$$
$$3° + x = 180°$$
$$-3° + 3° + x = -3° + 180°$$
$$x = 177°$$

*These are solutions to questions changed in or added to the *1992 Edition.*

7. $x° + (140° - x°) + y = 180°$
   $x° + 140° + -x° + y = 180°$
   $x° + -x° + 140° + y = 180°$
   $140° + y = 180°$
   $-140° + 140° + y = -140 + 180°$
   $y = 40°$

8. $4 \cdot 90° = 360°$

9. If a triangle had two obtuse angles, the sum of their measures would be more than 180° because the measure of each obtuse angle is greater than 90°. But the sum of the measures of all three angles is 180°.

10. m∠1 = 80° (∠1 and the 100° angle form a linear pair.); m∠2 = 100° (∠2 and the 100° angle are alternate interior angles, and $\overleftrightarrow{QS}$ // $\overrightarrow{RT}$.); m∠3 = 80° (By the markings, m∠3 = m∠ORQ. m∠ORQ = 80° because it forms a linear pair with ∠2.) m∠4 = 20° (m∠1 + m∠3 = 160°, so m∠4 = 180° - 160° by the Triangle-Sum Property.); m∠5 = m∠6 = m∠7 = 90° (∠5 and ∠7 are right angles because of the perpendicular lines. ∠5 and ∠6 are alternate interior angles.); m∠8 = 100° (∠8 and ∠3 form a linear pair.)

11. 90° (The measure of the right angle is 90°. This, plus the measures of the other two angles, must add to 180°.)

12. m∠1 = 75° (In triangle ABD, m∠B = 60° and m∠BAD = $\frac{90°}{2}$ = 45°. Apply the Triangle-Sum Property to find m∠1.); m∠2 = 105 (∠1 and ∠2 form a linear pair.)

13. (d) (Try special cases to verify.)

14. 74° (∠BAC forms a linear pair with the 116° angle, so m∠BAC = 180° - 116° = 64°. In △ABC, m∠ABC = 180° - (64° + 42°) = 74°.)

15. 146° (In triangle WYZ, m∠WYZ = 180° - (90° + 56°) = 34°. ∠XYZ forms a linear pair with ∠WYZ.)

16. m∠EIH = 88° (Apply the Triangle-Sum Property to triangle EIH.); m∠EIG = 39° (m∠EIG = m∠EIH - m∠GIH = 88° - 49°); m∠GHI = 101° (Apply the Triangle-Sum Property to triangle GHI.); m∠GHE = 49° (m∠GHE = m∠GHI - m∠EHI = 101° - 52°); m∠IFH = m∠EFG = 79° (These angles are vertical angles. Find m∠IFH by applying the Triangle-Sum Property to triangle IFH.); m∠IFE = m∠GFH (These angles are vertical angles. Each is supplementary to ∠IFH.)

17. $\overline{AD}$ and $\overline{BC}$ are parallel.

18. $\overline{AB}$ and $\overline{AD}$ are perpendicular.

19. m∠B = m∠BCD

20. The angles have the same measure.

21. a. Line segment AB is parallel to ray CD.
    b.
    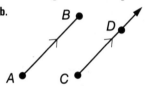

22. a. Line EF is perpendicular to line segment GH.
    b.
    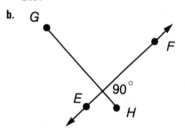

23. a. true (A square is a rectangle with four sides of equal length.)
    b. true (A square is a rhombus with four right angles.)

24. a. Richard: 62.8 kg − 65.3 kg =
  62.8 kg + -65.3 kg = -2.5 kg;
  Marlene: 54.3 kg − 53.4 kg = .9 kg;
  Evelyn: 55.1 kg − 58.6 kg =
  55.1 kg + -58.6 kg = -3.5 kg;
  Daniel: 72.0 kg − 71.1 kg = .9 kg
b. Marlene and Daniel (Each gained .9 kg)
c. Evelyn (She lost 3.5 kg)

25. $a − b + c − d$
  $= 0 − -10 + -100 − -1000$
  $= 0 + 10 + -100 + 1000$
  $= 0 + 10 + 1000 + -100$
  $= 910$

26. $a − b + c − d$
  $= 43 − 2 + 5 − 11$
  $= -43 + -2 + 5 + -11$
  $= -43 + -2 + -11 + 5$
  $= -51$

27. $-5 = 15.4 − x$
      $-5 = 15.4 + -x$
  $-15.4 + -5 = -15.4 + 15.4 + -x$
      $-20.4 = -x$
      $20.4 = x$

28. $x − 3 = -3$
      $x + -3 = -3$
  $x + -3 + 3 = -3 + 3$
      $x = 0$

29. a. $m\angle A = 109°$, $m\angle D = 56°$; $m\angle Q = 38°$,
  $m\angle U = 157°$
b. $109° + 56° + 38° + 157° = 360°$

30. (c) (For a triangle, $n = 3$. So $180 (n − 2) =$
  $180 (3 − 2) = 180 · 1 = 180$. For a
  quadrilateral, $n = 4$. So $180 (n − 2) = 180$
  $(4 − 2) = 180 · 2 = 360$. These results
  agree with the Triangle-Sum Property and
  Question 29.)

CHAPTER 7 PROGRESS SELF-TEST (p. 329)

1. $-6 + -22 = -28$

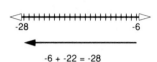
$-6 + -22 = -28$

2. $45 + -110 = -65$

3. $5 − x + 2 − y$
  $= 5 − 13 + 2 − -11$
  $= 5 + -13 + 2 + 11$
  $= 5 + 2 + 11 + -13$
  $= 5$

4. $y − 14 = -24$
    $y + -14 = -24$
  $y + -14 + 14 = -24 + 14$
    $y = -10$

5. $-50 = 37 − x$
    $-50 = 37 + -x$
  $-37 + -50 = -37 + 37 + -x$
    $-87 = -x$
    $87 = x$

6. $g − 3.2 = -2$
    $g + -3.2 = -2$
  $g + -3.2 + 3.2 = -2 + 3.2$
    $g = 1.2$

7. $c − a = b$
    $c + -a = b$
  $c + -a + a = b + a$
    $c = b + a$
    $-b + c = -b + b + a$
    $-b + c = a$, or $a = c − b$

8. 155° (Angles ABE and ABD are a linear pair,
  so their measures add to 180°.)

9. 65° ($m\angle CBD = 90° − m\angle ABD =$
  $90° − 25° = 65°$)

10. 106° ($\angle 5$ and $\angle 6$ are corresponding angles, so
  they have the same measure 74°. $\angle 7$ forms a
  linear pair with $\angle 6$, so $m\angle 7 =$
  $180° − 74° = 106°$.)

11. $\angle 5$ (a corresponding angle); $\angle 3$ (a vertical angle); and $\angle 4$ (the vertical angle to $\angle 5$)

12. angles 1, 8, 2, and 7 (Angles 1 and 8 each form a linear pair with $\angle 5$. Angles 2 and 7 have the same measures as angles 1 and 8.)

13. The sum of 3 right angles is 270°, which is greater than the triangle-sum of 180°.

14. $$55° + 4° + x = 180°$$
$$59° + x = 180°$$
$$-59° + 59° + x = -59° + 180°$$
$$x = 121°$$

15. $\angle CBE$ (an alternate interior angle)

16. In a parallelogram, two angles have measure x, and two angles have measure $180° - x$, with opposite angles having the same measure.
$180° - 50° = 130°$

17. Rhombuses have all sides equal in length.

18. $x + -y + 5$

19. (c) (Suppose $x = 40$ and $y = 140$. Then these numbers work in formulas a, b, and d which are all forms of $x + y = 180$. These numbers do not work in c.)

20. $V - N = L$ (Valleyview had the greater score. Subtract Newton's score and the result is the number of points by which Newton lost.), or $N + L = V$

21. $5 \text{ m} - 0.4 \text{ m} = 4.6 \text{ m}$

22. $Z - 67$ inches (Verify with a special case: If Ray is 69 in., then he is 2 in. taller than Fay: $69 - 67 = 2$)

23. $x° - 7° = -3°$

24. $$x - 7° = -3°$$
$$x + -7° = -3°$$
$$x + -7° + 7° = -3° + 7°$$
$$x = 4°$$

25. 48 m² (area of outer square $= (8 \text{ m})^2 = 64 \text{ m}^2$; area of inner square $= (4 \text{ m})^2 = 16 \text{ m}^2$; area of shaded region $= 64 \text{ m}^2 - 16 \text{ m}^2 = 48 \text{ m}^2$

CHAPTER 7 REVIEW (pp. 330-333)

1. $40 - 360 = 40 + -360 = -320$

2. $-4 - -12 = -4 + 12 = 8$

3. $x - y - z$
$= 10.5 - 3.8 - -7$
$= 10.5 + -3.8 + 7$
$= 10.5 + 7 + -3.8$
$= 13.7$

4. $a - (b - c)$
$= -2 - (-3 - 4)$
$= -2 + -(-3 + -4)$
$= -2 + -(-7)$
$= -2 + 7$
$= 5$

5. $$x - 64 = 8$$
$$x + -64 = 8$$
$$x + -64 + 64 = 8 + 64$$
$$x = 72$$

6. $$6 = y - \frac{1}{5}$$
$$6 = y + -\frac{1}{5}$$
$$6 + \frac{1}{5} = y + -\frac{1}{5} + \frac{1}{5}$$
$$6\frac{1}{5} = y \text{ (or } y = 6.2)$$

7. $$-4.2 = V - -3$$
$$-4.2 = V + 3$$
$$-4.2 + -3 = V + 3 + -3$$
$$-7.2 = V$$

8. $$2 + m - 5 = 4$$
$$2 + m + -5 = 4$$
$$-3 + m = 4$$
$$3 + -3 + m = 3 + 4$$
$$m = 7$$

9.
$$e = c - 4.5$$
$$e = c + \text{-}4.5$$
$$e + 4.5 = c + \text{-}4.5 + 4.5$$
$$e + 4.5 = c$$

10.
$$200 - b = 3$$
$$200 + \text{-}b = 3$$
$$\text{-}200 + 200 + \text{-}b = \text{-}200 + 3$$
$$\text{-}b = \text{-}197$$
$$b = 197$$

11.
$$\text{-}28 = 28 - z$$
$$\text{-}28 = 28 + \text{-}z$$
$$\text{-}28 + \text{-}28 = \text{-}28 + 28 + \text{-}z$$
$$\text{-}56 = \text{-}z$$
$$56 = z$$

12.
$$223 - x = 215$$
$$223 + \text{-}x = 215$$
$$\text{-}223 + 223 + \text{-}x = \text{-}223 + 215$$
$$\text{-}x = \text{-}8$$
$$x = 8$$

13.
$$\frac{4}{9} - y = \frac{5}{18}$$
$$\frac{4}{9} + \text{-}\ y = \frac{5}{18}$$
$$\text{-}\frac{4}{9} + \frac{4}{9} + \text{-}y = \text{-}\frac{4}{9} + \frac{5}{18}$$
$$\text{-}y = \text{-}\frac{4}{9} + \frac{5}{18}$$
$$\text{-}y = \text{-}\frac{8}{18} + \frac{5}{18}$$
$$\text{-}y = \text{-}\frac{3}{18}$$
$$y = \frac{3}{18}$$
$$y = \frac{1}{6}$$

14.
$$180 - y = x$$
$$180 + \text{-}y = x$$
$$180 + \text{-}y + y = x + y$$
$$180 = x + y$$
$$\text{-}x + 180 = \text{-}x + x + y$$
$$\text{-}x + 180 = y$$
$$180 + \text{-}x = y$$
$$180 - x = y$$

15. 90

16. 60° (∠2 and ∠4 are vertical angles.)

17. 180° − x° (∠4 and ∠5 form a linear pair.)

18. 35° (The angle formed by angles 1 and 3, and ∠5 are vertical angles. So m∠1 + m∠3 = 125°. Since m∠1 = 90°, m∠3 = 125° − 90° = 35°.)

19. angles 7, 1, and 3 (∠6 and ∠7 are vertical angles; ∠6 and ∠1 are corresponding angles; ∠7 and ∠3 are alternate interior angles.)

20. 43° (∠3 and ∠7 are corresponding angles.)

21. 180° − y° (m∠5 = y° because ∠2 and ∠5 are corresponding angles. ∠7 and ∠5 form a linear pair.)

22. 45° (m∠4 = 135° because ∠8 and ∠4 are corresponding angles. ∠1 and ∠4 form a linear pair.)

23. 38° (180° − (118° + 24°) = 180° − 142° = 38°)

24.
$$y° + (150° - y°) + x° = 180°$$
$$y° + (150° + \text{-}y°) + x° = 180°$$
$$y° + \text{-}y° + 150° + x° = 180°$$
$$150° + x° = 180°$$
$$\text{-}150° + 150° + x° = \text{-}150° + 180°$$
$$30° = x$$

25. 50° (∠B is a right angle, so m∠B = 90°. m∠BCA = 40° because ∠BCA and ∠ECF are vertical angles. So in triangle ABC, m∠A + 90° + 40° = 180°. Thus, m∠A = 50°.)

26. 162° (In triangle ABC, 72° + 90° + m∠BCA = 180°. So m∠BCA = 18°. ∠BCA and ∠ECB form a linear pair, so m∠ECB = 180° − 18° = 162°.)

27. Yes, 10 cm (All sides have same length; 4 · 2.5 = 10)

28. 90° (Each angle is a right angle.)

29. 4 (Draw parallelogram ABCD. The vertices are named in order, so $\overline{AB}$ and $\overline{BC}$ are opposite sides. In a parallelogram, opposite sides have the same length.)

30. 75° (The angles have measure $x°$ or $180 - x°$. Opposite angles have the same measure, but $\angle A$ and $\angle D$ are not opposite. So m$\angle A = 180° - 105° = 75°$.)

31. ⁻3

32. ⁻535

33. $a + c = b$ (Suppose $a = 10$, $c = 7$, and $b = 3$. These values work in all of the other sentences.)

34. $3 - 8 = x$ (The solution to $3 - 8 = x$ is ⁻5. The solution to each of the other sentences is 11.)

35. $180° - 40° = 140°$

36. 40°

37. $180° - x°$

38. 4

39. 1, 8, 4, and 5

40. 7

41. 1, 7, 5, and 3 ($\angle 1$ and $\angle 7$ each form a linear pair with $\angle 8$. $\angle 3$ and $\angle 5$ are equal in measure to $\angle 1$ and $\angle 7$.)

42. rhombuses and squares

43. rectangles and squares (The angles are right angles.)

44. all (It is true of all parallelograms. Rectangles, rhombuses, and squares are parallelograms.)

45. all (See previous answer.)

46. The sum of the two measures would be 200°. But this is greater than 180°, the sum of the measures of the angles in any triangle.

47. yes; For example, the angles could have measures 40°, 60°, and 80°, which add to 180°.

48. 60 minutes $- 9\frac{1}{2}$ minutes =

60 minutes $- 9.5$ minutes $= 50.5$ minutes

49.
$$A - 2000 = 3500$$
$$A + {}^-2000 = 3500$$
$$A + {}^-2000 + 2000 = 3500 + 2000$$
$$A = 5500 \text{ sq ft}$$

50. $x - y = 100$ (Verify this with a special case. Suppose she had $600 and withdrew $500. Then $600 - $500 = $100.)

51. $AB + BC + CE = AE$
$$AB + 12 + 17 = 50$$
$$AB + 29 = 50$$
$$AB + 29 + {}^-29 = 50 + {}^-29$$
$$AB = 21$$

52. $x = {}^-13° - 5°$
$x = {}^-13° + {}^-5°$
$x = {}^-18°$ F

53. 1905 or 1904 ($1982 - 77 = 1905$. If he died during that part of 1982 before his birthday, then he was born in 1904.)

54. (b) (Try a special case to verify the expression $70 - x$. Suppose the person loses 2 kg. Then the resulting weight is 70 kg $- 2$ kg.)

55. 6.6 million $- 4.1$ million $= 2.5$ million

56. 13 points too high (Subtract the estimated value minus the actual value: $12 - {}^-1 = 12 + 1 = 13$.)

57. $F - R = L$ (Try a special case. Suppose the original fare is $400. If it is reduced $50, then the lower fare is $350. $400 - $50 = $350)

58. ⁻8

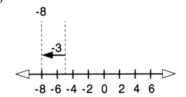

59. ⁻2

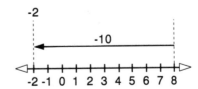

LESSON 8-1 (pp. 336–340)

1. 1 hour

2. vertical

3. Several possible answers. Sample: relaxation time

4. 100,000 people

5. horizontal

6. Filipino (Filipinos: 782,000; Japanese: 716,000)

7. Los Angeles and Houston (For these cities, the 1980 bar is longer than the 1970 bar.)

8. New York City (The 1980 bar is shorter than the 1970 bar by a greater amount than any of the other cities.)

9. 2 million people

10. 1 billion dollars   [*4 billion dollars]

11. **a.** 1981 [*1989]
    b. $-4.9 billion (This represents a loss.) [*$-20.7 billion]

12. **a.** 1979   [*1985]
    b. $3.6 billion (This represents a gain.) [*$3.7 billion]

13. vertical

14. **a.** yes   **b.** 2

15. **a.** yes   **b.** 3

16. **a.** no; **b.** The first two intervals have different lengths.

17. **a.** no
    b. The numbers are not equally spaced.

18. 3.4 (Write the numbers in thousandths: 3.390, 3.400, 3.391, 3.294. 3.400 is the greatest.)

19. 3.4 and 3.294 (The largest difference is between the greatest number and the least number.)

20. 1% or 0.5% (If the interval is too large, say 2%, the information cannot be graphed as accurately. If it is too small, say 0.1%, too many intervals would need to be shown.)

21. 100,000 or 200,000 votes

22. **a.** 100 miles
    b.
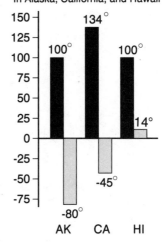

Miles of Coastline

23. All-time High and Low Temperatures In Alaska, California, and Hawaii

24. Alaska; $100° - {}^-80° = 100° + 80° = 180°$

25. $-2,200,000,000$

26. 7,200,000 people (7.2% of 100,000,000 = .072 · 100,000,000 = 7,200,000)

27. Lincoln: 1,900,000 (1,866,352 is between 1,800,000 and 1,900,000 and is nearer to 1,900,000.); Douglas: 1,400,000 (1,375,157 is between 1,300,000 and 1,400,000 and is nearer to 1,400,000.); Breckinridge: 800,000 (845,763 is between 800,000 and 900,000 and is nearer to 800,000.); Bell: 600,000 (589,581 is between 500,000 and 600,000 and is nearer to 600,000.)

28. a. $\frac{360°}{2} = 180°$

b. $\frac{360°}{3} = 120°$; $\frac{360°}{5} = 72°$

29. 144 (.4 · 360 = 144)

30. a.
$$150 + 45 + x = 180$$
$$150 + x = 180$$
$$^-150 + 150 + x = ^-150 + 180$$
$$x = 30$$

b. Several possible answers. Sample: A triangle has two angles with measures 105° and 45°. What is the measure of the third angle?

31. a. yes

b. The *1988 Information Please Almanac* gives the following populations: Bombay, India: 8,248,000; Cairo, Egypt: 12,560,000; Calcutta, India: 9,194,000; Jakarta, Indonesia: 7,636,000; Mexico City: 12,900,000; Moscow: 8,642,000; Peking (Beijing): 9,330,000; São Paulo, Brazil: 12,600,000; Seoul, South Korea: 9,600,000; Shanghai: 11,940,000; Tianjin (Tientsin), China: 7,850,000; Tokyo: 8,386,000

32. Answers will vary.

LESSON 8-2 (pp. 341-346)

1.

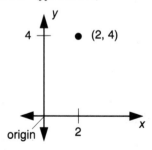

2. *B*

3. *E*

4. *P*

5. *C*

6. *I*

7. *H*

8. *R*

9. *F*

10. *K*

11. *R*

12. *L*

13. *J*

14.

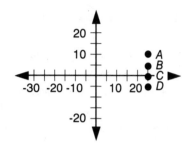

15.

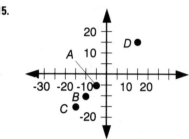

16. a. up

b. The point for 5 A.M. is higher.

17. 14.5° (14.5° is halfway between 11° (at 11:00 A.M.) and 18° (at noon).)

18.

Temperature

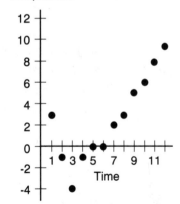

19. $^-3$

20. *y*

21. origin

22. *y*

23. 0

24. parentheses, comma

25. II (Go left for a negative *x*-coordinate; go up for a positive *y*-coordinate.)
26. IV (Go right for a positive *x*-coordinate; go down for a negative *y*-coordinate.)
27. III (Go left for a negative *x*-coordinate; go down for a negative *y*-coordinate.)
28. I (Go right for a positive *x*-coordinate; go up for a positive *y*-coordinate.)
29. III and IV (A point with 0 for the *x*-coordinate is on the *y*-axis; go down for a negative *y*-coordinate.)
30. I and IV (Go right for a positive *x*-coordinate; a point with 0 for the *y*-coordinate is on the *x*-axis.)
31. II and III (Go left for a negative *x*-coordinate; a point with 0 for the *y*-coordinate is on the *x*-axis.)
32. III and IV (A point with 0 for the *x*-coordinate is on the *y*-axis; go down for a negative *y*-coordinate.)
33. III (Refer to Question 27.)
34. IV (Refer to Question 26.)
35. II (Refer to Question 25.)
36. I (Refer to Question 28.)
37. Numbers on the scale should be 0, 2640, 5280, 7920, 10,560, 13,200, 15,840, 18,480, and 21,120. (Multiply 5280 ft by 0, then by .5, then by 1, and so on.) Change the label from miles to feet.

38. Unemployment Rates

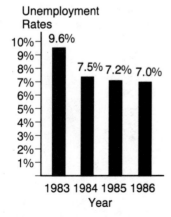

39. *1992 Edition:*

Unemployment Rates

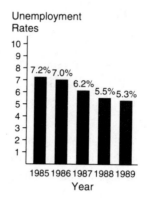

39.

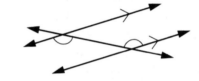

40. 20°
41. $y - x$

$$= -\frac{13}{16} - \frac{-17}{32}$$

$$= -\frac{13}{16} + \frac{17}{32}$$

$$= -\frac{26}{32} + \frac{17}{32}$$

$$= -\frac{9}{32}$$

42. $a + b = 9$
        $a + 15 = 9$
 $a + 15 + -15 = 9 + -15$
          $a = -6$

43. Answers will vary.

LESSON 8-3 (pp. 348-353)
1. Many possible answers. Samples: (10, 80), (2, 88), (45, 45)
2. line   3. $x + y = 90$
4. Many possible answers. Samples: (6, 2), (-1, -5), (4, 0)
5. line   6. 8

7. a.
$$x - y = 5$$
$$3 - y = 5$$
$$3 + {}^-y = 5$$
$${}^-3 + 3 + {}^-y = {}^-3 + 5$$
$${}^-y = 2$$
$$y = {}^-2$$

b. $(3, {}^-2)$

8. a.
$$x = 6 - y$$
$$40 = 6 - y$$
$$40 = 6 + {}^-y$$
$${}^-6 + 40 = {}^-6 + 6 + {}^-y$$
$$34 = {}^-y$$
$${}^-34 = y$$

b. $(40, {}^-34)$

9. Some points on this line: $(0, 10)$, $(5, 5)$, $(8, 2)$. (Find values for x and y such that $x + y = 10$.)

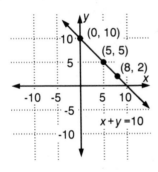

10. Some points on this line: $(6, 0)$, $(4, {}^-2)$, $(0, {}^-6)$ (Find values for x and y such that $x - y = 6$.)

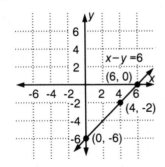

11. (c) ($x - y = 2 - 3 = {}^-1$, so it is on line a.
$-x - y = {}^-2 - 3 = {}^-5$, so it is on line b.
$x - y = 2 - 3 = {}^-1$, so it is not on line c.
$y - x = 3 - 2 = 1$, so it is on line d.)

12. (c) (The line in graph a contains $(0, 0)$, which does not work in $x + y = 10$. Neither point labeled in graph b works. Both labeled points in graph c work. In graph d, $({}^-10, 0)$ does not work.)

13. a. $x - y = 8$
b. some points on this line: $(0, {}^-8)$, $(8, 0)$, $(10, 2)$

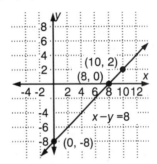

14. a. $x + y = 60$
b.

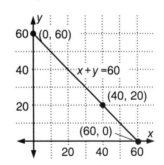

15. a.
$$y + x = {}^-7$$
$$y + x + {}^-x = {}^-7 + {}^-x$$
$$y = {}^-7 + {}^-x, \text{ or } y = {}^-x - 7$$

b. Many possible answers. Samples: $(0, {}^-7)$
(When $x = 0$, $-x - 7 = {}^-0 + {}^-7 = {}^-7$.),
$(2, {}^-9)$ (When $x = 2$, $-x - 7 = {}^-2 + {}^-7 = {}^-9$.), $({}^-10, 3)$ (When $x = {}^-10$, $-x - 7 = {}^-({}^-10) + {}^-7 = 10 + {}^-7 = 3$.)

16. a.
$$-x - y = 0$$
$$-x + -y = 0$$
$$x + -x + -y = x + 0$$
$$-y = x$$
$$y = -x$$

b. Many possible answers. Samples:
(0, 0) (When $x = 0$, $y = -x = -0 = 0$.),
(1, -1) (When $x = 1$, $y = -x = -1$.),
(-7.3, 7.3) (When $x = -7.3$, $y = -x = -(-7.3) = 7.3$.)

17. II (Move left for a negative x-coordinate; move up for a positive y-coordinate.)

18. II and III (Move left for a negative x-coordinate; a point with 0 for the y-coordinate is on the x-axis.)

19. a. $8.7\% + 16.4\% = 25.1\%$

b. 0.5% ($13.8\% + 25.2\% + 22.6\% + 12.8\% + 8.7\% + 16.4\% = 99.5\%$; $100\% - 99.5\% = 0.5\%$)

20. $180° - (5° + 10°) = 165°$

21. $10.50 (5.25% of $200 = .0525 \cdot 200 = 10.5$)

22. 1 liter $\approx$ 1.06 quarts

23. 99 (There are nine 2-digit palindromes: 11, 22, 33, 44, . . . , 99. Insert any digit between the 2 digits of a 2-digit palindrome, and you get a 3-digit palindrome. For example, insert a 5 between the two 3s in 33 and you get 353. Since there are 10 digits, each of the nine 2-digit palindromes can become ten 3-digit palindromes. So there are $9 \cdot 10 = 90$ 3-digit palindromes.)

24. a. Many possible answers. Samples: (-10, 70), (2.4, 57.6) (A negative number or a non-integral number is meaningless for counting students.)

b. x must be an integer between 0 and 60 inclusive.

25. a. The first four lines are:

X	Y
10	80
11	79
12	78

The values of X continue to increase by 1 while the values of Y decrease by 1. The last line is: 80   10

b. The values of X increase by 10 and the values of Y decrease by 10.

X	Y
10	80
20	70
30	60
40	50
50	40
60	30
70	20
80	10

c. Many possible answers. Sample: change line 20 to FOR X = 10 TO 100 STEP 5. Now the values of X increase by 5 and the values of Y decrease by 5. The last line is 100   -10.

LESSON 8-4 (pp. 354-357)

1. 1987-88
1992 Edition: 1988-1989

2. a. 12°   **b.** 5°   **c.** 32°
1992 Edition: **a.** 12°   **b.** 34°   **c.** 31°

3. a. 16°   **b.** 20°   **c.** -9°
1992 Edition: **a.** 16°   **b.** 10°   **c.** 31°

4. Overall, 1986–87 was warmer than the normal.
1992 Edition: Overall, both years were warmer than normal.

5. January (Read the "normal" broken line.)

6. January 6, 1988 (-14°)
1992 Edition: December 24, 1989 (-6°)

7. 1 day   **8.** 5° F

9. (Dec 24th, -20°)

10. Graphs can show a lot of information in a small space; graphs can also show trends.

11. Graphs can describe drawings and geometric figures.

12. Computers store the coordinates of key points and the order in which the points are to be connected.

13. circle

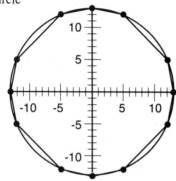

14. **a.** $B = (0, 12)$ (up 12 units along the y-axis), $C = (8, 12)$ (to the right 8 units, up 12 units), $D = (8, 2)$ (to the right 8 units, up 2 units), $E = (24, 2)$ (to the right 24 units, up 2 units), $F = (24, 0)$ (to the right 24 units along the x-axis)

b. $(24, 1)$ (to the right 24 units, up 1 unit)

c. near $(4, 9)$

15.

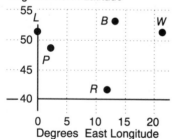

Degrees North Latitude

16. **a.** octagon   **b.** obtuse

c. four   **d.** four

(Trace the barrel to help answer these questions.)

17. some points on the line: $(0, -3)$, $(5, 2)$, $(3, 0)$ (Find values for x and y such that $x - y = 3$)

18. **a.** $x = y - 5$ (or $x + 5 = y$)

b. Many possible answers. Samples (graph not shown): $(67, 72)$, $(70, 75)$, $(85, 90)$, $(81, 86)$, $(75, 80)$. (Find values for x and y such that $x = y - 5$.)

19. $(3, 8)$

20. **a.** 69   **b.** 12

LESSON 8-5 (pp. 358-361)

1. The figure is moved 3 units to the right.

2. The figure is moved 10 units up.

3. The figure is moved 7 units down.

4. The figure is moved 6 units to the left.

5. translation

6. preimage, image

7. (Graph is not shown.) The image is a triangle with vertices $A' = (3, -5)$, $B' = (7, 2)$, and $C' = (-5, 4)$.

8. The image is a triangle with vertices $A'(-2, 0)$, $B'(2, 7)$, and $C'(-10, 9)$.

9. The graph is moved up k units.

10. The graph is moved h units to the left.

11. size, shape

12. true

13. **a., b.**

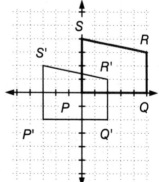

c. congruent

14. $A' = (-1, 9)$; $B' = (2, 9)$ (Compare C to C'. -1 was added to the first coordinate of C, and 9 was added to the second coordinate of C, to get the coordinates of C'.)

15. Many possible answers. Samples:

   a. image of (0, 0) is (4, −5),

      image of (3, −1) is (7, −6),

      image of (−2, 3) is (2, −2)

   b.

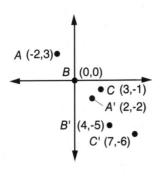

16. $B' = (320, 0)$, $C' = (320, 100)$,
$D' = (280, 100)$, $E' = (260, 40)$,
$F' = (60, 40)$, $G' = (40, 100)$,
$H' = (0, 100)$. (Compare A to A'.
160 was added to the first coordinate of A, and
the second coordinate of A was unchanged, to
get the coordinates of A'.)

17. some points on the line: (2, −2), (−5, 5),
(0, 0). (Find values for x and y such that
$x + y = 0$.)

18. World Population
(billions)

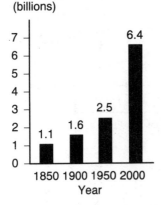

19. **a.** World Population
(billions)

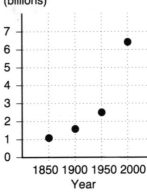

   b. It is easier to insert additional points.

20. Many possible answers. Sample:

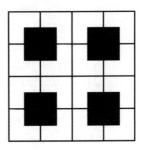

21. Answers will vary. (See page 373 for a sample
figure.)

LESSON 8-6 (pp. 362-366)

  1. reflecting line or mirror

  2. perpendicular

  3. distance

  4. coincides

  5. false

  6. true

  7. transformations

  8.

9.

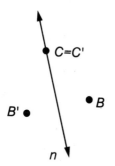

10.

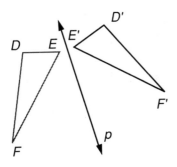

11.

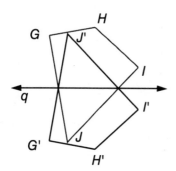

12. (2, −4)

13. a.-b.

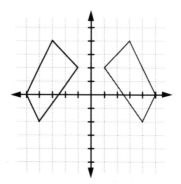

c. over the *y*-axis

14. a. Many possible answers. Samples:
The image of (1, 4) is (4, 1),
the image of (6, −2) is (−2, 6),
the image of (3, 0) is (0, 3).

b. The graph (not shown) of these points and
their images show a reflection over the line
$y = x$.

15. TOMATO

16. WHY

17. CHEEK

18. BIKE

19. $B = (150, 0)$ (150 units to the right along the
x-axis), $C = (150, 50)$ (150 units to the right,
up $225 - 175 = 50$ units), $D = (50, 50)$ (50
units to the right, up 50 units), $E = (50, 225)$
(50 units to the right, up 225 units), $F =
(0, 225)$ (up 225 units along the *y*-axis)

20. some points on the line: (0, −10), (10, 0),
(5, −5) (Find values for *x* and *y* such that
$x - y = 10$.)

21. a. 5%

b. $-7\% - -19\% = -7\% + 19\% = 12\%$

c. telephone/telegraph

22. Answers will vary. (First, list the letters that
could work. For example, A and M work with
a vertical line, E and K work with a horizontal
line. Then try to make words.)

LESSON 8-7 (pp. 367-371)

1. A figure has line symmetry when it coincides with its reflection image over some line.

2. two

3. Many possible answers. Sample:

4. Many possible answers. Sample:

5. Many possible answers. Sample:

6. Many possible answers. Sample:

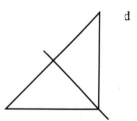

7. infinitely many
8. B, C, D, E, H, I, O, X
9. A, H, I, M, O, T, U, V, W, X, Y
10. perhaps O and Q
11. 8
12. 6

13.

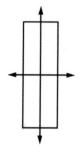

14.

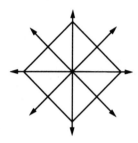

15.

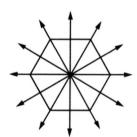

16.

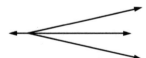

17.

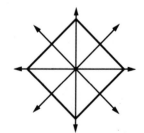

*These are solutions to questions changed in or added to the *1992 Edition.*

18.

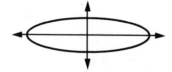

19. Many possible answers. Sample:

20. Many possible answers. Sample:

21.

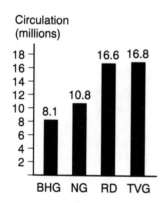

Circulation
(millions)

```
18
16           16.6 16.8
14
12     10.8
10  8.1
8
6
4
2
   BHG  NG   RD  TVG
```

1992 Edition:

Circulation
(millions)

```
18           16.3
16               15.8
14
12     10.1
10  8.0
8
6
4
2
   BHG  NG   RD  TVG
```

22.

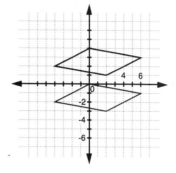

23. some points on this line: (−2, −2), (5, −9), and (0, 4) (Find values for x and y such that x + y = −4.)

24. (−3, −8) (Graph (−3, 8) and reflect it over the x-axis to find the image.)

25. $a + 3(b + 4(c + 5))$
$= 1 + 3(2 + 4(3 + 5))$
$= 1 + 3(2 + 4 \cdot 8)$
$= 1 + 3(2 + 32)$
$= 1 + 3 \cdot 34$
$= 1 + 102$
$= 103$

26. Yes, 90° (Trace the figure and rotate it over the figure in the book about the "center" point. Stop when your tracing coincides with the figure in the book. How much did you turn your tracing?)

LESSON 8-8 (pp. 372-375)

1. A tessellation is a filling up of space by congruent copies of a figure that do not overlap.

2. The fundamental region is the figure whose copies fill up the space.

3. a regular hexagon

4. A regular polygon is a convex polygon whose sides have the same length and whose angles have the same measure.

5. equilateral triangles, squares, regular hexagons

6. yes (For example, parallelograms tessellate.)
7. yes (Consider Escher's tessellations.)
8. Several arrangements are possible. For a sample, see page 372. In 9–13, sample tessellations are shown.

9.

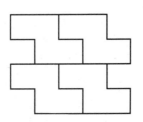

10.

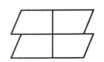

11.

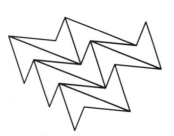

12.

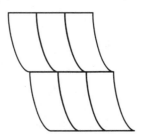

13.

14. **a.** octagon   **b.** no
15. **a.** A sheet of stamps is a tessellation; rectangles tessellate, so no paper is wasted.
   b. Many possible answers. Sample: Unusual stamps are popular with collectors and can be a source of income for a country.

16. $\dfrac{180°}{3} = 60°$

17. square

18. Some points on the line are: (0, 5), (-2, 3), (-5, 0). (Find values for x and y such that $y = x + 5$.)

19.

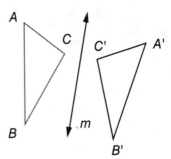

20.

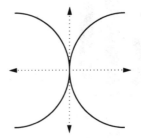

21. There are no symmetry lines.

22. (−4, 8), (2, 5); (Reflect the given points over the y-axis.)

23. 2×10^{-8} (Write 2. The decimal point must move 8 places to the left to get 0.00000002, so the exponent of 10 is −8.)

24. $A + B + C + D = 360$
$A + -A + B + -B + C + D + -D$
$\qquad = 360 + -A + -B + -D$
$\qquad C = 360 - A - B - D$

25. (c) (This expression works for triangles and quadrilaterals. When $n = 3$, $180(n - 2)/n = 180(3 - 2)/3 = 180/3 = 60$. When $n = 4$, $180(n - 2)/n = 180(4 - 2)/4 = 360/4 = 90$.)

26. Answers will vary.

27. a. Granada, Spain **b.** a palace
   c. Moorish kings **d.** 1248–1354

CHAPTER 8 PROGRESS SELF-TEST (p. 378)

1. the week of November 9

2. about 3 million barrels

3. 0.4 million barrels

4.

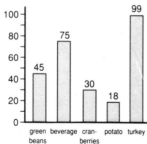

Cost of a Thanksgiving Meal, 1988
Cost (in pennies)

green beans 45, beverage 75, cranberries 30, potato 18, turkey 99

5. a. *E* **b.** *A*

6. *E*

7. *B* (The values of −4 for *x* and 2 for *y* work in the sentence $x + y = -2$: $-4 + 2 = -2$.)

8. (2, 15) (Add 10 to the second coordinate.)

9.

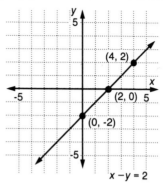

$x - y = 2$

(4, 2), (2, 0), (0, -2)

10. $M = (3, 6)$ (*M* is 3 units below (3, 9), so the first coordinate of *M* is 3 and the second coordinate is 9 − 3 or 6.)

11. Hole = (9, 10.5). (The hole is directly above (9, 3) so its first coordinate is 9. Its second coordinate is halfway between 9 and 12, so it is 10.5.)

12. Many possible answers. Sample:

13. Many possible answers. Sample:

14.

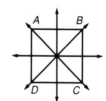

A *B*
D *C*

15.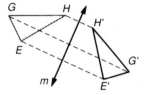

16. A sample tessellation is shown.

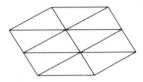

17.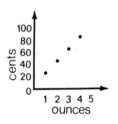

18. 72°

19. List any two: Graphs can show a lot of information in a small place. Graphs can picture relationships. Graphs show trends. Graphs can picture geometric figures.

20. Two figures are congruent when they have the same size and shape.

CHAPTER 8 REVIEW (pp. 379-381)

1-2.

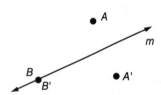

3-4.

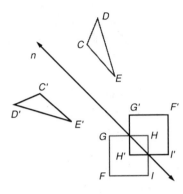

5.

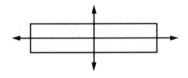

6. There are no lines of symmetry.

7.

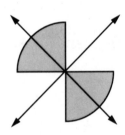

8.

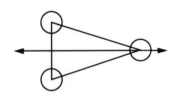

Sample tessellations are shown for 9 and 10.

9.

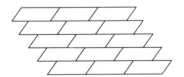

10.

11. 90° (Line t is perpendicular to $\overline{PP'}$.)

12. 14 (P and P' are the same distance from t.)

13. yes

14. yes

15. 2″

16. 16 (The lengths of the two bars differ the most at age 16.)

17. 4′ 11″

18. boys (Notice that the gap between boys and girls at age 12 decreases at age 13. The boys grow more, nearly closing the gap.)

19. 10 calories

20.

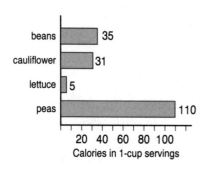

21. 1 million

22.

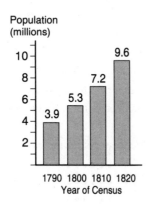

23. The number of personal computers increased rapidly from 1982 through 1987.

24. 1983

25. 1985

26. 1985 to 1987

1992 Edition: 1987 to 1989

27.

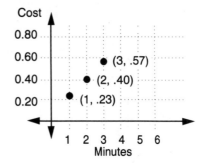

28.

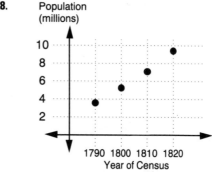

29. List any two: Graphs show trends. Graphs can picture geometric figures. Graphs can picture relationships between numbers. Graphs can show a lot of information in a small space.

30. $A = (3, 1); D = (5, -5)$

31. $B = (-2, 4); C = (-2, 0)$

32.

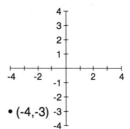

33.

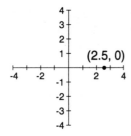

(2.5, 0)

34.

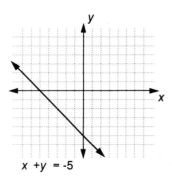

$x + y = -5$

35.

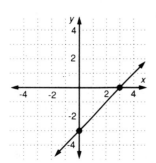

36.

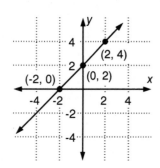

(2, 4)

(-2, 0)   (0, 2)

37. $x - y = 3$ (The value of -2 for x and -5 for y works in the sentence $x - y = 3$: $-2 - -5 = -2 + 5 = 3$.)

38. (4, 5) (The x-coordinate stays the same; the y-coordinate increases by 5.)

39. (-2, -3) (Graph (2, -3) and reflect it over the y-axis.)

40. (5, -6) (Graph (5, 6) and reflect it over the x-axis.)

41. (9, 3); (7, 7); (10, 5)

(Add 7 to each x-coordinate;

subtract 2 from each y-coordinate.)

CHAPTER 9   PATTERNS LEADING TO MULTIPLICATION

LESSON 9-1   (pp. 384-388)

1. 3 cm $\cdot$ 4 cm = 12 cm^2

2.

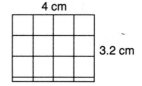

4 cm

3.2 cm

The entire rectangle has area 3.2 $\cdot$ 4 cm^2.

Within it is a rectangle with area 3 $\cdot$ 4 cm^2.

3. cm^2 (square centimeters)

4. The area of a rectangle with length ℓ and width w is ℓw.

5. 2 in. $\cdot$ 1 in. = 2 sq in.

6. 6 units $\cdot$ 4 units = 24 square units

7. **a.** 3   **b.** 20   **c.** 3 $\cdot$ 20 = 60

8. **a.** The array has 5 dots across, 7 dots up and down in each column; **b.** 7 $\cdot$ 5 = 35

9. For any numbers a and b, $ab = ba$.

10. Switching dimensions of a rectangle keeps its area.

11. Several possible answers. Samples:

12. Many possible answers. Samples: 1 in. and 15 in., 2.5 in. and 6 in.

13. $cr = d$ (Check this with the special cases in Questions 7 and 8.)

14. A: $15 \cdot 23 = 345$ seats;
B: 15 mm $\cdot 23$ mm $= 345$ mm^2

15. (b) (The area of store $1 = 60$ ft $\cdot 120$ ft $= 7200$ ft^2; the area of store $2 = 90$ ft $\cdot 90$ ft $= 8100$ ft^2.)

16. 1262.5 ft^2 ($55 \cdot 37.5 - 40 \cdot 20 = 2062.5 - 800 = 1262.5$)

17. true (This illustrates the Commutative Property of Multiplication. It is true for any value of x.)

18. 18 square units (The horizontal dimension is 3 units, from (2, 4) to (5, 4). The vertical dimension is 6 units, from (2, 4) to (2, 10). (3 units $\cdot$ 6 units $= 18$ square units)

19. **a.** yes ($357 \cdot 246 = 87,822$; $246 \cdot 357 = 87,822$); **b.** yes ($.5 \cdot .4 = .2$; $.4 \cdot .5 = .2$)
c. yes ($67.92 \cdot 0.00043 = 0.0292056$; $0.00043 \cdot 67.92 = 0.0292056$)

20.
$$x + \frac{22}{7} = -\frac{3}{2}$$
$$x + \frac{22}{7} + -\frac{22}{7} = -\frac{3}{2} + -\frac{22}{7}$$
$$x = -\frac{3}{2} + -\frac{22}{7}$$
$$x = -\frac{21}{14} + -\frac{44}{14}$$
$$x = -\frac{65}{14}$$

21.

22. 1 kg $\approx$ 2.2 lb

23. $14 - 3(x + 3y)$
$= 14 - 3(-2 + 3 \cdot 5)$
$= 14 - 3(-2 + 15)$
$= 14 - 3(13)$
$= 14 - 39$
$= 14 + -39$
$= -25$

24. **a.** 48 (48.49 is between 48 and 49 and is nearer to 48.)
b. $\frac{4849}{100}$ ($48.49 = 48\frac{49}{100} = \frac{4849}{100}$)

25. **a.** $4 \cdot 6$ miles $= 24$ miles
b. 6 miles $\cdot$ 6 miles $= 36$ square miles

26. about 1,380,000 students (58% of 2,380,000 $= .58 \cdot 2,380,000 = 1,380,000$)

27. 0.270901 cm^3 (Volume of larger cube $= (3.01)^3 = 27.270901$; volume of smaller cube $= 3^3 = 27$. $27.270901 - 27 = 0.270901$)

28. 714 square units (There are 2 squares with side length 1 unit. The other squares, in increasing size, have side lengths of 2 units, 3 units, 5 units, 8 units, 13 units, and 21 units. So the total area $= 2 \cdot 1^2 + 2^2 + 3^2 + 5^2 + 8^2 + 13^2 + 21^2 = 2 + 4 + 9 + 25 + 64 + 169 + 441 = 714$.)

*29 *1992 Edition only:* **a.** HHH, HHT, HTH, THH, HTT, THT, TTH, TTT

b.

Number of Tosses	1	2	3
Number of Outcomes	2 or 2^1	4 or 2^2	8 or 2^3

c. For n tosses, the number of possible outcomes is 2^n.

LESSON 9-2 (pp. 389-392)

1. rectangular solid

2. rectangle   **3.** 6

4. The surface area of a solid is the sum of the areas of its faces.

5. **a.**

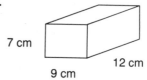

7 cm

9 cm

12 cm

b.

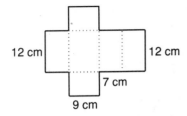

c. 510 cm² (12 · 7 + 12 · 7 + 12 · 9 +
12 · 9 + 9 · 7 + 9 · 7 = 84 + 84 +
108 + 108 + 63 + 63 = 510)

6. a.

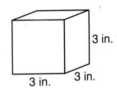

b.

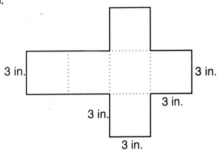

c. 54 square inches (3 · 3 + 3 · 3 + 3 · 3
+ 3 · 3 + 3 · 3 + 3 · 3 = 6 · 9 = 54)

7. 1116 square inches (Change 2 ft to 24 in.
Surface area = 24 · 3 + 24 · 3 + 18 · 3 +
18 · 3 + 18 · 24 + 18 · 24 = 72 + 72 +
54 + 54 + 432 + 432 = 1116)

8. $2\ell w + 2\ell h + 2hw$ (Check this with the
special cases in Questions 5c, 6c, and 7.)

9. 367 square inches ($2\ell w + 2\ell h + 2hw$ =
2 · 14 · 9 + 2 · 14 · 2.5 + 2 · 9 · 2.5 =
252 + 70 + 45 = 367)

10. Move one of the top rectangles to the bottom.

11. Construct a box. (Start with a flat pattern like
the one shown on page 389.)

12. a. 34 cm by 42 cm (5 + 24 + 5 = 34; 5 +
16 + 5 + 16 = 42)

b. 260 cm² (Area of rectangular sheet of
cardboard = 34 cm · 42 cm = 1428 cm²;
surface area of box, as found on page 390,
= 1168 cm². 1428 cm² − 1168 cm² =
260 cm²)

13. 150 square units (6 · 5² = 6 · 25 = 150)

14. 1360 cm² (24 · 20 + 2 · 24 · 10 +
2 · 20 · 10 = 480 + 480 + 400 = 1360)

15. 4 · 13 = 52

16. a. 0

b. 0.12 · 3.4 + 3.4 · 0.12 − 0.12 · 3.4
= 0.12 · 3.4 + 3.4 · 0.12 + ⁻(0.12 ·
3.4)
= 3.4 · 0.12
= 0.408

17. Commutative Property of Addition

18. $\frac{1}{6} - \frac{3}{18} - \frac{2}{3} + \frac{5}{9}$

$= \frac{1}{6} + \frac{-3}{18} + \frac{-2}{3} + \frac{5}{9}$

$= \frac{3}{18} + \frac{-3}{18} + \frac{-12}{18} + \frac{10}{18}$

$= \frac{-12}{18} + \frac{10}{18}$

$= \frac{-2}{18}$

$= \frac{-1}{9}$

19. 34 + 57 = 91
91 − 57 = 34
91 − 34 = 57

20. $x - y = 34$
$x + {}^-y = 34$
$x + {}^-y + y = 34 + y$
$-34 + x = -34 + 34 + y$
$-34 + x = y$, or $y = x - 34$

21. a. $n - 2$

b. $2 < n$

c. $2 - n$

22. 40 + 60 + 40 + 60 = 200 units

23. $(5 \text{ units})^3 = 125$ cubic units

24.

There are 10 possible patterns.

LESSON 9-3 (pp. 393-397)

1. counting, using a formula

2. 6 cm • 3 cm • 4 cm = 72 cm³

3. 12 in. • 6 in. • 2.25 in. = 162 in.³

4. 10 meters • w meters • d meters = 10wd cubic meters

5. $V = Bh = 40 \text{ cm}^2 \cdot 4 \text{ cm} = 160 \text{ cm}^3$

6. 10 in. • 12 in. • 1.5 in. = 180 in.³

7. Ah

8. For any numbers a, b, and c: $a(bc) = (ab)c = abc$

9. Many possible answers. Sample: $3 \cdot (4 \cdot 0.5) = 3 \cdot 2 = 6$ and $(3 \cdot 4) \cdot 0.5 = 12 \cdot 0.5 = 6$

10. 4370 (Multiply the 5 and 2 first.)

11. 0 (Notice that the minuend and subtrahend are the same number.)

12. 67 (Find 50% of 2 first: half of 2 is 1.)

13. 9 ft • 12 ft • 8 ft = 864 ft³

14. Many possible answers. Sample: 12, 12, and 1; 12, 4, and 3. (The product of the three numbers must be 144.)

15. **a.**

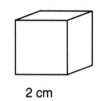

2 cm

b. cube

c. Many possible answers. Sample:

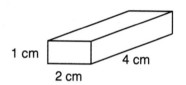

1 cm   2 cm   4 cm

16. **a.** 24 in. • 9 in. • 5 in. = 1080 in.³

b. 762 in.² (2 • 24 • 9 + 2 • 24 • 5 + 2 • 9 • 5 = 432 + 240 + 90 = 762)

17. 364 • 720 = 262,080 dots

18. $2WL + 2LD + 2WD$ (2 rectangles have dimensions W by L, 2 have dimensions L by D, and 2 have dimensions W by D.)

19.
$$83 - x = 110$$
$$83 + {}^-x = 110$$
$${}^-83 + 83 + {}^-x = {}^-83 + 110$$
$${}^-x = 27$$
$$x = {}^-27$$

20. **a.** $180° - (100° + 32\frac{1}{2}°) = 47\frac{1}{2}°$

b. two   **c.** one

21. **a.** 132.678 is shown on the display.

b. 132.678 is shown on the display.

c. Both displays are the same; Commutative Property of Multiplication

22. $<$ ($^-4 - 4 = ^-4 + ^-4 = ^-8$, and
$^-4 + 4 = 0$; $^-8 < 0$)

23. $<$ ($^-7.352$ is to the left of $^-7.351$ on a
horizontal number line.)

24. $>$ ($\frac{2}{3} = .\overline{6}$. So in the ninth decimal place of
$\frac{2}{3}$ there is a 6, while there is a zero in the ninth
decimal place of .66666666.)

25. **a.** fourth (Go right 4 units, then 1 unit down.)
   b. Many possible answers. Sample: $y = x - 5$
   (Substituting 4 for x and $^-1$ for y in this
   equation yields $^-1 = 4 - 5$. This is a true
   sentence.)

26. $(3n + 5)(2n - 3)$
   $= (3 \cdot 10 + 5)(2 \cdot 10 - 3)$
   $= (30 + 5)(20 - 3)$
   $= 35 \cdot 17$
   $= 595$

27. 2.6 km $= 2.6 \cdot 1000$ m $= 2600$ meters

28. 8

29. three places to the right

30. **a.** $6 \cdot 6 = 36$
   b.

X	3.0	3.2	3.4	3.6	3.8	4.0
7.0	21.0	22.4	23.8	25.2	26.6	28.0
7.2	21.6	23.04	24.48	25.92	27.36	28.8
7.4	22.2	23.68	25.16	26.64	28.12	29.6
7.6	22.8	24.32	25.84	27.36	28.88	30.4
7.8	23.4	24.96	26.52	28.08	29.64	31.2
8.0	24.0	25.6	27.2	28.8	30.4	32.0

   c. Many possible answers. Samples: In any
   column, the difference between an entry and
   the one above it is the same number. Every
   number ends in an even digit. Products
   increase as you go down or to the right.

LESSON 9-4 (pp. 398-402)

1. cm

2. cm^3

3. cm^2

4. cm^2

5. area

6. volume

7. perimeter

8. surface area

9. **a.** miles
   b. square miles

10. Many possible answers. Sample:

11. false (They are only numerically equal.)

12. Many possible answers. Sample: 24 by 2 by 1
   (volume $= 24 \cdot 2 \cdot 1 = 48$ cubic units and
   surface area $= 2 \cdot 24 \cdot 2 + 2 \cdot 24 \cdot 1 +$
   $2 \cdot 2 \cdot 1 = 96 + 48 + 4 = 148$ units) and
   6 by 4 by 2 (volume $= 6 \cdot 4 \cdot 2 =$
   48 cubic units and surface area $= 2 \cdot 6 \cdot 4 +$
   $2 \cdot 6 \cdot 2 + 2 \cdot 4 \cdot 2 = 48 + 24 + 16$
   $= 88$ units)

13. 5 in. $\cdot$ 7 in. $= 35$ in.^{2}; 7 in. $\cdot$ 14 in. $=$
   98 in.^{2}; 5 in. $\cdot$ 14 in. $= 70$ in.^{2}

14. **a.** $4 \cdot 11$ mm $+ 4 \cdot 12$ mm $+ 4 \cdot 13$ mm $=$
   144 mm
   b. $2 \cdot 11$mm $\cdot 12$ mm $+$
   $2 \cdot 11$ mm $\cdot 13$ mm $+$
   $2 \cdot 12$mm $\cdot 13$ mm $= 862$ mm^2
   c. 11mm $\cdot 12$ mm $\cdot 13$ mm $= 1716$ mm^3

15. $\ell + \ell + \ell + \ell + w + w + w + w + h$
   $+ h + h + h$ (or $4\ell + 4w + 4h$)

16. **a.** yes
   b. Many possible answers. Sample: 200 in. by
   0.001 in. (200 in $\cdot$ 0.001 in. $= 0.2$ in^2)

17. surface area

18. volume

19. volume

20. (a)

21. (c)

22.

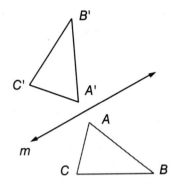

23. 133 square units (The horizontal dimension is 7 units, from (−3, −8) to (4, −8), and the vertical dimension is 19 units, from (4, −8) to (4, 11). 7 units · 19 units = 133 square units.)

24. some points on the line: (3, 3), (0, 0), (−1.5, −1.5)

25. 3 mi = 3 · 5280 ft = 15,840 feet

26. 130° (∠1 forms a linear pair with the angle between ∠1 and ∠2, so this angle has measure 180° − 140° = 40°. This angle and ∠2 form an alternate interior angle with ∠3. Since the lines are parallel, the alternate interior angles have the same measure. So m∠3 = 40° + 90° = 130°.)

27. (8, −14) (Subtract 10 from the *y*-coordinate.)

28. a. 3×10^{12} (Write 3. The decimal point must move 12 places to the right to get 3 trillion, which is a 3 followed by 12 zeros. So the exponent of 10 is 12.)

b. 3×10^{-12} (Write 3. The decimal point must move 12 places to the left to get 3 trillionths, which is written .00000 00000 03. So the exponent of 10 is −12.)

29. a. $33.\overline{3}\%$ or $33\frac{1}{3}$ ($\frac{1}{3} = .\overline{3}$)

b. $66.\overline{6}\%$ or $66\frac{2}{3}\%$ ($\frac{2}{3} = .\overline{6}$)

c. 80% ($\frac{4}{5} = .8$)

30.

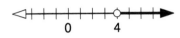

31. a. A * B * C (on line 30), 2 * A * B + 2 * B * C + 2 * A * C (on line 40)

b. SIDES OF BOX
? 2, 3, 4
VOLUME   SURFACE AREA
24   52

c. Many possible answers. Sample:
SIDES OF BOX
? 10, 15, 7.5
VOLUME   SURFACE AREA
1125   675

32. a. no

b. Each lens of the glasses is a different color and blacks out part of the picture. Each eye sees a slightly different image, so the brain thinks the viewer is seeing 3-D.

LESSON 9-5 (pp. 403-407)

1. a. 67.8 $\boxed{\times}$ 3.00 $\boxed{=}$ or
67.8 $\boxed{+}$ 67.8 $\boxed{+}$ 67.8 $\boxed{=}$

b. yes

2. a. The calculator will display the reciprocal of 16 in decimal form.

b. Multiply her answer by 16; she should get 1.

3. 953 + 953 + 953 + 953 = 3812; the answer does not check.

4. a. The multiplicative identity is 1.

b. The additive identity is 0.

5. a. For any number n, $n \cdot 1 = 1 \cdot n = n$.

b. For any number n, $n + 0 = 0 + n = n$.

6. a. $\frac{1}{20}$ **b.** −20

c. −20   **d.** $\frac{1}{20}$

7. a. $\frac{1}{x}$ **b.** −*x*

c. −*x*   **d.** $\frac{1}{x}$

8. $3x$

9. $2L + 2W$

10. $4 \cdot 25 + 5 \cdot 20 = 100 + 100 = 200$

11. They can represent the length and width of a rectangle; the result is the perimeter.

12. $y + y + y + y + y + y$

13. $x + x + z + z + z + z$

14. $6 \cdot \$1.19$ or $\$1.19 + \$1.19 + \$1.19 + \$1.19 + \$1.19 + \$1.19$

15. $\$1.19c$

16. $3e$ $(e + e + e + e - e = e + e + e + e + -e = e + e + e = 3e)$

17. (c) (The multiplicative identity is 1. $\frac{7}{7} = 1$; .6 · $\frac{5}{3} = \frac{3}{5} \cdot \frac{5}{3} = 1$; $x - x = 0$; .3 + .7 = 1)

18. (a), (b), (c), (d), (g) (In these pairs, the product is 1.

In (e), $3.5 \cdot \frac{3}{5} = 3.5 \cdot .6 = 2.1$;

in (f), $16 \cdot -16 = -256$, as can be verified on the calculator; and in (h), $3 \cdot .3 = .9$)

19. (f)

20. $1 + 0 = 1$

21. $12.5 = 12\frac{1}{2} = \frac{25}{2}$; its reciprocal is $\frac{2}{25}$.

22. a. $\ell w - ab$;   **b.** no

23. a. Associative Property of Addition (The order of the grouping is changed.)

    b. Associative Property of Multiplication (The order of the grouping is changed.)

    c. Add-Opp Property of Subtraction

24. a. area $= 3$ ft $\cdot 4$ ft $= 12$ ft^2; perimeter $= 2 \cdot 4$ ft $+ 2 \cdot 3$ ft $= 14$ ft

    b. surface area $= 2 \cdot 2 \cdot 3 + 2 \cdot 3 \cdot 4 + 2 \cdot 2 \cdot 4 = 12 + 24 + 16 = 52$ ft^2; volume $= 2$ ft $\cdot 3$ ft $\cdot 4$ ft $= 24$ ft^3

25. a. 1 point too low ($4 - 5 = 4 + -5 = -1$)

    b. $w - z$ points (subtract the estimated value minus the actual value.)

26. true (Since both numbers are greater than 1, the product is greater than either of the numbers.)

27. $m\angle 1 = m\angle 3 = m\angle 4 = 145°$; $m\angle 2 = 35°$ ($\angle 1$ and the $35°$ angle form a linear pair, so $m\angle 1 = 180 \cdot 35 = 145°$. $\angle 1$ and $\angle 3$ are corresponding angles, so $m\angle 1 = m\angle 3$, and $\angle 3$ and $\angle 4$ are vertical angles, so $m\angle 3 = m\angle 4$. $m\angle 2 = 35°$ because $\angle 2$ and the $35°$ angle are vertical angles.)

28. a. 5

    b. The calculator has taken the reciprocal of the reciprocal of 5.

    c. You will get 0.2, the reciprocal of 5.

    d. If you press the reciprocal key an even number of times, you will get the original number. If you press the key an odd number of times, you will get its reciprocal.

LESSON 9-6 (pp. 408-412)

1. a. 4.4 cm

---

    b. $2 \cdot 4.4$ cm $= 8.8$ cm; the line segment drawn should be 8.8 cm.

    c. $3 \cdot 4.4$ cm $= 13.2$ cm

    d. $3.5 \cdot 4.4$ cm $= 15.4$ cm

2. $1.5 \cdot 1.9$ cm $= 2.85$ cm; The line segment drawn should be 2.85 cm.

3. a.-b.

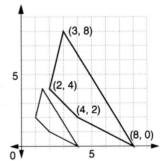

    c. They are twice as long.

    d. They are the same.

116

4. similar **5.** similar

6. true

7.

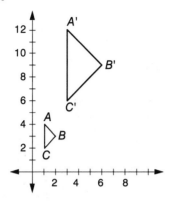

8. (kx, ky)

9. a. 3

  b. $3 \cdot \$25.50 = \$76.50$

10. a. $1.5 \cdot \$1.50 = \$2.25$;

  b. $3 \cdot \$1.50 + 1 \cdot \$2.25 = \$4.50 + \$2.25$
    $= \$6.75$)

11. $150 \cdot 0.1 \text{ mm} = 15 \text{ mm}$

12. no (The width in the drawing is $2\frac{1}{8}$ in. The

  width of the actual bookcase $= 40 \cdot 2\frac{1}{8}$ in. $=$

  $40 \cdot 2.125$ in. $= 85$ in. 85 in. $= 7\frac{1}{12}$ ft, so

  the actual bookcase is more than 2 ft too long.)

13. 3 $(3 \cdot 4 = 12)$

14. 2 **15.** 5

16. 8 **17.** 4

18. $10 \cdot \$3.95 = \$39.50$

19. 1 **20.** 100

21. a. $2 \cdot 200 \text{ m} + 2 \cdot 5 \text{ m} = 500 \text{ m}$

  b. 500 m

  c. $200 \text{ m} \cdot 50 \text{ m} = 10,000 \text{ m}^2$

22. a. 750 in.^{2} $(2 \cdot 9 \cdot 10 + 2 \cdot 10 \cdot 15 +$
    $2 \cdot 9 \cdot 15 = 180 + 300 + 270 = 750)$

  b. $9 \text{ in.} \cdot 10 \text{ in.} \cdot 15 \text{ in.} = 1350 \text{ in.}^3$

23. Associative Property of Multiplication (The
order of the grouping is changed.)

24. Cummutative Property of Multiplication (The
order of the factors is changed.)

25. Equal Fractions Property

26.
$$3.8 = E - 0.09$$
$$3.8 = E + \text{-}0.09$$
$$3.8 + 0.09 = E + \text{-}0.09 + 0.09$$
$$3.89 = E$$

27. Electron microscopes come with different
powers. Their magnifications may be as high
as 1,000,000. So the size change magnitude is
1,000,000.

LESSON 9-7 (pp. 413-417)

1. a. 3.5 cm

  b. $0.3 \cdot 3.5 \text{ cm} = 1.05 \text{ cm}$

  _____

  c. 0.3

2. 0,1

3. (3, 2) (Multiply each coordinate by 0.5.)

4. (4.5, 3) (Multiply each coordinate by 0.75.)

5. (1.5, 1) (Multiply each coordinate by 0.25.)

6. a., b.

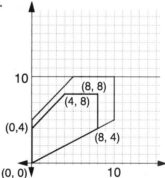

  c. The lengths of the sides of the image are
  0.8 times the lengths of the sides of the
  preimage.

d. The corresponding angles have the same measure.

7. If a quantity is multiplied by a size change factor k, the result is a quantity that is k times as big.

8. $455 (One adult pays $210. One adult pays $\frac{2}{3}$ of $210: $\frac{2}{3}$ of $210 \approx 0.6666666 \cdot \$210 \approx$ 139.99999, which rounds to $140. The child pays $\frac{1}{2}$ of $210: $\frac{1}{2} \cdot \$210 = 0.5 \cdot \$210 =$ $105. The total is $210 + $140 + $105 = $455.)

9. .077 $\cdot$ 240,000,000 = 18,480,000
   1992 Edition:
   .078 $\cdot$ 250,000,000 = 19,500,000

10. 7.7% or .077
    1992 Edition: 7.8% or .078

11. about 2.25 cm (.5 $\cdot$ 4.5cm) or .875 in. (.5 $\cdot$ 1.75 in.)

12. They will get equal values.

13. $(12k, 5k)$

14. (b) (0.05 $\cdot$ $7000 = $350)

15. (d) (The offered price is $7000 $-$ $350 = $6650. 0.95 $\cdot$ $7000 = $6650)

16. **a.** 2 (When switched, the lengths in the image are twice the lengths in the preimage.)
    b. The magnitude of the new size change is the reciprocal of the magnitude of the original size change.

17. 10 m

18. 300 (First multiply 3 $\cdot$ $\frac{1}{3}$ = 1 and 20 $\cdot$ 5 = 100.)

19. 2 m (First multiply $4m \cdot 0.25 = 1m = m$.)

20. $\frac{1}{40}$

21. -40

22. $\frac{1}{40}$

23. 1

24. 1

25. (c) (Solve the equation for y by adding $-x$ to both sides. $180 + -x$ is the same as $180 - x$ or $-x + 180$, but is not the same as $-180 + x$.)

26. **a.** $-\frac{14}{5} - -\frac{3}{10} - \frac{2}{15} - -50$

   $= -\frac{14}{5} + \frac{3}{10} + -\frac{2}{15} + 50$

   $= -\frac{84}{30} + \frac{9}{30} + -\frac{4}{30} + \frac{1500}{30}$

   $= \frac{9}{30} + \frac{1500}{30} + \frac{-84}{30} + \frac{-4}{30}$

   $= \frac{1421}{30}$, or $47.3\overline{6}$

   b. Add-Opp Property of Subtraction: $x - y = x + -y$

27. The temperature dropped 22°. $(-2° - 20° = -2° + -20° = -22°)$

28. $R + 0.8$ (Try $R = 10$. Then $R + 0.8 = 10 + 0.8 = 10.8$, but $0.8R = 0.8 \cdot 10 = 8$.)

29. **a.** $(7 \text{ cm})^3 = 343 \text{ cm}^3$
    b. $6 \cdot (7 \text{ cm})^2 = 294 \text{ cm}^2$
    c. $12 \cdot 7 \text{ cm} = 84 \text{ cm}$

30. Answers will vary.

31. Check your drawing by connecting the right hand and the left foot. This segment should be 2.5 times the length of the segment joining the right hand and the left foot on the original drawing.

LESSON 9-8 (pp. 418-422)
1. 2
2. n
3. $\frac{2}{3}$
4. $\frac{a}{b}$

5. 2 $(\frac{1}{8} \cdot 16 = \frac{16}{8} = 2)$

6. $\frac{5}{x}$

7. 0.5 m $(\frac{5}{10} = 0.5)$

8. $\frac{1}{3} \cdot \frac{1}{4} = \frac{1}{3 \cdot 4} = \frac{1}{12}$

9. $\frac{1}{5} \cdot \frac{1}{5} = \frac{1}{5 \cdot 5} = \frac{1}{25}$

10. $\frac{1}{40x}$

11. $\frac{1}{ab}$

12. **a.** $\frac{1}{4} \cdot \frac{1}{2} = \frac{1}{8}$

 b. $\frac{1}{8}$ of $\$100 = \frac{1}{8} \cdot \$100 = \frac{\$100}{8} = \$12.50$

13. **a.** $\frac{1}{50}$ **b.** $\frac{1}{75}$

 c. $\frac{1}{50} \cdot \frac{1}{75} = \frac{1}{50 \cdot 75} = \frac{1}{3750}$

14. A unit fraction is a fraction with 1 in the numerator and a natural number in the denominator.

15. $\frac{1}{6} \cdot \frac{1}{3} = \frac{1}{18}$

16. $\frac{1}{4} \cdot \frac{1}{5} = \frac{1}{20}$

17. $\frac{1}{DH}$

18. **a.** $\frac{1}{2}$ **b.** $\frac{1}{6}$ **c.** $\frac{1}{n}$

19. $\frac{W}{5}$ dollars

20. (c) $\left(8 \text{ times the reciprocal of } 3 = 8 \cdot \frac{1}{3} = \frac{8}{3}\right)$

21. **a.** $\frac{1}{7} \cdot \frac{1}{23} = \frac{1}{161}$

 b. $1 \div 161 = 0.0062112$

 c. $0.142857 \cdot 0.0434783 = 0.0062112$

 d. A number may be substituted for its equal without affecting the answer. (Substitution Principle).

22.

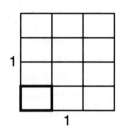

23.

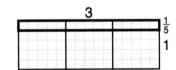

$3 \cdot \frac{1}{5} = \frac{3}{5}$

24. $\frac{1}{2} \cdot \frac{1}{3} \cdot \frac{1}{4}$

 $= \frac{1}{6} \cdot \frac{1}{4}$

 $= \frac{1}{24}$

25. $\frac{1}{2} \cdot \frac{1}{2} \cdot \frac{1}{2} \cdot \frac{1}{2}$

 $= \frac{1}{4} \cdot \frac{1}{2} \cdot \frac{1}{2}$

 $= \frac{1}{8} \cdot \frac{1}{2}$

 $= \frac{1}{16}$

26. 4

27. a. $\frac{8}{30}, \frac{1}{3}, \frac{3}{8}$ ($\frac{8}{30} = .2\overline{6}; \frac{1}{3} = .\overline{3}, \frac{3}{8} = .375$)

b. $-\frac{3}{8}, -\frac{1}{3}, -\frac{8}{30}$ (On a horizontal number line, $-\frac{3}{8}$ or $-.375$, is farthest to the left.)

28. $4a$ ($3a + a = a + a + a + a$)

29. $2a$ ($3a - a = a + a + a + -a$)

30. $5.1 \text{ m} \cdot 6.2 \text{ m} = 31.62 \text{ m}^2 \approx 32 \text{ m}^2$

31. perimeter   **32.** similar

33. The smallest possible volume is 8.5 cm $\cdot$ 14.5 cm $\cdot$ 19.5 cm $\approx$ 2403 cm³. (If the dimensions were smaller, they would be rounded down to 8 cm, 14 cm, and 19 cm.) The largest possible volume is 9.5 cm $\cdot$ 15.5 cm $\cdot$ 20.5 cm $\approx$ 3019 cm³. (If the dimensions were larger, they would be rounded up to 10 cm, 16 cm, and 21 cm.)

*34. *1992 Edition only:* **a.** $\frac{1}{45}$ (the order in which the 2 numbers are guessed does not matter so the probability of guessing both numbers correctly is $2\left(\frac{1}{10} \cdot \frac{1}{9}\right) = \frac{1}{45}$.)

b. Worse; if returned, the chance of guessing both numbers correctly is $2\left(\frac{1}{10} \cdot \frac{1}{10}\right) = \frac{1}{50}$.

LESSON 9-9 (pp. 423-427)

1. $\frac{6}{5} \cdot \frac{2}{9} = \frac{6 \cdot 2}{5 \cdot 9} = \frac{12}{45}$, or $\frac{4}{15}$ (Divide numerator and denominator of $\frac{12}{45}$ by 3.)

2. $\frac{3}{5} \cdot \frac{5}{3} = \frac{3 \cdot 5}{5 \cdot 3} = \frac{15}{15} = 1$

3. $\frac{1}{9} \cdot \frac{9}{2} = \frac{1 \cdot 9}{9 \cdot 2} = \frac{1 \cdot 9 \,(1/9)}{9 \cdot 2 \,(1/9)} = \frac{1}{2}$

4. $7 \cdot \left(\frac{1}{12}\right) \cdot \left(3 \cdot \frac{1}{4}\right) = \frac{7}{12} \cdot \frac{3}{4} = \frac{7 \cdot 3}{12 \cdot 4} = \frac{21}{48}$, or $\frac{7}{16}$ (Divide numerator and denominator of $\frac{21}{48}$ by 3.)

5. $\frac{a}{b} \cdot \frac{c}{d} = \frac{ac}{bd}$

6. $12 \cdot \frac{3}{4} = \frac{12}{1} \cdot \frac{3}{4} = \frac{12 \cdot 3}{1 \cdot 4} = \frac{36}{4} = 9$

7. $12 \cdot 0.75 = 9$

8. $1.2 \cdot .\overline{2} = .2\overline{6}; \frac{12}{45} = .2\overline{6}$ **9.** $\frac{6}{5}$

10. 6 in 20, or 3 in 10 $\left(\frac{3}{4} \cdot \frac{2}{5} = \frac{6}{20}, \text{ or } \frac{3}{10}\right)$

11. $0.625 \cdot 1.6 = 1$

12. a. $\frac{5}{7}$ **b.** $\frac{5}{7} \cdot \frac{5}{7} = \frac{25}{49}$

13. $4 \cdot \frac{1}{5} + 3 \cdot \frac{1}{15} = \frac{4}{5} + \frac{3}{15} = \frac{4}{5} + \frac{1}{5} = \frac{5}{5} = 1$

14. $\frac{6}{10} \cdot \frac{1}{26} = \frac{6}{260}$, or $\frac{3}{130}$

15. 3 square miles ($4 \cdot \frac{3}{4} = \frac{4}{1} \cdot \frac{3}{4} = \frac{3}{1} = 3$)

16. a.    **b.** $\frac{24}{35}$

17. a. $\frac{1}{2} \cdot \frac{1}{3} \cdot \frac{1}{4} = \frac{1}{6} \cdot \frac{1}{4} = \frac{1}{24}$

b. All of the factors are between 0 and 1.

18. a. $\frac{3}{2} \cdot \frac{5}{4} \cdot \frac{7}{6} = \frac{15}{8} \cdot \frac{7}{6} = \frac{105}{48} = \frac{35}{16}$, or $2\frac{3}{16}$

b. All of the factors are greater than 1.

19. a. $3\frac{1}{2} \cdot 2\frac{3}{4} = \frac{7}{2} \cdot \frac{11}{4} = \frac{77}{8}$, or $9\frac{5}{8}$

b. Several possible answers. Sample: Change everything to decimals and multiply.

20. $4 \cdot \frac{1}{3} \cdot 6 = 24 \cdot \frac{1}{3} = \frac{24}{3} = 8$

21. $\frac{3}{4}$ ($3 \cdot \frac{1}{4} = \frac{3}{4}$)

22. **a., b.**

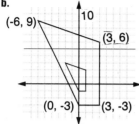

23. contraction ($\frac{5}{6}$ is between 0 and 1.)

24. m∠SRT = 23° (135° + m∠SRT + 22° = 180°); m∠S = 135° (alternate interior angles); m∠T = 22° (alternate interior angles)

25.

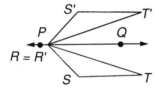

26. **a.** 2 · 50 cm · 40 cm + 2 · 40 cm · 36 cm + 2 · 50 cm · 36 cm = 10,480 cm²
b. 50 cm · 40 cm · 36 cm = 72,000 cm³

27. Many possible answers. Sample: Six people share a pizza equally. Mary ate only $\frac{2}{3}$ of her share. What part of the whole pizza did she eat?

*28. *1992 Edition only:* **a.** $\frac{9}{12}$ **b.** $\frac{2}{12}$

Shirts: A,   B,   C,   D* (* stains)
Slacks: X,   Y#, Z#   (# holes)
Array: AX   BX   CX   D*X
        AY# BY# CY# D*Y#
        AZ# BZ# CZ# D*Z#

CHAPTER 9 PROGRESS SELF-TEST (pp. 429-430)

1. $\frac{6}{25}$

2. $3y + 3$

3. $4 \cdot \frac{1}{3} \cdot \frac{5}{4} = \frac{4}{3} \cdot \frac{5}{4} = \frac{5}{3}$

4. $\frac{7}{16x}$

5. Associative Property of Multiplication (The order of the grouping is changed.)

6. Property of Reciprocals

7. There are rs seats broken or unbroken; there are $rs - 5$ seats to sit in.

8. Area = 17.3 m · 6.8 m = 117.64 m²; perimeter = 2 · 17.3 m + 2 · 6.8 m = 34.6 m + 13.6 m = 48.2 m.

9. 2 · 6cm · 11 cm + 2 · 6 cm · 3 cm + 2 · 3 cm · 11 cm = 234 cm²

10. 6 cm · 3 cm · 11 cm = 198 cm³

11. square kilometers or km² (Area measures fishing room.)

12. Many possible answers. Samples: 8 and 2, 16 and 1, 10 and 1.6

13. The reciprocal is 1/38 = 0.02631 . . . ≈ 0.026

14. $1.29 + $1.29 + $1.29 or 3 · $1.29 = $3.87

15. $\frac{2}{3} \cdot \frac{2}{5} = \frac{4}{15}$

16. (32, 8) (Multiply each coordinate by 4.)

17. 1.5 · $5.80 = $8.70

18.

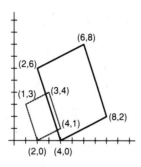

19. contraction (the magnitude is between zero and one), similar

20. 102 students $\left(\frac{3}{25} \cdot 850 = \frac{3}{25} \cdot \frac{850}{1} = \frac{2550}{25} = 102\right)$

21. $56000 $\left(\frac{2}{3} \cdot 8400 = \frac{2}{3} \cdot \frac{8400}{1} = \frac{16800}{3} = 5600\right)$

22. Your chances are 1 in 1000. $\left(\frac{1}{10} \cdot \frac{1}{10} \cdot \frac{1}{10} = \frac{1}{1000}\right)$

23. Your chances are 4 in 15. $\left(\frac{2}{3} \cdot \frac{2}{5} = \frac{4}{15}\right)$

24. Example: Make the rectangle very thin as shown here.

This rectangle has length 3 in. and width $\frac{1}{8}$ in. for a perimeter of 6.25 in. and an area of $\frac{3}{8}$ sq. in.

25. (c) $\left(\frac{1}{1.25} = 0.8\right)$

CHAPTER 9 REVIEW (pp. 431-433)

1. $3 \cdot \frac{1}{6} = \frac{3}{6} = \frac{1}{2}$

2. $\frac{4}{5} \cdot \frac{4}{3} = \frac{16}{15}$

3. $\frac{300}{8}$, or $\frac{75}{2}$

4. $\frac{2}{5} \cdot \frac{2}{5} \cdot \frac{2}{5} = \frac{4}{25} \cdot \frac{2}{5} = \frac{8}{125}$

5. $10\frac{1}{8} \cdot 10 = \frac{81}{8} \cdot \frac{10}{1} = \frac{810}{8} = \frac{405}{4}$, or $101\frac{1}{4}$

6. $2\frac{1}{2} \cdot 3\frac{2}{3} = \frac{5}{2} \cdot \frac{11}{3} = \frac{55}{6}$, or $9\frac{1}{6}$

7. area $= 7 \cdot 3.5 = 24.5$ square units;
perimeter $= 2 \cdot 7 + 2 \cdot 3.5 = 21$ units

8. area $= 5w$ square units;
perimeter $= 2 \cdot 5 + 2w = 10 + 2w$ units

9. surface area $= 2 \cdot 25 \cdot 10 + 2 \cdot 10 \cdot 7.5 + 2 \cdot 25 \cdot 7.5 = 1025$ square units;
volume $= 25 \cdot 10 \cdot 7.5 = 1875$ cubic units

10. surface area $= 2xy + 2yz + 2xz$; xyz

11. $n \cdot 1 = n$.

12. Mult-Rec Prop. of Division

13. $\frac{3}{2}$

14. Associative Property of Multiplication (Order of grouping is changed.)

15. 0 $(ab - ba = ab - ab = ab + {}^-ab = 0)$

16. $y + 1$

17. $4m$

18. $\frac{x}{2}$ (First multiply $\frac{1}{5} \cdot 5 = 1$)

19. Multiply in the reverse order.
$6.54 \cdot 2.48 \neq 16.1292$; it does not check.

20. $7.98 + $7.98 + $7.98 + $7.98 + $7.98 = $39.90; it does check.

21. $\frac{1}{8} \cdot \frac{1}{5} = \frac{1}{40}$; $0.125 \cdot 0.2 = 0.025$ and $\frac{1}{40} = 0.025$, so it checks.

22. square feet

23. square inches

24. Many possible answers. Samples:
cubic centimeters, liters, cubic feet

25. $6 \cdot 8 = 48$

26. 900 ft² (Area of restaurant $= 42$ ft $\cdot$ 25 ft $=$ 1050 ft²; area of kitchen $= 15$ ft $= 10$ ft $=$ 150 ft²; seating area $= 1050$ ft² $- 150$ ft² $=$ 900 ft²)

27. $2 \cdot 11.5$ cm $\cdot 3$ cm $+ 2 \cdot 3$ cm $\cdot 3$ cm $+$ $2 \cdot 11.5$ cm $\cdot 3$ cm $= 156$ cm²

28. 11.5 cm $\cdot 3$ cm $\cdot 3$ cm $= 103.5$ cm³

29. no (surface area of top and sides $=$

$7' \cdot 6' + 2 \cdot 7' + \frac{3}{4}' + 2 \cdot 6' \cdot \frac{3}{4} =$

42 ft² $+ 10\frac{1}{2}$ ft² $+ 9$ ft² $= 61\frac{1}{2}$ ft²)

30. yes ($V = Bh = 72 \cdot 14 = 1008$ cm³; 1 L $= 100$ cm³)

31. $\frac{1}{4} \cdot \$150 = \frac{\$150}{4} = \$37.50$

32. $3x$ dollars

33. $1.5 \cdot \$3.50 = \$5.25$

34. \$2600 (per week: $\frac{1}{10} \cdot \$500 = \frac{\$500}{10} = \$50$; per year: $52 \cdot \$50 = \$2600$)

35. $\frac{1}{3} \cdot \frac{1}{3} = \frac{1}{9}$

36. $\frac{5}{7} \cdot \frac{1}{25} = \frac{5}{175}$, or $\frac{1}{35}$

37.

38.

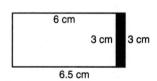

39.

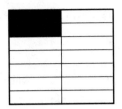

40.

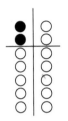

41.

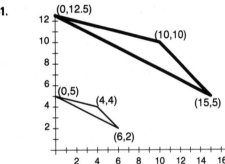

42. $(1000x, 1000y)$

43. contraction ($\frac{3}{7}$ is between 0 and 1.)

44.

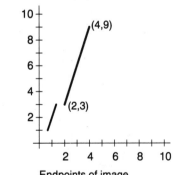

Endpoints of image are (2/3, 1) and (4/3, 3).

Endpoints of image are $(\frac{2}{3}, 1)$ and $(\frac{4}{3}, 3)$.

CHAPTER 10   MORE MULTIPLICATION PATTERNS

LESSON 10-1   (pp. 436-439)

1. (a) ($5/x$ means "five divided by x.")

2. An equation is in the form $ax = b$ when one number is multiplied by an unknown to get a second number.

3. **a.** yes ($7 \cdot 4 = 28$)
   b. no ($7 \neq 4 \cdot 28$)
   c. no ($28 \cdot 4 \neq 7$)
   d. no ($.28 \neq 0.7 \cdot 4$)
   e. no ($7 + 4 \neq 28$)

4. 2 ($18 \cdot 2 = 36$)

5. 1 ($.798 \cdot 1 = .798$)

6. 50 ($3 \cdot 50 = 150$)

7. $\frac{72}{9} = 8$, and $\frac{72}{8} = 9$

8. $\frac{17.02}{37} = 0.46$, and $\frac{17.02}{0.46} = 37$

9. If $xy = P$, then $\frac{P}{x} = y$ and $\frac{P}{y} = x$

10. **a.** $\frac{901}{t} = 53$, and $\frac{901}{53} = t$

    b. $t = \frac{901}{53}$
    $t = 17$
    check: $53 \cdot 17 = 901$

11. $n = \frac{6}{0.8}$
    $n = 7.5$
    check: $0.8 \cdot 7.5 = 6$

12. $n = \frac{6}{0.7}$
    $n \approx 8.57$
    check: $0.7 \cdot 8.57 = 5.999 \approx 6$

13. $\frac{222,300}{325} = 684$ (or $\frac{222,300}{684} = 325$); correct

14. $\frac{1.2}{0.4} = 3$ (or $\frac{1.2}{0.3} = 4$); not correct

15. $\frac{1152}{.72} = 1600$ (or $\frac{1152}{1600} = .72$); correct

16. $\frac{9}{12} = .75 = \frac{3}{4}$ (or $9 \div \frac{3}{4} = 9 \div .75 = 12$); correct

17. **a.** Answers may vary depending on calculator. Sample: 1.1052632
    b. 1.11
    c. $3.8x = 4.2$

18. $x + x + x = 801$
    $3x = 801$
    $x = \frac{801}{3}$
    $x = 267$

19. $t + t = 4.5$
    $2t = 4.5$
    $t = \frac{4.5}{2}$
    $t = 2.25$

20. You are likely to repeat any mistakes made.

21. **a.** $\frac{1}{6}$ **b.** $\frac{12}{5}$

22. 8 ($xy = 1$, so $3xy + 5 = 3 \cdot 1 + 5 = 8$)

23. x (First multiply $4 \cdot \frac{1}{4} = 1$.)

24. **a.** $-\frac{31}{6}$

    b.
    $\frac{31}{6} + m = -\frac{5}{8}$
    $-\frac{31}{6} + \frac{31}{6} + m = -\frac{31}{6} + -\frac{5}{8}$
    $m = -\frac{31}{6} + -\frac{5}{8}$
    $m = -\frac{124}{24} + -\frac{15}{24}$
    $m = -\frac{139}{24}$

25. reciprocal and multiplicative inverse; opposite and additive inverse

26. $.4H$ (40% $= .4$)
    *1992 Edition: $.65H$ (65% $= .65$)

27. **a.** $A = \ell w = L \cdot 6 = 6L$ square feet

 b. $P = 2\ell + 2w = 2L + 2 \cdot 6 =$ $12 + 2L$ feet

28. 157°

29. $1 - 5 - 4 = 1 + {}^-5 + {}^-4 =$ $1 + {}^-9 = {}^-8$

30. **a.** 0.000001   **b.** 10^{-6}

31. 12 ft, or 144 in. (An area of 1 sq ft is equivalent to the area of a square 1 ft by 1 ft, or 12 in. by 12 in. Since 12 in. $\cdot$ 12 in. = 144 sq in., 1 sq ft = 144 sq in. So, for the rectangle, 144 sq in. $= \ell \cdot 1$, which means $\ell = 144$ in., or 12 ft.)

LESSON 10-2 (pp. 440-444)

1. $6y$

2. Multiplication Property of Equality

3. **a.** $\frac{1}{5}$

 b. $5x = 80$

 $\frac{1}{5} \cdot 5x = \frac{1}{5} \cdot 80$

 $1 \cdot x = \frac{80}{5}$

 $x = 16$

4. **a.** $\frac{25}{6}$

 b. $\frac{6}{25} \cdot A = \frac{2}{9}$

 $\frac{25}{6} \cdot \frac{6}{25} \cdot A = \frac{25}{6} \cdot \frac{2}{9}$

 $1 \cdot A = \frac{50}{54}$

 $A = \frac{50}{54}$, or $\frac{25}{27}$

5. **a.** $\frac{1}{3}$

 b. $3x = 0.12$

 $\frac{1}{3} \cdot 3x = \frac{1}{3} \cdot 0.12$

 $1 \cdot x = \frac{0.12}{3} \cdot$

 $x = 0.04$

 c. $3x = 0.12$

 $x = \frac{0.12}{3}$

 $x = 0.04$

6. yes $(\frac{2}{3} \cdot \frac{15}{2} = \frac{30}{6} = 5)$

7. $7x = 413$

 $\frac{1}{7} \cdot 7x = \frac{1}{7} \cdot 413$

 $1 \cdot x = \frac{413}{7}$

 $x = 59$

8. $.07 \cdot n = 84$

 $\frac{1}{.07} \cdot .07n = \frac{1}{.07} \cdot 84$

 $1 \cdot n = \frac{84}{.07}$

 $n = 1200$

9. $.4 \cdot n = 25$

 $\frac{1}{.4} \cdot .4n = \frac{1}{.4} \cdot 25$

 $1 \cdot n = \frac{25}{.4}$

 $n = 62.5$

10. $\frac{10}{3} \cdot n = 30$

 $\frac{3}{10} \cdot \frac{10}{3}n = \frac{3}{10} \cdot 30$

 $1 \cdot n = \frac{3}{10} \cdot \frac{30}{1}$

 $n = \frac{90}{10}$

 $n = 9$

11. Step 1: Multiplication Property of Equality;
Step 2: Associative Property of Multiplication;
Step 3: Property of Reciprocals; Step 4:
Multiplication of Fractions and Multiplication
Identity Property of 1

12. a. $x \cdot \frac{1}{6} = \frac{4}{25}$

b. $x \cdot \frac{1}{6} = \frac{4}{25}$

$x \cdot \frac{1}{6} \cdot 6 = \frac{4}{25} \cdot 6$

$x \cdot 1 = \frac{4}{25} \cdot \frac{6}{1}$

$x = \frac{24}{25}$

c. $\frac{24}{25} \cdot \frac{1}{6} = \frac{24}{150} = \frac{4}{25}$

13. $16.56 = 7.2y$

$\frac{1}{7.2} \cdot 16.56 = \frac{1}{7.2} \cdot 7.2y$

$\frac{16.56}{7.2} = 1 \cdot y$

$2.3 = y$

check: $16.56 = 7.2 \cdot 2.3$

14. $\frac{2}{3}k = 62\%$

$\frac{3}{2} \cdot \frac{2}{3}k = \frac{3}{2} \cdot 62\%$

$1 \cdot k = 1.5 \cdot .62$

$k = .93$, or 93%

check: $\frac{2}{3} \cdot 93\% = \frac{2}{3} \cdot .93 = \frac{2}{3} \cdot \frac{.93}{1} = $

$.62 = 62\%$

15. $3.2 + 4.8 = (3.6 + 2.4)x$

$8 = 6x$

$\frac{1}{6} \cdot 8 = \frac{1}{6} \cdot 6x$

$\frac{8}{6} = 1 \cdot x$

$\frac{4}{3} = x$, or $x = 1.\overline{3}$

check: $3.2 + 4.8 = (3.6 + 2.4)\frac{4}{3}$

$8 = 6 \cdot \frac{4}{3}$

16. c, (The solution to a, b, and d is $x = 90$; the solution to c is $\frac{1}{90}$. Notice in a, b, and d, x is multiplied by 0.2, $\frac{1}{5}$, or 20%, all of which are equal, to give a product of 18.)

17. $x - 7 = 50$

$x + {}^-7 = 50$

$x + {}^-7 + 7 = 50 + 7$

$x = 57$

18. $7 - n = 50$

$7 + {}^-n = 50$

${}^-7 + 7 + {}^-n = {}^-7 + 50$

${}^-n = 43$

$n = {}^-43$

19. $3H + 20$ meters (Add the lengths of all the sides.)

20. $1.08^1 = 1.08$; $1.08^2 = 1.1664$; $1.08^3 = 1.259712$; $1.08^4 = 1.360489 \dots$;
$1.08^5 = 1.469328 \dots$

21. 320,000,000,000 (Move the decimal point 11 places to the right.)

22. $7.7\% = .077 = \frac{77}{1000}$

1992 Edition:

$4.9\% = .049 = \frac{49}{1000}$

23. 80 cm (Since 1 cm $= .01$ m, 80 cm $= \frac{1}{100}$ of 80 m)

24. 10

25. 5.499 (Round each factor to the nearest ten thousandth: $1.0123 \cdot 5.4321 \approx 5.499$)

*These are solutions to questions changed in or added to the *1992 Edition.*

26.

number of rows	number of seats in a row
1	144
2	72
3	48
4	36
6	24
8	18
9	16
12	12
16	9
18	8
24	6
36	4
48	3
72	2
144	1

LESSON 10-3 (pp. 445-449)

1. Read the question carefully to be sure you understand it.
2. You might have made an error when you set up the equation.
3. $22\ell = 330$

$$\ell = \frac{330}{22}$$

$$\ell = 15 \text{ ft}$$

4. $\frac{1}{12} \cdot \ell = 3.25$

$$12 \cdot \frac{1}{12}\ell = 12 \cdot 3.25$$

$$\ell = 39 \text{ in.}$$

5. $1\frac{1}{2} \cdot W = \$3.60$

$$1.5W = \$3.60$$

$$W = \frac{\$3.60}{1.5}$$

$$W = \$2.40$$

6. $.51v = 1{,}297{,}737$

$$v = \frac{1{,}297{,}737}{.51}$$

$$v \approx 2{,}540{,}000 \text{ people}$$

7. **a.** $0.0002 \, h = 11$

$$h = \frac{11}{0.0002}$$

$$h = 55{,}000 \text{ cm}$$

b. $55{,}000 \text{ cm} = 550 \text{ m}$

8. $\frac{1}{3}h = 6$

$$3 \cdot \frac{1}{3}h = 3 \cdot 6$$

$$h = 18 \text{ ft}$$

The adult is 18 ft. This is 12 ft taller than the newborn.

9. $8 \cdot 10.5 \cdot h = 600$

$$84h = 600$$

$$h = \frac{600}{84}$$

$$h \approx 7.14 \text{ cm}$$

10. $.7p = \$489.95$

$$p = \frac{\$489.95}{.7}$$

$$p \approx \$699.93, \text{ or about } \$700$$

11. $3s = \$110{,}000$

$$s = \frac{\$110{,}000}{3}$$

$$s \approx \$37{,}000$$

12. $x + x + x + x + x = 32$

$$5x = 32$$

$$x = \frac{32}{5}$$

$$x = 6.4$$

13. $75c = 3000$

$$c = \frac{3000}{75}$$

$$c = 40 \text{ columns}$$

14. $.41 \cdot 1066 \approx 437 \text{ votes}$

15. $40 - 20 \cdot 3 + 200/5 + 5/1$

$$= 40 - 60 + 40 + 5$$

$$= 40 + {}^{-}60 + 40 + 5$$

$$= 25$$

16. $1 \text{ ft} = 12 \text{ in.} = 12 \cdot 2.54 \text{ cm} = 30.48 \text{ cm}$

17. polygon, quadrilateral, parallelogram, rectangle, square

18. **a., b.**

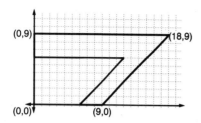

19. $\pi \cdot 2$ cm $\approx 3.14 \cdot 2$ cm ≈ 6.28 cm^2 ≈ 6 cm^2

20. $8 \cdot 8 = 64$ pieces

21. $\frac{4}{3} x = 1200$

$\frac{3}{4} \cdot \frac{4}{3} x = \frac{3}{4} \cdot 1200$

$x = 900$

The number is 900.

$\frac{3}{4}$ of $900 = \frac{3}{4} \cdot \frac{900}{1} = 675$.

22. Many possible answers. Sample:

$\frac{1}{2}$ mile by $\frac{3}{4}$ mile $\left(\frac{1}{2} \cdot \frac{3}{4} = \frac{3}{8} \right)$

LESSON 10-4 (pp. 450-454)

1. **a.** For the game only <u>4 tickets per student</u> are available.

b. 4 tickets/student

c. $4 \frac{\text{tickets}}{\text{student}}$

2. **a.** The speed limit there is <u>45 miles per hour</u>.

b. 45 miles/hour

c. $45 \frac{\text{miles}}{\text{hour}}$

3. **a.** 150 miles

b. Many possible answers. Sample: How far will a person travel driving 50 miles per hour for 3 hours?

4. **a.** $18.78 (rounded up to the next cent)

b. Many possible answers. Sample: What is the cost of 8.2 pounds of ribs at $2.29 a pound?

5. **a.** $16 \frac{\text{games}}{\text{season}}$ (The units "week" and "weeks" cancel.)

b. Many possible answers. Sample: A team plays 2 games a week during an 8-week season. How many games will the team play per season?

6. **a.** about 5.68 miles;

b. Many possible answers. Sample: Convert 30,000 ft to miles.

7. 7 months $\cdot 1.5 \frac{\text{kg}}{\text{month}} = 10.5$ kg

8. 20 minutes $\cdot 40 \frac{\text{words}}{\text{minute}} = 800$ words

9. 35,000 ft $\cdot \frac{1 \text{ mile}}{5280 \text{ ft}} \approx 6.63$ miles

10. 50 rows $\cdot 20 \frac{\text{seats}}{\text{row}} = 1000$ seats; 1000 people can be seated.

11. When a rate is multiplied by another quantity, the unit of the product is the "product" of the units, multiplied like fractions. The product has meaning whenever the unit has meaning.

12. **a.** 3750 questions (The units "classes" and "class" cancel, and the units "students" and "student" cancel.);

b. Many possible answers. Sample: A teacher has 5 classes, each with 25 students. If each student takes a test with 30 questions, how many questions must the teacher grade?

13. **a.** 6.36 quarts

b. Many possible answers. Sample: Convert 6 liters to quarts.

14. 10 cm $\cdot \frac{1 \text{ in.}}{2.54 \text{ cm}} \approx 3.94$ in.

15. $24 \frac{\text{hours}}{\text{day}} \cdot 60 \frac{\text{minutes}}{\text{hour}} \cdot 70 \frac{\text{beats}}{\text{minute}} = $

$100,800 \frac{\text{beats}}{\text{day}}$

16. 4 hours · x = 120 miles

$$x = \frac{120 \text{ miles}}{4 \text{ hours}}$$

$$x = 30 \frac{\text{miles}}{\text{hour}}, \text{ or } 30 \text{ miles/hour}$$

17. 10 dollars · $9 \frac{\text{francs}}{\text{dollar}}$ · $8 \frac{\text{pesetas}}{\text{franc}}$ = 720 pesetas

18. 14 gallons · $25 \frac{\text{miles}}{\text{gallons}}$ = 350 miles, how far

the Chevy can go on a tank of gas

19. $74x = 47$

$$x = \frac{47}{74}$$

$$x \approx 0.6$$

20. $.3c = \$12$

$$c = \frac{\$12}{.3}$$

$$c = \$40$$

21. $1.6\ell = 42$

$$\ell = \frac{42}{1.6}$$

$$\ell \approx 26 \text{ mm}$$

22. $\frac{2}{5}t = 44$

$$\frac{5}{2} \cdot \frac{2}{5}t = \frac{5}{2} \cdot 44$$

$$t = \frac{5}{2} \cdot \frac{44}{1}$$

$$t = 110$$

23. $-\frac{2}{3} - \frac{2}{3} = -\frac{2}{3} + -\frac{2}{3} = -\frac{4}{3}$

24. lb   **25.** kg   **26.** mL

27. 55 ft $(25 - -30 = 25 + 30 = 55)$

28. $-|x + 5|$

$$= -|-3 + 5|$$
$$= -|2|$$
$$= -2$$

29. some points on the line: $(0, -4)$, $(2, -2)$, and $(4, 0)$

30. **a.** $x + 1$;   **b.** $x - 1$;   **c.** $x - 10$

31. **a.** Count the words on a page. Multiply by the number of pages.

b. Many possible estimates. Sample: about 275 words on page 453; about 45 pages in the chapter (combining partial pages); $275 \cdot 45 = 12,375$. Estimate is 12,000 words.

LESSON 10-5   (pp. 455-458)

1. A woman loses 3.8 pounds per month for 3 months.

2. **a.** $-3 \frac{\text{pounds}}{\text{month}}$ · 2 months;

b. -6 pounds; The person loses 6 pounds in all.

3. **a.** $-5 \frac{\text{pounds}}{\text{month}}$ · 4 months;

b. -20 pounds; The person will be 20 pounds lighter.

4. **a.** $-6 \frac{\text{pounds}}{\text{month}}$ · -2 months;

b. 12 pounds; The person was 12 pounds heavier.

5. changes   **6.** keeps

7. -32 **8.** -3285

9. 18   **10.** -2.9

11. -64 **12.** 500

13. positive   **14.** negative

15. negative   **16.** positive

17. **a.** $-5x = -5 \cdot 2 = -10$;

b. $-5x = -5 \cdot 1 = -5$;

c. $-5x = -5 \cdot 0 = 0$;

d. $-5x = -5 \cdot -1 = 5$;

e. $-5x = -5 \cdot -2 = 10$

18. $3 + -7a + 2b$

$$= 3 + -7 \cdot -4 + 2 \cdot -10$$
$$= 3 + 28 + -20$$
$$= 31 + -20$$
$$= 11$$

19. $-3 \cdot 4 \cdot -5$
$= -12 \cdot -5$
$= 60$

20. $-6 \cdot -6 \cdot -6 \cdot -6$
$= 36 \cdot -6 \cdot -6$
$= -216 \cdot -6$
$= 1296$

21. $-\frac{2}{3} \cdot -\frac{9}{10}$
$= \frac{18}{30}$
$= \frac{3}{5}$

22. (b) ($2500 in debt is represented by -2500; spending $200 is represented by -200; 5 weeks ago is represented by -5.)

23. $2400\,x = 60$
$x = \frac{60}{2400}$
$x = 0.025$, or $\frac{1}{40}$

24. $\frac{1}{2}y = 54$
$2 \cdot \frac{1}{2}y = 2 \cdot 54$
$y = 108$

25. 0.45 pounds $\cdot$ $5.98/pound = $2.691
$\approx $2.69

26. **a.** 3% of $80,000 $= .03 \cdot $80,000 = $2400
b. $.03x = $25,000
$x = \frac{$25,000}{.03}$
$x \approx $833,333
1992 Edition: **a.** 3% of $98,400 $= 0.3 \cdot$ 98,400 $= $2,952. **b.** same as **26b** above.

27.

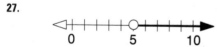

28. **a.** km/sec; g/cm³
29. Many possible answers. Sample: $-2 + 3 = 1$

30. Supplementary angles are two angles whose measures add to 180°.

31. Answers will vary.

LESSON 10-6 (pp. 459-463)

1. $(-8, -10)$ (Multiply each coordinate by -2.)
2. $(50, -35)$ (Multiply each coordinate by -5.)
3. similar   **4.** 3
5. parallel
6. For a change of magnitude -3, the image is rotated 180°.

7.

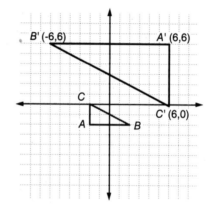

8. reverses
9. 180°

10.

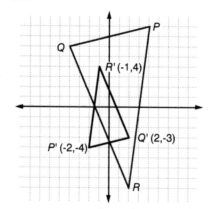

11. true (Preimage and image points lie on a line that goes through the origin.)

12. **a.** yes
b. They are both 2 times the size of *ABCD*. (They have the same size and shape.)

13. 2 (Since k is negative, the figure will be rotated 180°.)

14. **a.** -$50/day **b.** 4 days

 c. -4 days

 d. -$50/day · 4 days = -$200

 e. -$50/day · -4 days = $200

15. 8 in. · 10.5 in. = 84 in.²

16.

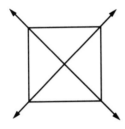

17. $-5x + 6$
 $= -5 \cdot -9 + 6$
 $= 45 + 6$
 $= 51$

18. $3a + 2a$
 $= 5a$
 $= 5 \cdot -7$
 $= -35$

19. $\frac{y}{7} = 30$

  $\frac{1}{7} \cdot y = 30$

 $7 \cdot \frac{1}{7} y = 7 \cdot 30$

   $y = 210$

20. $1260 = \frac{3}{4} x$

 $\frac{4}{3} \cdot 1260 = \frac{4}{3} \cdot \frac{3}{4} x$

 $\frac{4}{3} \cdot \frac{1260}{1} = x$

  $1680 = x$

21. Since $75\% = \frac{3}{4}$, the solution is the same as in

 Question 20. Or solve as follows:

 $1260 = .75x$

 $\frac{1260}{.75} = x$

 $1680 = x$

22. 75% of 1260 = .75 · 1260 = 945

23. 9,765,625 (Use the key sequence 5 $\boxed{y^x}$ 10 $\boxed{=}$)

24. $\frac{1}{3} \cdot \frac{1}{7} = \frac{1}{21}$ ($\frac{1}{3}$ of the earth's surface is land;

 $\frac{1}{7}$ of the days is Sunday.)

25. -0.6 ($-\frac{2}{3} = -0.666 \ldots$; of -0.666 … ,

 -0.6, and -0.66, -0.6 is farthest to the right.)

26. $-3n + 4n = n$

27 **a.** $0 \cdot -4 = 0$ **b.** yes

  $-1 \cdot -4 = 4$

  $-2 \cdot -4 = 8$

  $-3 \cdot -4 = 12$

  $-4 \cdot -4 = 16$

28. **a.** Output:

  4 TIMES ⁻4 EQUALS ⁻16
  3 TIMES ⁻4 EQUALS ⁻12
   • • •
  ⁻10 TIMES ⁻4 EQUALS 40

 b. Many possible answers. Sample:

  10 FOR X = 10 TO ⁻2 STEP ⁻3
  20 PRINT X "TIMES ⁻5 EQUALS", ⁻5∗X
  30 NEXT X
  40 END
  RUN
  10 TIMES ⁻5 EQUALS ⁻50
   7 TIMES ⁻5 EQUALS ⁻35
   4 TIMES ⁻5 EQUALS ⁻20
   1 TIMES ⁻5 EQUALS ⁻5
  ⁻2 TIMES ⁻5 EQUALS 10

LESSON 10-7 (pp. 464-468)

1. For any number x, $x \cdot 0 = 0$

2. For any number x, $-1 \cdot x = -x$.

3. 7   **4.** -8

5. -1 (There are 3 negative factors. Since 3 is odd, the product is negative.)

6. 0   **7.** 0   **8.** 0

9. -1   **10.** y

11. ab (Refer to Example 4 on page 466.)

12. $5x$ **13.** one ($x = 0$)

14. infinitely many (y can be any number.)

15. none (There is no number that can be multiplied by 0 to give a product of 10.)

16. negative (There are 7 negative factors. Since 7 is odd, the product is negative.)

17. negative (There are 3 negative factors. Since 3 is odd, the product is negative.)

18. positive; There are an even number of negative factors.

19. 0 (The product is 0 because one of the factors is 0.)

20. $xy + {^-1}xy$
$= xy + {^-xy}$
$= 0$

21. ${^-1} \cdot c + 0 \cdot c$
$= {^-c} + 0$
$= {^-c}$

22. $1 \cdot {^-1} \cdot A$
$= {^-1} \cdot A$
$= {^-A}$

23. $e + 0 \cdot e + 1 \cdot e + 2e + {^-e} + {^-1} \cdot e$
$= e + 0 + e + 2e + {^-e} + {^-e}$
$= e + e + e + e + {^-e} + {^-e}$
$= 2e$

24. **a.**

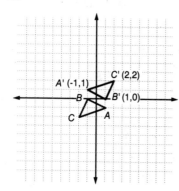

b. They are congruent; corresponding sides are parallel; $\triangle ABC$ has been rotated 180° to get $\triangle A'B'C'$.

25. If you could apply a size change with magnitude 0 to a figure, all image points would be (0, 0) and the original figure would be wiped out.

26. **a.** yes;
b. The product of a number and its reciprocal is 1: ${^-1} \cdot {^-1} = 1$.

27. **a.** no;
b. $0 \cdot 0 \neq 1$

28. -36

29. ${^-1} - {^-2} - {^-3} - {^-4} - {^-5} - {^-6} - {^-7} - {^-8}$
$= {^-1} + 2 + 3 + 4 + 5 + 6 + 7 + 8$
$= {^-1} + 35$
$= 34$

30. $- xy$ dolars
$= \frac{4}{9} - {^-\frac{2}{3}} \cdot \frac{5}{4}$
$= \frac{4}{9} - {^-\frac{5}{6}}$
$= \frac{4}{9} + \frac{5}{6}$
$= \frac{8}{18} + \frac{15}{18}$
$= \frac{23}{18}$

31. For any number x, $x + 0 = x$.

32. For any number x, $x \cdot 1 = x$.

33.
$$57 - x = 4.6$$
$$57 + {^-x} = 4.6$$
$${^-57} + 57 + {^-x} = {^-57} + 4.6$$
$${^-x} = {^-52.4}$$
$$x = 52.4$$

34. $C = 5(F - 32)/9$
$= 5(98.6 - 32)/9$
$= 5 \cdot 66.6/9$
$= 37$

35. 14 (Draw a heptagon, a polygon with 7 sides, and draw its diagonals.)

36. $\frac{4}{7}x = 56$
$\frac{7}{4} \cdot \frac{4}{7}x = \frac{7}{4} \cdot 56$
$x = \frac{7}{4} \cdot \frac{56}{1}$
$x = 98$

37. 50 hours $\cdot$ 25 $\frac{\text{miles}}{\text{hour}} = 1250$ miles

38. (Sample key sequences: 5 $\boxed{y^x}$ .5 $\boxed{=}$;
5 $\boxed{y^x}$ .4 $\boxed{=}$)

x	5^x
0.5	2.2360680
0.4	1.9036539
0.3	1.6206566
0.2	1.3797297
0.1	1.1746189
0.01	1.0162246
0.001	1.0016167
0.0001	1.0001610
0.00001	1.0000161

The value of 5^x is getting closer to 1. It seems that $5^0 = 1$.

LESSON 10-8 (pp. 469-472)

1. $-\frac{1}{8}$ or -0.125 **2.** -3

3. $-\frac{5}{9}$ or $-0.\overline{5}$ **4.** $-.08\overline{3}$ or $-\frac{5}{6}$

5. $-\frac{1}{x}$ **6.** $-x$

7.
$$-4x = 8$$
$$-\frac{1}{4} \cdot -4x = -\frac{1}{4} \cdot 8$$
$$x = -2$$
check: $-4 \cdot -2 = 8$

8.
$$-4y = -52$$
$$-\frac{1}{4} \cdot -4y = -\frac{1}{4} \cdot -52$$
$$y = 13$$
check: $-4 \cdot 13 = -52$

9.
$$-1.2A = 84$$
$$-\frac{1}{1.2} \cdot -1.2A = -\frac{1}{1.2} \cdot 84$$
$$A = -\frac{84}{1.2}$$
$$A = -70$$
check: $-1.2 \cdot -70 = 84$

10.
$$1.2 = -1.2B$$
$$-\frac{1}{1.2} \cdot 1.2 = -\frac{1}{1.2} \cdot -1.2B$$
$$-\frac{1.2}{1.2} = B$$
$$-1 = B$$
check: $1.2 = -1.2 \cdot -1$

11.
$$-\frac{2}{15} = -\frac{5}{3}t$$
$$-\frac{3}{5} \cdot -\frac{2}{15} = -\frac{3}{5} \cdot -\frac{5}{3}t$$
$$\frac{6}{75} = t$$
$$\frac{2}{25} = t$$
check: Does $-\frac{2}{15} = -\frac{5}{3} \cdot \frac{2}{25}$?

Yes: $-\frac{5}{3} \cdot \frac{2}{25} = -\frac{10}{75} = -\frac{2}{15}$

12.
$$1.2C = -0.3$$
$$\frac{1}{1.2} \cdot 1.2C = \frac{1}{1.2} \cdot -0.3$$
$$C = -\frac{0.3}{1.2}$$
$$C = -0.25$$
check: $1.2 \cdot -0.25 = -0.3$

13. Multiplication Property of Equality

14. $-\frac{1}{a}$

15. $-\frac{2}{5}\frac{\text{inches}}{\text{day}} \cdot d \text{ days} = -6 \text{ inches}$
$$-\frac{2}{5}d = -6$$
$$-\frac{5}{2} \cdot -\frac{2}{5}d = -\frac{5}{2} \cdot -6$$
$$d = \frac{30}{2}$$
$$d = 15$$
It will take about 15 days.

16.

$$-4.5x = -100 \quad (1 \text{ m} = 100 \text{ cm})$$
$$-\frac{1}{4.5} \cdot -4.5x = -\frac{1}{4.5} \cdot -100$$
$$x = \frac{100}{4.5}$$
$$x = 22.\overline{2}$$

$22.\overline{2}$ years

17.

$$-800 \, m = -4500$$
$$-\frac{1}{800} \cdot -800 \, m = -\frac{1}{800} \cdot -4500$$
$$m = \frac{4500}{800}$$
$$m = 5.625$$

about 5.6 months

18. negative (t is multiplied by a negative number. To yield a positive product, t must be negative.)

19. y is positive (y is multiplied by a negative number. To yield a negative product, y must be positive.)

20.

$$-3 + x = -12$$
$$3 + -3 + x = 3 + -12$$
$$x = -9$$

21. $a + 0 \cdot a - b + 1 \cdot b + -1 \cdot a - a$
$$= a + 0 - b + b + -a - a$$
$$= a + 0 + -b + b + -a + -a$$
$$= -a$$

22. $-7x + 2y - 3z$
$$= 7 \cdot -\frac{5}{3} + 2 \cdot 4 - 3 \cdot -2$$
$$= \frac{35}{3} + 8 - -6$$
$$= 11\frac{2}{3} + 8 + 6$$
$$= 25\frac{2}{3} \text{ or } \frac{77}{3}$$

23. 30% of 600 students $= .3 \cdot 600$ students $=$ 180 students

24. $.3x = 600$
$$x = \frac{600}{.3}$$
$$x = 2000 \text{ students}$$

25. $(6 - |3 - 7|)/36$
$$= (6 - |3 + -7|)/36$$
$$= (6 - |-4|)/36$$
$$= (6 - 4)/36$$
$$= 2/36$$
$$= \frac{1}{18}$$

26. $180° - x$ (The angles form a linear pair.)

27. $m\angle HEG = 98°$ ($180° - (50° + 32°)$);
$m\angle H = 50°$ (alternate interior angles);
$m\angle G = 32°$ (alternate interior angles)

28.

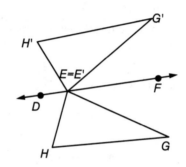

29. 1000 (Since $-11x + -111 = -11,111$, first look for a quantity which, when added to -111, gives $-11,111$. This quantity is $-11,000$ since $-11,000 + -111 = -11,111$. So $-11x = -11,000$. Solve this equation: $x = 1000$)

LESSON 10-9 (pp. 473-477)

1. a. -25

b.
$$4x + 25 = 85$$
$$4x + 25 + -25 = 85 + -25$$
$$4x = 60$$
$$\frac{1}{4} \cdot 4x = \frac{1}{4} \cdot 60$$
$$x = 15$$

2. a. 8

b.
$$3v - 8 = -50$$
$$3v + -8 = -50$$
$$3v + -8 + 8 = -50 + 8$$
$$3v = -42$$
$$\frac{1}{3} \cdot 3v = \frac{1}{3} \cdot -42$$
$$v = -14$$

3. If you cannot solve a sentence, convert it to one you can solve.

4. a. Add 3 and 5.

b.
$$3 + 4x + 5 = 6$$
$$8 + 4x = 6$$
$$-8 + 8 + 4x = -8 + 6$$
$$4x = -2$$
$$\frac{1}{4} \cdot 4x = \frac{1}{4} \cdot -2$$
$$x = -\frac{1}{2}$$

5.
$$2y + 7 = 41$$
$$2y + 7 + -7 = 41 + -7$$
$$2y = 34$$
$$\frac{1}{2} \cdot 2y = \frac{1}{2} \cdot 34$$
$$y = 17$$

6.
$$300 + 120t = -1500$$
$$-300 + 300 + 120t = -300 + -1500$$
$$120t = -1800$$
$$\frac{1}{120} \cdot 120t = \frac{1}{120} \cdot -1800$$
$$t = -15$$

7.
$$60 - 9x = 48$$
$$60 + -9x = 48$$
$$-60 + 60 + -9x = -60 + 48$$
$$-9x = -12$$
$$-\frac{1}{9} \cdot -9x = -\frac{1}{9} \cdot -12$$
$$x = \frac{12}{9}$$
$$x = \frac{4}{3}, \text{ or } 1.\overline{3}$$

8.
$$17 + 60m + 3 = 100$$
$$20 + 60m = 100$$
$$-20 + 20 + 60m = -20 + 100$$
$$60m = 80$$
$$\frac{1}{60} \cdot 60m = \frac{1}{60} \cdot 80$$
$$m = \frac{80}{60}$$
$$m = \frac{4}{3}, \text{ or } 1.\overline{3}$$

9. $4 \cdot 80 + 180 + 10 \cdot 11 = 610$ calories

10. $4 \cdot 80 + 180 + 11F = 500 + 11F$ calories

11.
$$500 + 11F = 900$$
$$-500 + 500 + 11F = -500 + 900$$
$$11F = 400$$
$$\frac{1}{11} \cdot 11F = \frac{1}{11} \cdot 400$$
$$F = 36.\overline{36}$$

about 36 french fries

12. $80h + 11F$

13.
$$80h + 180 + 11 \cdot 20 = 1000$$
$$80h + 400 = 1000$$
$$80h + 400 + -400 = 1000 + -400$$
$$80h = 600$$
$$\frac{1}{80} \cdot 80h = \frac{1}{80} \cdot 600$$
$$h = 7.5$$

7.5-ounce hamburger

14. a. $-n$

b.
$$mx + n = p$$
$$mx + n + -n = p + -n$$
$$mx = p - n$$
$$\frac{1}{m} \cdot mx = \frac{1}{m} \cdot (p - n)$$
$$x = \frac{p - n}{m}$$

15. no $(400 - 12 \cdot -17 = 400 - -204 = 400 + 204 = 604)$

16.
$$2y + 1 = 0$$
$$2y + 1 + \text{-}1 = 0 + \text{-}1$$
$$2y = \text{-}1$$
$$\tfrac{1}{2} \cdot 2y = \tfrac{1}{2} \cdot \text{-}1$$
$$y = \text{-}\tfrac{1}{2}$$
check: $2 \cdot \text{-}\tfrac{1}{2} + 1 = 0$

17.
$$\tfrac{3}{2} - 14z + \tfrac{7}{8} = 0$$
$$\tfrac{3}{2} + \text{-}14z + \tfrac{7}{8} = 0$$
$$\tfrac{19}{8} + \text{-}14z = 0$$
$$\text{-}\tfrac{19}{8} + \tfrac{19}{8} + \text{-}14z = \text{-}\tfrac{19}{8} + 0$$
$$\text{-}14z = \text{-}\tfrac{19}{8}$$
$$\text{-}\tfrac{1}{14} \cdot \text{-}14z = \text{-}\tfrac{1}{14} \cdot \text{-}\tfrac{19}{8}$$
$$z = \tfrac{19}{112}$$
check: $\tfrac{3}{2} - 14 \cdot \tfrac{19}{112} + \tfrac{7}{8} =$
$$\tfrac{3}{2} - \tfrac{19}{8} + \tfrac{7}{8} = \tfrac{12}{8} + \text{-}\tfrac{19}{8} + \tfrac{7}{8} = 0$$

18.
a. Addition Property of Equality
b. Associative Property of Addition
c. Property of Opposites
d. Additive Identity Property of Zero
e. Multiplication Property of Equality
f. Associative Property of Multiplication
g. Property of Reciprocals and Multiplication of Fractions Property
h. Multiplicative Identity Property of 1

19.
$$\text{-}\tfrac{2}{3} t = \tfrac{5}{4}$$
$$\text{-}\tfrac{3}{2} \cdot \text{-}\tfrac{2}{3} t = \text{-}\tfrac{3}{2} \cdot \tfrac{5}{4}$$
$$t = \text{-}\tfrac{15}{8}$$

20.

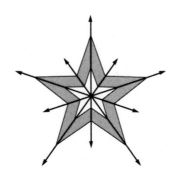

21. 25 inches $\cdot \dfrac{1 \text{ meter}}{39.37 \text{ inches}} \approx .635$ meter

22. $\text{-}4 (3 + \text{-}2 \cdot 6 - 1)$
$= \text{-}4 (3 + \text{-}12 + \text{-}1)$
$= \text{-}4 \cdot \text{-}10$
$= 40$

23. $1 \cdot x + 0 \cdot y + \text{-}1 \cdot \text{-}2z$
$= x + 0 + 2z$
$= x + 2z$

24. There is no such number.

25.
$$.39v = 248{,}000$$
$$\tfrac{1}{.39} \cdot .39v = \tfrac{1}{.39} \cdot 248{,}000$$
$$v = 635897.43 \ldots$$
about 635,900 people

26. a. $61{,}250 \dfrac{\text{words}}{\text{book}}$ (Multiply the numbers; cancel "page" and "pages.")
b. Many possible answers. Sample: There are about 350 words on a printed page. Estimate how many words would appear in a 175-page book.

27. $2500 - D + B - S = 2300$

28. $131.40 (9 ft $\cdot$ 12 ft = 3 yd $\cdot$ 4 yd = 12 square yards; 12 $\cdot$ $10.95 = $131.40)

29. a. $25¢ + 20¢ \cdot 1 = 45¢$
b. $25¢ + 20¢ \cdot 2 = 65¢$
c. $25¢ + 20¢ \cdot 3 = 85¢$
d. $25 + 20(n - 1)$ cents

30. **a.** $(-32 \cdot 1 + 128)$ ft/sec $= 96$ ft/sec

b. $(-32 \cdot 2 + 128)$ ft/sec $= 64$ ft/sec

c. The projectile is falling.

31. The prices are described with positive and negative halves, quarters, and eighths.

CHAPTER 10 PROGRESS SELF-TEST (p. 479)

1. $\frac{3}{5}n = 15$

$\frac{5}{3} \cdot \frac{3}{5}n = \frac{5}{3} \cdot 15$

$n = 25$

2. If $x = y$, then $ax = ay$.

3. $10w = 5$

$w = \frac{5}{10}$

$w = \frac{1}{2}$ ft

4. $2000 = .08L$

$\frac{1}{.08} \cdot 2000 = \frac{1}{.08} \cdot .08L$

$\$25{,}000 = L$

5. $13x = 1001$

$x = \frac{1001}{13}$

$x = 77$

6. $13x = 1001$

$\frac{1}{13} \cdot 13x = \frac{1}{13} \cdot 1001$

$x = 77$

7. 37.5 hours $\cdot \dfrac{\$8.50}{\text{hr}} = \$318.75$

8. 4 hours $\cdot -3\,\dfrac{\text{cm}}{\text{hr}} = -12$ cm

9. -45

10. $-3 \cdot -3 + -2 \cdot -2$

$= 9 + 4$

$= 13$

11. $2 \cdot -3 \cdot 4 \cdot -5 \cdot 6 \cdot -7$

$= -(2 \cdot 3 \cdot 4 \cdot 5 \cdot 6 \cdot 7)$

$= -5040$

(There are 3 negative factors, so the product is negative.)

12. $6x - 3yz$

$= 6 \cdot 0 - 3 \cdot -1 \cdot 5$

$= 0 - -15$

$= 0 + 15$

$= 15$

13. $a + 1 \cdot a + b + 0 \cdot b + -1 \cdot c + c$

$= a + a + b + 0 + -c + c$

$= 2a + b$

14. d must be positive.

15.

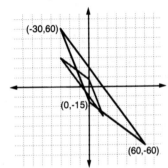

16. Many possible answers. Samples: Things that are the same: Figures have same shape, same angle measure, and corresponding sides are parallel. Things that are different: lengths of sides of image are 2.5 times lengths of sides of preimage; preimage is rotated 180° to get image.

17. All are equal.

18. $\dfrac{39.37 \text{ inches}}{1 \text{ meter}}$, $\qquad \dfrac{1 \text{ meter}}{39.37 \text{ inches}}$

19. 1200 inches $\cdot \dfrac{1 \text{ meter}}{39.37 \text{ inches}} \approx 30.48$ meters

(Multiply $1200 \cdot \frac{1}{39.37}$ and cancel "inches.")

20.
$$-x = -4$$
$$-1 \cdot {-}x = -1 \cdot -4$$
$$x = 4$$

21.
$$35.1 = -9t$$
$$-\frac{1}{9} \cdot 35.1 = -\frac{1}{9} \cdot -9t$$
$$-3.9 = t$$

22.
$$-\frac{2}{5}m = -\frac{3}{4}$$
$$-\frac{5}{2} \cdot -\frac{2}{3}m = -\frac{5}{2} \cdot -\frac{3}{4}$$
$$m = \frac{15}{8}$$

23. k can be any number
(Any number times $0 = 0$.)

24.
$$2 + 3A = 17$$
$$-2 + 2 + 3A = -2 + 17$$
$$3A = 15$$
$$\frac{1}{3} \cdot 3A = \frac{1}{3} \cdot 15$$
$$A = 5$$

25.
$$12 - 4h - 15 = 10$$
$$12 + {-}4h + {-}15 = 10$$
$$-3 + {-}4h = 10$$
$$3 + {-}3 + {-}4h = 3 + 10$$
$$-4h = 13$$
$$-\frac{1}{4} \cdot -4h = -\frac{1}{4} \cdot 13$$
$$h = -\frac{13}{4}$$

CHAPTER 10 REVIEW (pp. 480-481)

1. 16

2. $3 + {-}10 \cdot 4$
$= 3 + {-}40$
$= -37$

3. 400 (There are 2 negative factors, so product is positive.)

4. $5x - 2y$
$= 5 \cdot -3 - 2 \cdot -16$
$= -15 - -32$
$= -15 + 32$
$= 17$

5. 3

6. -1

7. $-x = 7$
$x = -7$

8. $10y = 0$
$$y = \frac{0}{10}$$
$$y = 0$$

9. positive (The product of a negative number and a positive number is negative.)

10. no $\left(\frac{3}{8} \cdot \frac{1}{3} = \frac{1}{8} \right)$

11.
$$40t = 3000$$
$$\frac{1}{40} \cdot 40t = \frac{1}{40} \cdot 3000$$
$$t = 75$$
check: $40 \cdot 75 = 3000$

12.
$$-22 = 4A$$
$$\frac{1}{4} \cdot -22 = \frac{1}{4} \cdot 4A$$
$$-5.5 = A$$
check: $-22 = 4 \cdot -5.5$

13.
$$0.02v = 0.8$$
$$\frac{1}{0.02} \cdot 0.02v = \frac{1}{0.02} \cdot 0.8$$
$$v = 40$$
check: $0.02 \cdot 40 = 0.8$

14.
$$\frac{2}{3}x = 18$$
$$\frac{3}{2} \cdot \frac{2}{3}x = \frac{3}{2} \cdot 18$$
$$x = 27$$
check: $\frac{2}{3} \cdot 27 = 18$

15.
$$-49 = -7y$$
$$-\frac{1}{7} \cdot -49 = -\frac{1}{7} \cdot 7y$$
$$7 = y$$
check: $-49 = -7 \cdot 7$

16.
$$2.4 + 3.6 = (5 - 0.2)x$$
$$6 = 4.8x$$
$$\frac{1}{4.8} \cdot 6 = \frac{1}{4.8} \cdot 4.8x$$
$$1.25 = x$$
check: Does $2.4 + 3.6 = (5 - 0.2) \cdot 1.25$?
Yes: $2.4 + 3.6 = 6$ and $(5 - 0.2) \cdot 1.25 = 4.8 \cdot 1.25 = 6$

17.
$$8m + 2 = 18$$
$$8m + 2 + -2 = 18 + -2$$
$$8m = 16$$
$$\frac{1}{8} \cdot 8m = \frac{1}{8} \cdot 16$$
$$m = 2$$
check: $8 \cdot 2 + 2 = 16 + 2 = 18$

18.
$$-2.5 + .5y = 4.2$$
$$2.5 + -2.5 + .5y = 2.5 + 4.2$$
$$.5y = 6.7$$
$$\frac{1}{.5} \cdot .5y = \frac{1}{.5} \cdot 6.7$$
$$y = 13.4$$
check: $-2.5 + .5 \cdot 13.4 = -2.5 + 6.7 = 4.2$

19.
$$11 - 6u = -7$$
$$11 + -6u = -7$$
$$-11 + 11 + -6u = -11 + -7$$
$$-6u = -18$$
$$-\frac{1}{6} \cdot -6u = -\frac{1}{6} \cdot -18$$
$$u = 3$$
check: $11 - 6 \cdot 3 = 11 - 18 = -7$

20.
$$23 + 4x - 10 = -39$$
$$23 + 4x + -10 = -39$$
$$13 + 4x = -39$$
$$-13 + 13 + 4x = -13 + -39$$
$$4x = -52$$
$$\frac{1}{4} \cdot 4x = \frac{1}{4} \cdot -52$$
$$x = -13$$
check: $23 + 4 \cdot -13 - 10 =$
$23 + -52 + -10 = -39$

21. $\frac{3}{11}$ **22.** -12

23. $-1 \cdot -x = x$

24. $0 \cdot a + 1 \cdot b + -1 \cdot c$
$= 0 + b + -c$
$= b + -c, \text{or } b - c$

25. no solutions (Any number times $0 = 0$.)

26. $t = \frac{16}{6.4}$ and $6.4 = \frac{16}{t}$

27. $\frac{13,261.6}{48.4} = 274$ (or $\frac{13,261.6}{274} = 48.4$); answer checks

28. $9x = 819$
$$x = \frac{819}{9}$$
$$x = 91$$

29. a. $2 \frac{\text{cookies}}{\text{day}} \cdot 365 \frac{\text{days}}{\text{year}} = 730 \frac{\text{cookies}}{\text{year}}$

b. Many possible answers. Sample: If you eat 2 cookies a day, how many will you eat in a year?

30. a. $5 \text{ hours} \cdot 25 \frac{\text{miles}}{\text{hour}} = 125 \text{ miles}$

b. Many possible answers. Sample: If you travel 25 miles an hour, how many miles will you travel in 5 hours?

31. $20,475

$(10.50 \frac{\text{dollars}}{\text{hour}} \cdot 37.5 \frac{\text{hours}}{\text{week}} \cdot 52 \frac{\text{weeks}}{\text{year}} = 20,475 \frac{\text{dollars}}{\text{year}})$

32. 360 people (6 rooms $\cdot$ 60 $\frac{\text{people}}{\text{room}} = 360$ people)

33. She weighed 9.2 kg more. (-4 months $\cdot$ $-2.3 \frac{\text{kg}}{\text{month}} = 9.2$ kg)

34. $\frac{1 \text{ foot}}{30.48 \text{ cm}}$ and $\frac{30.48 \text{ cm}}{1 \text{ foot}}$

35. about 16.4 ft (500 cm $\cdot$ $\frac{1 \text{ foot}}{30.48 \text{ cm}} \approx 16.4$ ft)

36. 6.25 days (150 hours $\cdot$ $\frac{1 \text{ day}}{24 \text{ hours}} = 6.25$ days)

37. $20s = 500$

$s = \frac{500}{20}$

$s = 25$ seats

38. $3500 = 40d$

$\frac{3500}{40} = d$

$87.5 \text{ ft} = d$

39. $8 \cdot 25 \cdot h = 2400$

$200\,h = 2400$

$h = \frac{2400}{200}$

$h = 12$ cm

40. $6n = \frac{1}{3}$

$\frac{1}{6} \cdot 6n = \frac{1}{6} \cdot \frac{1}{3}$

$n = \frac{1}{18}$

41. $.12x = 240$

$\frac{1}{.12} \cdot .12x = \frac{1}{.12} \cdot 240$

$x = 2000$

42. $.8p = \$40$

$\frac{1}{.8} \cdot .8p = \frac{1}{.8} \cdot \$40$

$p = \$50$

43. $1.5w = \$12$

$\frac{1}{1.5} \cdot 1.5w = \frac{1}{1.5} \cdot \$12$

$w = \$8$ per hour

44. $\frac{7}{8}x = 112$

$\frac{8}{7} \cdot \frac{7}{8}x = \frac{8}{7} \cdot 112$

$x = 128$

45. $(-8, 16)$ (Multiply each coordinate by -0.2.)

46. Many possible answers. Samples: Same features: They will have the same shape and angle measures. Different features: The image will have lengths 5 times those in the preimage; the preimage will be rotated 180° to get the image.

47.

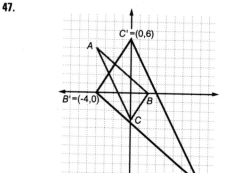

48. 180°

CHAPTER 11   PATTERNS LEADING TO DIVISION

LESSON 11-1   (pp. 484-487)

1. (or 50 miles/hour, $\frac{+or}{p_A}$ $\frac{}{p_A}$ = 0

    50 mph)

2. $\frac{400 \text{ miles}}{8.5 \text{ hours}} \approx 47.1 \frac{\text{miles}}{\text{hour}}$

3. $\frac{600 \text{ km}}{9 \text{ hr}} \approx 66.7 \text{ km/hr}$

4. $\frac{d}{m}$ meters per minute

5. $\frac{28 \text{ boys}}{14 \text{ girls}} = 2$ boys per girl

6. $\frac{150 \text{ students}}{7 \text{ classes}} \approx 21$ students/class

7. $\frac{120 \text{ acres}}{6 \text{ people}} = 20$ acres per person

8. If a and b are quantities with different units, then $\frac{a}{b}$ is the amount of quantity a per quantity b.

9. a. $\frac{129¢}{12 \text{ oz}} = 10.75¢$ per ounce $\approx 10.7¢$ or 10.8¢ per ounce

    b. $\frac{173¢}{18 \text{ oz}} \approx 9.6¢$ per ounce

    c. the 18-oz box

10. a. $\frac{119 \text{ nails}}{9 \text{ nannies}} \approx 13$ nails per nanny

    b. 2 nails ($119 \div 9 = 13$ R2)

11. $\frac{m}{h}$ miles per hour

12. $\frac{\$222}{34 \text{ hr}} \approx \$6.53$ per hour

13. $\frac{\$20}{80 \text{ hr}} = \$0.25$ per hour

14. California (Rate in Hawaii is $\frac{2743 \text{ doctors}}{964,691 \text{ people}} \approx$ .0028 doctors per person. Rate in California is $\frac{72,089 \text{ doctors}}{23,667,764} \approx$ .0030 doctors per person.)

15. $\frac{140 \text{ bandages}}{15 \text{ days}} = 9\frac{1}{3}$ bandages per day (1 school week = 5 days)

16. Many possible answers. Sample: 84 sheets in 10 days ($84 \div 10 = 8.4 = 8\frac{2}{5}$)

17. a. $\frac{43}{6}$ (To find the numerator, calculate $7 \cdot 6 + 1$)

    b. $\frac{6}{43}$

18. For any numbers x and y, when $y \neq 0$, $\frac{x}{y} = x \cdot \frac{1}{y}$.

19.
$$-5 - 5m = 5$$
$$-5 + -5m = 5$$
$$5 + -5 + -5m = 5 + 5$$
$$-5m = 10$$
$$-\frac{1}{5} \cdot -5m = -\frac{1}{5} \cdot 10$$
$$m = -2$$

20. $|a - b + c| - |a|$
$$= |-2 - 5 + 1| - |-2|$$
$$= |-2 + -5 + 1| - 2$$
$$= |-6| - 2$$
$$= 6 - 2$$
$$= 4$$

21. angles 3 and 7; angles 2 and 6

22. angles 8 and 6; angles 1 and 3; angles 2 and 4; angles 7 and 5

23. 75° (m$\angle 3$ = 75° because $\angle 3$ and $\angle 5$ are vertical angles; m$\angle 1$ = 75° because $\angle 1$ and $\angle 3$ are corresponding angles.)

24. 180° $- x$ (m$\angle 2$ = x because $\angle 2$ and $\angle 4$ are corresponding angles; m$\angle 7$ = 180° $- x$ because $\angle 2$ and $\angle 7$ form a linear pair.)

25. 8, 8, 20 (Draw an octagon and its diagonals. Count the diagonals.)

26. a. For ages 11-18: males should have 45-56 grams per day; females should have 46 grams per day.

b. about 69 people per square mile

c. Many possible answers. Sample: A Toyota Tercel gets about 39 miles per gallon.

d. about 343 sunny days per year

LESSON 11-2 (pp. 488-491)

1. $\dfrac{12 \text{ dollars}}{\frac{5}{2} \text{ hours}}$

$= 12 \cdot \dfrac{2}{5} \dfrac{\text{dollars}}{\text{hour}}$

$= \dfrac{24}{5} \dfrac{\text{dollars}}{\text{hour}}$

$= \$4.80$ per hour

2. For any numbers a and b, when $b \neq 0$, $\dfrac{a}{b} = a \cdot \dfrac{1}{b}$.

3. $\dfrac{\frac{8}{9}}{\frac{4}{3}} = \dfrac{8}{9} \cdot \dfrac{3}{4} = \dfrac{24}{36} = \dfrac{2}{3}$

4. $\dfrac{\frac{2}{5}}{7} = \dfrac{2}{5} \cdot \dfrac{1}{7} = \dfrac{2}{35}$

5. $\dfrac{\frac{17}{6}}{\frac{2}{3}} = \dfrac{17}{6} \cdot \dfrac{3}{2} = \dfrac{51}{12} = \dfrac{17}{4}$ or $4\frac{1}{4}$

6. $\dfrac{66 \text{ games}}{\frac{2}{3} \text{ season}}$

$= 66 \cdot \dfrac{3}{2} \dfrac{\text{games}}{\text{season}}$

$= 99$ games per season

7. $\dfrac{12 \text{ games}}{\frac{1}{5} \text{ season}}$

$= 12 \cdot \dfrac{5}{1} \dfrac{\text{games}}{\text{season}}$

$= 60$ games per season

8. a. $\dfrac{4\frac{1}{4}}{3\frac{2}{5}} = \dfrac{\frac{17}{4}}{\frac{17}{5}} = \dfrac{17}{4} \cdot \dfrac{5}{17} = \dfrac{5}{4}$ or $1\frac{1}{4}$

b. $3\frac{2}{5}$ is smaller than $4\frac{1}{4}$.

c. $\dfrac{4.25}{3.4} = 1.25 = 1\frac{1}{4}$

9. a. $\dfrac{1\frac{2}{3}}{5\frac{4}{7}} = \dfrac{\frac{5}{3}}{\frac{39}{7}} = \dfrac{5}{3} \cdot \dfrac{7}{39} = \dfrac{35}{117}$

b. $5\frac{4}{7}$ is greater than $1\frac{2}{3}$.

c. $\dfrac{1.6666667}{5.5714285} = 0.299145 \ldots$ and

$\dfrac{35}{117} = 0.299145 \ldots$

d. The decimals are infinite, so it is easier to work with the fractions.

10. a. $\dfrac{\frac{1}{3} \text{ mile}}{\frac{1}{6} \text{ hour}}$

$= \dfrac{1}{3} \cdot \dfrac{6}{1} \dfrac{\text{miles}}{\text{hour}}$

$= 2$ miles per hour

b. 2 miles

11. $\dfrac{\frac{2}{x}}{\frac{1}{y}} = \dfrac{2}{x} \cdot \dfrac{y}{1} = \dfrac{2y}{x}$

12. $\dfrac{\frac{a}{b}}{\frac{c}{d}} = \dfrac{a}{b} \cdot \dfrac{d}{c} = \dfrac{ad}{bc}$

13.
$$7\frac{1}{2}n = 375$$
$$\frac{15}{2}n = 375$$
$$\frac{2}{15} \cdot \frac{15}{2}n = \frac{2}{15} \cdot 375$$
$$n = 50$$

14. $\dfrac{21.12 \text{ dollars}}{3.3 \text{ hours}}$

$= \dfrac{21.12}{3.3} \dfrac{\text{dollars}}{\text{hour}}$

$= \$6.40 \text{ per hour}$

15.
$$-4 + G = -3$$
$$4 + -4 + G = 4 + -3$$
$$G = 1$$

16.
$$-4 - G = -3$$
$$-4 + -G = -3$$
$$4 + -4 + -G = 4 + -3$$
$$-G = 1$$
$$G = -1$$

17.
$$-4G = -3$$
$$-\frac{1}{4} \cdot -4G = -\frac{1}{4} \cdot -3$$
$$G = \frac{3}{4}$$

18. $x + y$

$= \frac{5}{4} + \frac{1}{2}$

$= \frac{5}{4} + \frac{2}{4}$

$= \frac{7}{4}$

19. $x - y$

$= \frac{5}{4} - \frac{1}{2}$

$= \frac{5}{4} - \frac{2}{4}$

$= \frac{3}{4}$

20. $8xy$

$= 8 \cdot \frac{5}{4} \cdot \frac{1}{2}$

$= 10 \cdot \frac{1}{2}$

$= 5$

21. $\dfrac{1}{10,000} \cdot \dfrac{1}{10,000} = \dfrac{1}{100,000,000}$ (1 in 100 million)

22. 21 in. $\cdot$ 10 in. $\cdot$ 35 in. $= 7350$ in.^{3}

23. $2 \cdot 10$ in. $\cdot 21$ in. $+ 2 \cdot 10$ in. $\cdot 35$ in. $+ 2 \cdot 21$ in. $\cdot 35$ in. $= 420$ in.$^2 + 700$ in.$^2 + 1470$ in.$^2 = 2590$ in.^{2}

24. $2 \cdot 35$ in. $+ 2 \cdot 21$ in. $= 70$ in. $+ 42$ in. $= 112$ in.

25.

$$\dfrac{\dfrac{1\frac{1}{2} \text{ eggs}}{1\frac{1}{2} \text{ hens}}}{1\frac{1}{2} \text{ days}}$$

$$= \dfrac{\dfrac{1\frac{1}{2} \dfrac{\text{egg}}{\text{hen}}}{1\frac{1}{2}}}{1\frac{1}{2} \text{ days}}$$

$$= \dfrac{1 \text{ egg per hen}}{1\frac{1}{2} \text{ days}}$$

$$= \dfrac{1}{1\frac{1}{2}} \dfrac{\text{egg per hen}}{\text{day}}$$

$$= 1 \cdot \frac{2}{3} \dfrac{\text{egg per hen}}{\text{day}}$$

$$= \frac{2}{3} \text{ egg per hen per day}$$

24 hens $\cdot$ 24 days $\cdot \frac{2}{3}$ egg per hen per day $=$

$24 \cdot 24 \cdot \frac{2}{3}$ eggs $= 384$ eggs

LESSON 11-3 (pp. 492-496)

1. -2

2. $-\frac{1}{3}$

3. 7

4. -30

5. $\dfrac{40 + 60 + 80 + 100}{4} = \dfrac{280}{4} = 70$

6. $\dfrac{-40 + -60 + -80 + -100}{4} = \dfrac{-280}{4} = -70$

7. $\dfrac{-11 + 14 + -17 + -20 + 6 + -30}{6} = \dfrac{-58}{6} =$

$-9\frac{2}{3}$ or $-9.\overline{6}$

8. positive (The quotient is negative. Two negative factors yield a positive product.)

9. positive (The quotient is negative. The opposite of a negative number is a positive number.)

10. negative (The quotient is positive. The opposite of a positive number is a negative number.)

11. positive (Each quotient is negative. Two negative factors yield a positive product.)

12. $-\frac{1}{2} = \frac{-1}{2} = \frac{1}{-2} = -\frac{-1}{-2}; \frac{-1}{-2} = \frac{1}{2} = -\frac{-1}{2}$

13. a. $\dfrac{-4 \text{ pounds}}{2 \text{ days}} = -2$ pounds per day

b. $\dfrac{-4 \text{ pounds}}{2 \text{ days}}$; divide $\dfrac{-4}{2}$

c. 2, 4, more

d. $\dfrac{4 \text{ pounds}}{-2 \text{ days}}$; divide $\dfrac{4}{-2}$

14. a. $\dfrac{9,000,000 \text{ people}}{20 \text{ years}} = 450,000$ people per year

b. 20, less

c. $\dfrac{-9,000,000}{-20 \text{ years}} = 450,000$ people per year

15. 1. Change subtractions to additions. Change divisions to multiplications.   2. Think of an application using negative numbers to help find the answer.

16. $x + y = -10 + 5 = -5;$

$x - y = -10 - 5 = -10 + -5 = -15;$

$xy = -10 \cdot 5 = -50;$

$\dfrac{x}{y} = \dfrac{-10}{5} = -2$

17. $x + y = -6 + -9 = -15;$

$x - y = -6 - -9 = -6 + 9 + 3;$

$xy = -6 \cdot -9 = 54;$

$\dfrac{x}{y} = \dfrac{-6}{-9} = \dfrac{2}{3},$ or $.\overline{6}$

18. $x + y = 1 + -1 = 0;$

$x - y = 1 - -1 = 1 + 1 = 2;$

$xy = 1 \cdot -1 = -1;$

$\dfrac{x}{y} = \dfrac{1}{-1} = -1$

19. $x + y = -12 + -12 = -24;$

$x - y = -12 - -12 = -12 + 12 = 0;$

$xy = -12 \cdot -12 = 144; \dfrac{x}{y} = \dfrac{-12}{-12} = 1$

20. $C = 5(F - 32)/9$

$= 5(-40 - 32)/9$

$= 5(-40 + -32)/9$

$= 5 \cdot -72/9$

$= -360/9$

$= -40$

The temperature is $-40°C$. This is the one temperature at which $F = C$.

21. $\dfrac{15}{-8} \cdot \dfrac{2}{-3} = -\dfrac{15}{8} \cdot -\dfrac{2}{3} = \dfrac{30}{24} = \dfrac{5}{4}$

22. $\dfrac{350}{-6} = -58.\overline{3} \approx -58$

23. a. $(\frac{1}{4}, 5)$ $(x = \dfrac{-8 + -15 + 12 + 12}{4} =$

$\dfrac{-23 + 24}{4} = \dfrac{1}{4};$

$y = \dfrac{-10 + 10 + 30 + -10}{4} = \dfrac{20}{4} = 5)$

b.

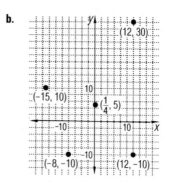

144

24. $\dfrac{\frac{10}{3}}{\frac{5}{6}} = \dfrac{10}{3} \cdot \dfrac{6}{5} = \dfrac{60}{15} = \dfrac{4}{1}$

25. (−6, 3) (Subtract 20 from first coordinate; subtract 3 from second coordinate.)

26. $\dfrac{100 \text{ miles}}{3.5 \text{ days}} = \dfrac{100}{3.5} \dfrac{\text{miles}}{\text{day}} \approx 28.6$ miles per day

27. **a.** 0.44 (Move the decimal point 2 places to the left.)

 b. $44\% = \dfrac{44}{100} = \dfrac{11}{25}$

28. 40% of 500 = .4 • 500 = 200

29. $.4x = 500$

$\dfrac{1}{.4} \cdot .4x = \dfrac{1}{.4} \cdot 500$

$x = 1250$

30. **a.** Several possible answers depending on calculator used. Sample: $\boxed{\text{E}}$, meaning error

 b. 5000

 c. −5000

 d. Many possible answers. Samples: $\dfrac{5}{0.000001}$

 $= 5{,}000{,}000;\ \dfrac{5}{-0.0000003} \approx 16{,}666{,}666.$ If the dividend stays the same, the closer the divisor is to zero, the greater the absolute value of the quotient.

*31. *1992 Edition only:* **a.** −2°

 b. Many possible answers. Sample: 110, 96, 87, 16, 11; Median 87, mean 64.

LESSON 11-4 (pp. 497-500)

1. $\dfrac{12}{30} = .4 = 40\%$ **2.** $\dfrac{\$0.64}{\$16.00} = .04 = 4\%$

3. **a.** $\dfrac{\$0.35}{\$5.83} \approx .06 \approx 6\%$

 b. about 6% (This question is equivalent to part a: $\dfrac{0.35}{5.83} = \dfrac{35}{583} \approx 6\%$)

4. You can divide 6 by 25, or you can divide 25 by 6.

5. $\dfrac{6}{25} = .24 = 24\%$ **6.** $\dfrac{6}{12} = .5 = 50\%$

7. $\dfrac{6}{6} = 1 = 100\%$ **8.** $\dfrac{6}{3} = 2 = 200\%$

9. $\dfrac{41}{300} = .13\overline{6} \approx 14\%$ **10.** $\dfrac{250}{300} = .8\overline{3} \approx 83\%$

11. **a.** 3% $\left(\dfrac{90{,}000}{3{,}000{,}000} = .03 = 3\%\right)$

 b. about 33 $\left(\dfrac{3{,}000{,}000}{90{,}000} = 33.\overline{3}\right)$

12. Ratios do not have units. Rates have units.

13. **a.** $\dfrac{14}{25} = .56 = 56\%$

 b. $\dfrac{11}{25} = .44 = 44\%$

 (Or subtract 100% − 56% = 44%.)

14. 12% of 90 = .12 • 90 = 10.8

15. **a.** $\dfrac{36}{40} = .9 = 90\%$

 b. 36% of 40 = .36 • 40 = 14.4

 c. $40 = .36n$

 $\dfrac{1}{.36} \cdot 40 = \dfrac{1}{.36} \cdot .36n$

 $111.\overline{1} = n$

16. $\dfrac{\$13.50}{\$60} = .225 = 22.5\%$

17. $\dfrac{7000}{350{,}000} = .02 = 2\%$

18. $\dfrac{-6}{-2} = 3$

19. $\dfrac{x}{y} = \dfrac{\frac{2}{5}}{\frac{-2}{15}} = \dfrac{2}{5} \cdot -\dfrac{15}{2} = -\dfrac{3}{1}$

20. 2.5 hours $\cdot$ 2.5 $\frac{\text{miles}}{\text{hour}}$ = 6.25 miles

21.
$$1\tfrac{3}{4}w = \$17.15$$
$$1.75w = \$17.15$$
$$\tfrac{1}{1.75} \cdot 1.75w = \tfrac{1}{1.75} \cdot \$17.15$$
$$w = \$9.80$$

22. $12C - 200$ dollars

23. $90 - x = 90 - 43 = 47$

24. $\frac{3}{5} + \frac{3}{4} = \frac{12}{20} + \frac{15}{20} = \frac{27}{20}$

25. $\frac{a - c}{b - d}$

$= \frac{10 - 30}{20 - 40}$

$= \frac{10 + {}^{-}30}{20 + {}^{-}40}$

$= \frac{{}^{-}20}{{}^{-}20}$

$= 1$

26. a. Many possible answers. Sample: 24 heads

b. Many possible answers. Sample: $\frac{24}{50}$.

(Answer should be $\frac{n}{50}$ where n heads is the answer to part **a**.)

c. Many possible answers. Sample: 48%.
(Answer should be $2n\%$ where n heads is answer to part **a**. This is equivalent to changing the fraction in part **b** to a percent.)

LESSON 11-5 (pp. 501-505)

1. 1, 0

2. 0

3. 1

4. A $(\frac{1}{2} > \frac{1}{3})$

5. precipitation tomorrow $(70\% = .7; \frac{3}{5} = .6)$

6. 20% $(1 - 80\% = 100\% - 80\% = 20\%)$

7. $\frac{9}{10}$ $(1 - \frac{1}{10} = \frac{10}{10} - \frac{1}{10} = \frac{9}{10})$

8. $1 - x$

9. One common way is to guess a probability; another way is to calculate a probability based on assumptions made about the probability of an associated event.

10. $\frac{1}{2}$ **11.** $\frac{1}{50}$ **12.** $\frac{3}{50}$

13. A probability is never negative. It is a number between 0 and 1 inclusive.

14. (b)

15. a. $\frac{45}{350}$, or $\frac{1}{8}$

b. B: $\frac{135}{360} = \frac{3}{8}$;

C: $\frac{90}{360} = \frac{1}{4}$;

D: $\frac{90}{360} = \frac{1}{4}$

16. $\frac{60}{80} = \frac{3}{4}$

17. $\frac{5}{n}$

18. a. The probability is taken from the results of an experiment.

b. Assume that 1 ticket has a probability of $\frac{1}{n}$, so 5 tickets have a probability of $\frac{5}{n}$.

19. $\frac{7}{100}$ (The prime numbers ending in 3 are: 3, 13, 23, 43, 53, 73, and 83.)

20. $\frac{14 \text{ less cars}}{7 \text{ days ago}} = \frac{{}^{-}14 \text{ cars}}{{}^{-}7 \text{ days}} = 2$ cars per day

21. $\frac{35}{82} = .426 \ldots \approx 43\%$ (There are $35 + 47$, or 82 third-graders in all.)

22. **a.** 3% of 32 $= .03 \cdot 32 = .96$

b. $\frac{3}{32} = .09375 = 9.375\%$

c.
$$3 = .32n$$
$$\frac{1}{.32} \cdot 3 = \frac{1}{.32} \cdot .32n$$
$$9.375 = n$$

23. $\frac{-9x}{y}(x + 2)$

$$= \frac{-9 \cdot 5}{-3}(5 + 2)$$
$$= \frac{-45}{-3}(5 + 2)$$
$$= 15 \cdot 7$$
$$= 105$$

24. $2 \cdot 3^4 = 2 \cdot 81 = 162$

25. Answers will vary. (Some objects to try are paper cups, plastic flower pots, funnels, corks, or number cubes.)

26. Answers will vary, but the probability of a commercial phone number ending in 0 is greater than the probability of a residential number ending in 0. A yellow-pages customer representing a business or service often requests a phone number ending in one, two, or three 0s.

LESSON 11-6 (pp. 506-510)

1. 1, 3

2. 600

3. A proportion is a statement that two fractions are equal.

4. (b) (In (a), $\frac{50 \cdot 2}{3 \cdot 5 \cdot 2} = \frac{100}{7}$;

in (b), $\frac{1}{3} = .\overline{3}$, but $\frac{33}{100} = .33$;

in (c), $\frac{24}{60} = \frac{2}{5}$ and $\frac{14}{35} = \frac{2}{5}$)

5. (c) (The left side in (c) is not a single fraction.)

6. **a.** $15t$

b. $15t \cdot \frac{40}{t} = \frac{21}{15} \cdot 15t$
$$600 = 21t$$
(On the left, the ts cancel; on the right, the 15s cancel.)

c. $600 = 21t$
$$\frac{600}{21} = t$$
$$\frac{200}{7} = t$$

d. $\frac{40}{\frac{200}{7}} = 40 \cdot \frac{7}{200} = \frac{280}{200} = \frac{7}{5}$, and $\frac{21}{15} = \frac{7}{5}$,

so solution checks.

7.
$$\frac{8}{7} = \frac{112}{Q}$$
$$7Q \cdot \frac{8}{7} = \frac{112}{Q} \cdot 7Q$$
$$8Q = 784$$
$$Q = \frac{784}{8}$$
$$Q = 98$$

8.
$$\frac{200}{8} = \frac{x}{22}$$
$$8 \cdot 22 \cdot \frac{200}{8} = \frac{x}{22} \cdot 8 \cdot 22$$
$$440 = 8x$$
$$\frac{440}{8} = x$$
$$550 = x$$

9.
$$\frac{L}{24} = \frac{0.5}{4}$$
$$24 \cdot 4 \cdot \frac{L}{24} = 24 \cdot 4 \cdot \frac{0.5}{4}$$
$$4L = 12$$
$$L = \frac{12}{4}$$
$$L = 3$$

10. $\dfrac{3 \text{ boxes}}{4 \text{ minutes}} = \dfrac{b \text{ boxes}}{24 \text{ minutes}}$

$$\frac{3}{4} = \frac{b}{24}$$

$$4 \cdot 24 \cdot \frac{3}{4} = \frac{b}{24} \cdot 4 \cdot 24$$

$$72 = 4b$$

$$\frac{72}{4} = b$$

$$18 = b$$

18 boxes

11. $\dfrac{5 \text{ boxes}}{6 \text{ minutes}} = \dfrac{B \text{ boxes}}{45 \text{ minutes}}$

$$\frac{5}{6} = \frac{B}{45}$$

$$6 \cdot 45 \cdot \frac{5}{6} = \frac{B}{45} \cdot 6 \cdot 45$$

$$225 = 6B$$

$$\frac{225}{6} = B$$

$$37.5 = B$$

37.5 boxes, or 37 complete boxes

12. $\dfrac{\$25}{20 \text{ minutes}} = \dfrac{S \text{ dollars}}{45 \text{ minutes}}$

$$\frac{25}{20} = \frac{S}{45}$$

$$20 \cdot 45 \cdot \frac{25}{20} = \frac{S}{45} \cdot 20 \cdot 45$$

$$1125 = 20S$$

$$\frac{1125}{20} = S$$

$$\$56.25 = S$$

13. $\dfrac{300 \text{ km}}{40 \text{ L}} = \dfrac{450 \text{ km}}{x \text{ L}}$

$$\frac{300}{40} = \frac{450}{x}$$

$$40x \cdot \frac{300}{40} = \frac{450}{x} \cdot 40x$$

$$300x = 18{,}000$$

$$x = \frac{18{,}000}{300}$$

$$x = 60$$

No, 60 L of gas are needed.

14. $\dfrac{\frac{2}{3} \text{ teaspoon}}{6 \text{ people}} = \dfrac{t \text{ teaspoonsful}}{25 \text{ people}}$

$$\frac{\frac{2}{3}}{6} = \frac{t}{25}$$

$$6 \cdot 25 \cdot \frac{\frac{2}{3}}{6} = \frac{t}{25} \cdot 6 \cdot 25$$

$$\frac{50}{3} = 6t$$

$$\frac{1}{6} \cdot \frac{50}{3} = \frac{1}{6} \cdot 6t$$

$$\frac{50}{18} = t$$

$$\frac{25}{9} = t, \text{ or } t = 2\frac{7}{9}$$

$2\frac{7}{9}$ (almost 3) teaspoonsful

15. $\dfrac{583 \text{ goals}}{696 \text{ games}} = \dfrac{600 \text{ goals}}{g \text{ games}}$

$$\frac{583}{696} = \frac{600}{g}$$

$$696g \cdot \frac{583}{696} = \frac{600}{g} \cdot 696g$$

$$583g = 417{,}600$$

$$g = \frac{417{,}600}{583}$$

$$g \approx 716.3$$

717th game

1992 Edition:

$$\frac{691 \text{ goals}}{852 \text{ games}} = \frac{1000 \text{ goals}}{g \text{ games}}$$

$$\frac{691}{852} = \frac{1000}{g}$$

$$852g \cdot \frac{691}{852} = \frac{1000}{g} \cdot 852g$$

$$691g = 852{,}000$$

$$g = \frac{852{,}000}{691}$$

$$g \approx 1{,}232.9$$

1233rd game

16.

$$\frac{41 \text{ symphonies}}{35 \text{ years}} = \frac{s \text{ symphonies}}{70 \text{ years}}$$

$$\frac{41}{35} = \frac{s}{70}$$

$$35 \cdot 70 \cdot \frac{41}{35} = \frac{s}{70} \cdot 35 \cdot 70$$

$$2870 = 35s$$

$$\frac{2870}{35} = s$$

$$82 = s$$

82 symphonies

17. $\frac{17}{80}$ (7 appears in 17 digits: 7, 17, 27, 37, 47,

57, 67, 70, 71, 72, ... , 79)

18. $\frac{30}{15} = 2 = 200\%$

19. $\frac{15}{30} = .5 = 50\%$

20. neither; Both fold $\frac{4}{5}$ napkin per minute.

($\frac{32 \text{ napkins}}{40 \text{ minutes}} = \frac{32}{40} \frac{\text{napkins}}{\text{minute}} = \frac{4}{5}$ napkins per

minute; $\frac{20 \text{ napkins}}{25 \text{ minutes}} = \frac{20}{25} \frac{\text{napkins}}{\text{minute}} = \frac{4}{5}$ napkins

per minute)

21. $6s^2 = 6(30 \text{ cm})^2 = 6 \cdot 900 \text{ cm}^2 = 5400 \text{ cm}^2$

22. a.

$$\frac{\$5}{10 \text{ in.}} = \frac{c \text{ dollars}}{15 \text{ in.}}$$

$$\frac{5}{10} = \frac{c}{15}$$

$$10 \cdot 15 \cdot \frac{5}{10} = \frac{c}{15} \cdot 10 \cdot 15$$

$$75 = 10c$$

$$\frac{75}{10} = c$$

$$\$7.50 = c$$

b. While the *diameter* of the larger pizza is $1\frac{1}{2}$

times the diameter of the smaller, the *area*

of the larger pizza is more than $1\frac{1}{2}$ times the

area of the smaller. **c.** Answers will vary.

LESSON 11-7 (pp. 511–515)

1. t, 250 **2.** 15, 400

3. $250t = 400 \cdot 15$

4. a. $250t = 6000$

$$t = \frac{6000}{250}$$

$$t = 24$$

b. check: $\frac{15}{24} = \frac{5}{8}$, and $\frac{250}{400} = \frac{5}{8}$.

5. a. $\frac{8}{\$1.79} = \frac{10}{c}$

b. $8c = 17.9$

$$c = \frac{17.9}{8}$$

$$c = 2.2375$$

$$c \approx \$2.24$$

c. check: $\frac{8}{1.79} \approx 4.469$, and $\frac{10}{2.24} \approx 4.464$.

6. 2 is to 3 as 6 is to 9

7. It was difficult to remember which two

numbers to multiply.

8. $\frac{12 \text{ pieces}}{5 \text{ bags}} = \frac{p \text{ pieces}}{8 \text{ bags}}$

$$5p = 84$$

$$p = \frac{84}{5} = 19\frac{1}{5}$$

$19\frac{1}{5}$ silver pieces

9. Check the answer.

10. true **11.** false **12.** false **13.** true

14. yes

15. a. $\frac{47 \text{ deer}}{2 \text{ days}} = \frac{d \text{ deer}}{7 \text{ days}}$

$$2d = 329$$

$$d = \frac{329}{2} = 164.5$$

164 or 165 deer

b. Many possible answers. Sample: There

could be more hunters on the weekend.

16. $\dfrac{\$1.69}{5 \text{ cans}} = \dfrac{\$10}{c \text{ cans}}$

$1.69\,c = 50$

$c = \dfrac{50}{1.69}$

$c \approx 29.6$

29 cans

17. because the equation is not a proportion

18. $\dfrac{119}{240} = 49.58\overline{3} \approx 49.58\%$

19. 49.58% of 25,000 = .4958 • 25,000 = 12,395, or about 12,400 people

20. $\dfrac{1}{2}$ or .5 (.4958 ≈ .5)

21. $\dfrac{2}{3}$ **22.** $-\dfrac{2}{3}$ **23.** $\dfrac{2}{3}$ **24.** $-\dfrac{2}{3}$

25. $\dfrac{3\frac{1}{3} \text{ ft}}{16 \text{ years}} = \dfrac{3\frac{1}{3} \text{ ft}}{16 \text{ yr}} = \dfrac{10}{3} \cdot \dfrac{1}{16} \dfrac{\text{ft}}{\text{yr}} =$

$\dfrac{5}{24}$ feet per year, or 2.5 in. per year

26. $\dfrac{7}{10} \div \dfrac{2}{7} = \dfrac{7}{10} \cdot \dfrac{7}{2} = \dfrac{49}{20}$

27. $1\dfrac{4}{5} \div \dfrac{1}{15} = \dfrac{9}{5} \cdot \dfrac{15}{1} = 27$

28. $13^2 = 169$ squares

29. $\left(\dfrac{1}{8} \text{ in.}\right)^2 = \dfrac{1}{64} \text{ in.}^2$

30. $169 \cdot \dfrac{1}{64} \text{ in.}^2 = \dfrac{169}{64} \text{ in.}^2 \approx 2.64 \text{ in.}^2$

31. $4 \cdot \dfrac{1}{8} \text{ in.} = \dfrac{4}{8} \text{ in.} = \dfrac{1}{2} \text{ in.}$

32. 45.5 in. (There are 14 long horizontal segments and 14 long vertical segments. Each is $13 \cdot \dfrac{1}{8}$ in., or $\dfrac{13}{8}$ in. long. $28 \cdot \dfrac{13}{8}$ in. = $\dfrac{91}{2}$ in. = 45.5 in.)

33. Vexation means annoyance.

34. The Middle Ages were between about 500 and 1500 A.D.

LESSON 11-8 (pp. 516-520)

1. ratios of lengths of corresponding sides

2. a. $\dfrac{TY}{HE} = \dfrac{TI}{HU} = \dfrac{YN}{EG} = \dfrac{IN}{UG}$

b. $\dfrac{TY}{HE} = \dfrac{YN}{EG}$

$\dfrac{26}{HE} = \dfrac{16}{24}$

$16 \cdot HE = 624$

$HE = \dfrac{624}{16}$

$HE = 39$

3. $\dfrac{AD}{EH} = \dfrac{BC}{FG}$

$\dfrac{22}{EH} = \dfrac{8}{10}$

$8 \cdot EH = 220$

$EH = \dfrac{220}{8}$

$EH = 27.5$

4. $\dfrac{CD}{GH} = \dfrac{BC}{FG}$

$\dfrac{CD}{50} = \dfrac{8}{10}$

$10 \cdot CD = 400$

$CD = 40$

5. Many possible answers. Sample:

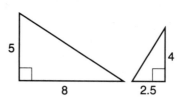

6. $\dfrac{2}{3} = \dfrac{5}{x}$

$2x = 15$

$x = \dfrac{15}{2}$

$x = 7.5$

7. Many possible answers. Samples: photographs, scale models, magnifications

8. **a.**

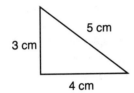

b. $\frac{3}{9} = \frac{4}{x}$ $\frac{3}{9} = \frac{5}{x}$

$3x = 36$ $3x = 45$

$x = 12$ $x = 15$

The other lengths are 12 cm and 15 cm.

c. The triangle should have a right angle formed by sides of 9 cm and 12 cm. The third side should have length 15 cm.

9. **a.** 12 cm long and 9 cm wide (60% of 20 = .6 · 20 = 12; 60% of 15 = .6 · 15 = 9)

b. yes (Each ratio, comparing sides in smaller drawing to sides in larger, is 60%.)

c. yes (Under a contraction, a figure and its image are similar.)

10. $\frac{11.7 \text{ mm}}{30 \text{ miles}} = \frac{26.5 \text{ mm}}{d \text{ miles}}$

$11.7d = 795$

$d = \frac{795}{11.7}$

$d \approx 67.9$

about 68 miles

11. $\frac{t}{40} = \frac{5}{16}$

$16t = 200$

$t = \frac{200}{16}$

$t = 12.5$

12. $\frac{300 \text{ miles}}{\frac{36}{60}\text{hr}} = \frac{300 \text{ mi}}{\frac{36}{60}\ \text{hr}}$

$= 300 \cdot \frac{60 \text{ mi}}{36 \text{ hr}}$

$= 500 \text{ mph}$

13. (c), (d), (e), and (f) ($x + y = 60 + {}^-10 = 50$;

$x - y = 60 - {}^-10 = 60 + 10 = 70$;

$y - x = {}^-10 - 60 = {}^-10 + {}^-60 = {}^-70$;

$xy = 60 \cdot {}^-10 = {}^-600; \frac{x}{y} = \frac{60}{-10} = {}^-6$;

$\frac{y}{x} = \frac{-10}{60} = {}^-\frac{1}{6}$)

14. $10A - 50 = 87$

$10A + {}^-50 = 87$

$10A + {}^-50 + 50 = 87 + 50$

$10A = 137$

$A = \frac{137}{10}$

$A = 13.7$

15. $.15b = \$2.25$

$\frac{1}{.15} \cdot .15b = \frac{1}{.15} \cdot \$2.25$

$b = \$15$

16. **a.** no (For example, does

$\frac{3}{4} = \frac{3+2}{4+2}$? No, since $\frac{3+2}{4+2} = \frac{5}{6} = .8\overline{3}$,

but $\frac{3}{4} = .75$.)

b. no (For example, does $\frac{9}{10} = \frac{9-2}{10-2}$? No,

since $\frac{9-2}{10-2} = \frac{7}{8} = .875$, but $\frac{9}{10} = .9$.)

c. yes (Dividing both numerator and denominator by the same number is equivalent to multiplying both by the reciprocal of the number. Hence, both numerator and denominator are multiplied by the same number.)

17. $u + v = \frac{8}{5} + \frac{7}{5} = \frac{15}{5} = 3$

18. $u - v = \frac{8}{5} - \frac{7}{5} = \frac{1}{5}$

19. $uv = \frac{8}{5} \cdot \frac{7}{5} = \frac{56}{25}$

20. $\frac{u}{v} = \frac{\frac{8}{5}}{\frac{7}{5}} = \frac{8}{5} \cdot \frac{5}{7} = \frac{8}{7}$

21. 3.8 · 10⁹ (Write 3.8. The decimal point must move 9 places to the right to get 3,800,000,000, so the exponent of 10 is 9.)

22. 5 and 6 $\left(\frac{41}{8} = 5.125\right)$

23. $\frac{41}{8} = 5.125$; $\frac{41}{8} = 5\frac{1}{8}$

24. $\frac{189}{11}$ (Multiply 17 · 11 and add 2 to find the numerator.); $17.\overline{18}$ ($\frac{2}{11} = .\overline{18}$, so $17\frac{2}{11} = 17.\overline{18}$.)

25.

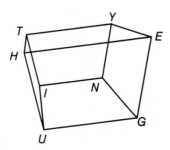

LESSON 11-9 (pp. 521-524)

1. Proportional thinking is getting or estimating an answer to a proportion without solving an equation.

2. Multiply by 3 (since 6 cans is 3 times as much as 2 cans) to get $7.50.

3. $\frac{2 \text{ cans}}{\$2.50} = \frac{6 \text{ cans}}{C \text{ dollars}}$

4. 640 acres

5. true (There are 1000 · 640 acres = 640,000 acres.)

6. 58,000 · 640 acres = 37,120,000 acres

7. 2 (90 = 45 · 2)

8. 10 (450 = 45 · 10)

9. Many possible answers. Sample: 4, 5 (45 · 4 = 180; 45 · 5 = 225)

10. $\frac{200 \text{ km}}{45 \frac{\text{km}}{\text{hr}}} = 200 \cdot \frac{1}{45}$ hr $= 44.\overline{4}$ hr, or $44\frac{4}{9}$ hr

(Notice that with simpler numbers in Questions 7 and 8, the answer can be found by dividing the distance by the rate.)

In 11-13, sample solutions are given.

11. a. $\frac{120 \text{ miles}}{55 \frac{\text{miles}}{\text{hour}}} = 120 \cdot \frac{1}{55}$ hours $= 2.\overline{18}$ hours

b. At 55 mph, you go 110 miles in 2 hours and 165 miles in 3 hours, so the answer seems right.

12. a. $\frac{100}{12} = 8\frac{1}{3}$ dozens

b. $\frac{12 \text{ eggs}}{1 \text{ dozen}} = \frac{100 \text{ eggs}}{d \text{ dozen}}$

$$12d = 100$$
$$d = \frac{100}{12}$$
$$d = 8\frac{1}{3}$$

13. a. $\frac{12,000}{640} = 18.75$ sq mi

b. There are 640 acres in a sq mi. So 1200 acres is less than 2 sq mi since 1200 < 2 · 640. Hence, multiplying by 10, 12,000 acres is less than 20 sq mi.

14. $\frac{30 \text{ words}}{45 \text{ seconds}} = \frac{w \text{ words}}{60 \text{ seconds}}$

$$45w = 1800$$
$$w = 40$$

40 words
(Or use proportional thinking: Since 60 seconds is $1\frac{1}{3}$ · 45 seconds, multiply $1\frac{1}{3}$ · 30 words = 40 words.)

15. 40 minutes (Each mows one of the two lawns during the 40 minutes.)

16. $\dfrac{100 \text{ stamps}}{2 \text{ weeks}} = \dfrac{s \text{ stamps}}{3 \text{ weeks}}$

$2s = 300$

$s = 150$

150 stamps

(Or use proportional thinking: Since 3 weeks is

$1\frac{1}{2} \cdot 2$ weeks, multiply $1\frac{1}{2} \cdot 100$ stamps $= 150$

stamps.)

17. $\dfrac{\$500}{4 \text{ people}} = \dfrac{c \text{ dollars}}{5 \text{ people}}$

$4c = 2500$

$c = 625$

$625 per month

(Or use proportional thinking: Since 5 people is

$1\frac{1}{4} \cdot 4$ people, multiply $1\frac{1}{4} \cdot \$500 = \$625$.)

18. $\dfrac{14}{21} = \dfrac{20}{x}$

$14x = 420$

$x = \dfrac{420}{14}$

$x = 30$

19. $\dfrac{14}{21} = \dfrac{23}{y}$

$14y = 483$

$y = \dfrac{483}{14}$

$y = 34.5$

20. 68 (Solve $.3x = 51$ to get 170. Then multiply
$.4 \cdot 170 = 68$)

21. $\dfrac{-3x}{2y}$

$= \dfrac{-3 \cdot -4}{2 \cdot -2}$

$= \dfrac{12}{-4}$

$= -3$

22. 14% of $200 = .14 \cdot 200 = 28$

23. $.14n = 200$

$n = \dfrac{200}{.14}$

$n \approx 1428.57$

24. $\dfrac{20 \text{ children}}{7 \text{ families}} = \dfrac{20}{7} \dfrac{\text{children}}{\text{family}} = 2\frac{6}{7}$ children per

family

25. $\dfrac{20 \text{ miles}}{7 \frac{\text{miles}}{\text{hour}}} = \dfrac{20}{7}$ hours $= 2\frac{6}{7}$ hours

26. a. more than doubled ($246.8 > 2 \cdot 116.3$)

b. $\dfrac{116.3 \text{ CPI}}{\$11,630} = \dfrac{246.8 \text{ CPI}}{d \text{ dollars}}$

$116.3d = 2,870,284$

$d = 24,680$

about $24,680

(Or use proportional thinking. In 1970, the car
cost 100 times the CPI. So multiply the 1980
CPI by 100: $100 \cdot 246.8 = 24,680$.)

1992 Edition:

a. more than tripled ($131.6 > 3 \cdot 38.8$)

b. $\dfrac{38.8}{11630} = \dfrac{131.6}{d \text{ dollars}}$

$38.8d = 1,530,508$

$d \approx 39,466.08$

about $39,400

27. a. 2 BAGS OF PEANUTS COST $.78
4 BAGS OF PEANUTS COST $1.56
. . .
20 BAGS OF PEANUTS COST $7.80

b. Change line 10 to FOR N = 2 TO 20

c. Answers will vary.

CHAPTER 11 PROGRESS SELF-TEST   (p. 526)

1. $\dfrac{30 \text{ words}}{5 \text{ minutes}} = 6$ words per minute

2. $\dfrac{m \text{ km}}{h \text{ hours}} = \dfrac{m}{h}$ kilometers per hour

3. $\dfrac{\frac{4}{9}}{\frac{1}{3}} = \dfrac{4}{9} \cdot \dfrac{3}{1} = \dfrac{12}{9} = \dfrac{4}{3}$

4. $\dfrac{7}{4}$ (A negative number divided by a negative

number yields a positive quotient.)

5. $\dfrac{\frac{3}{5}}{\frac{6}{5}} = \dfrac{3}{5} \cdot \dfrac{5}{6} = \dfrac{15}{30} = \dfrac{1}{2}$

6. $\dfrac{-2x}{8 + y} = \dfrac{-2 \cdot -5}{8 + -9} = \dfrac{10}{-1} = -10$

7. $\dfrac{7 + -17 + 3}{3} = \dfrac{-3}{3} = -1$

8. $\frac{a}{b}$ and $\frac{-a}{-b}$ (In these expressions, since a is negative, $-a$ is positive; since b is positive, $-b$ is negative.)

9. Many possible answers. Sample: If you lose 8 kilograms in 2 months, what is the rate at which your weight changed?

10. $\frac{40}{x} = \frac{8}{5}$

$8x = 200$

$x = \frac{200}{8}$

$x = 25$

11. $\frac{5}{12} = \frac{p}{3}$

$12p = 15$

$p = \frac{15}{12}$

$p = 1.25$ or $1\frac{1}{4}$

12. $\frac{14}{150} = .09\overline{3} \approx 9\%$

13. $\frac{0.30}{4.00} = 0.075 = 7.5\%$

14. $.60x = 30$

$x = \frac{30}{.60}$

$x = 50$

15. $\frac{189 \text{ miles}}{45 \frac{\text{miles}}{\text{hour}}} = 4.2$ hours

16. $10,000 \text{ sq mi} \cdot \frac{640 \text{ acres}}{1 \text{ sq mi}} = 6,400,000$ acres

17. b and c

18. If $\frac{a}{b} = \frac{c}{d}$, then $ad = bc$.

19. $\frac{x}{40} = \frac{144}{64}$

$64x = 5760$

$x = \frac{5760}{64}$

$x = 90$

20. $\frac{180}{y} = \frac{144}{64}$

$144y = 11,520$

$y = \frac{11,520}{144}$

$y = 80$

21. $\frac{12}{15} = \frac{n}{50}$

$15n = 600$

$n = \frac{600}{15}$

$n = 40$

22. $\frac{12}{15} = \frac{4}{5}$

23. $\frac{\frac{1}{3} \text{ teaspoon}}{4 \text{ people}} = \frac{x \text{ teaspoons}}{9 \text{ people}}$

$4x = 3$

$x = \frac{3}{4}$

$\frac{3}{4}$ teaspoon

24. $\frac{2}{3} = \frac{4}{A}$

$2A = 12$

$A = 6$

(This can easily be done mentally: $\frac{2}{3} = \frac{4}{6}$.)

25. $\frac{3}{n} = \frac{8}{1}$

$8n = 3$

$n = \frac{3}{8}$, or 0.375

CHAPTER 11 REVIEW (pp. 527-529)

1. $\frac{12}{\frac{2}{3}} = \frac{12}{1} \cdot \frac{3}{2} = \frac{36}{2} = 18$

2. $\frac{\frac{2}{3}}{\frac{4}{3}} = \frac{2}{3} \cdot \frac{3}{4} = \frac{6}{12} = \frac{1}{2}$

3. $\frac{\frac{7}{6}}{\frac{14}{3}} = \frac{7}{6} \cdot \frac{3}{14} = \frac{21}{84} = \frac{1}{4}$

4. $\frac{\frac{x}{y}}{\frac{a}{b}} = \frac{x}{y} \cdot \frac{b}{a} = \frac{xb}{ya}$, or $\frac{bx}{ay}$

5. $\frac{3\frac{3}{4}}{2\frac{1}{7}} = \frac{\frac{15}{4}}{\frac{15}{7}} = \frac{15}{4} \cdot \frac{7}{15} = \frac{105}{60} = \frac{7}{4}$

6. -5

7. positive

8. $\frac{2c}{d}$

$= \frac{2 \cdot 3}{-1}$

$= \frac{6}{-1}$

$= -6$

9. $\frac{-40}{-30} = \frac{4}{3}$, or $1.\overline{3}$

154

10. $\dfrac{40}{9} = \dfrac{12}{x}$

$40x = 108$

$x = \dfrac{108}{40}$

$x = 2.7$

11. $\dfrac{7}{G} = \dfrac{1}{3}$

$G = 21$

12. no $\left(\dfrac{7}{24} \text{ is less than } \dfrac{1}{2}; \dfrac{168}{192} \text{ is greater than } \dfrac{1}{2}.\right)$

13. $bd = ae$

14. $6x$

15. The left side is not a single fraction

16. (d) (**a**, **b**, and **c** are all equivalent to $-\dfrac{x}{y}$; **d** is

equivalent to $\dfrac{x}{y}$.)

17. negative

18. 1

19. $\dfrac{1}{3}$

20. $\dfrac{200 \text{ km}}{4 \text{ hr}} = 50$ km per hour

21. $\dfrac{5 \text{ pounds}}{16 \text{ hamburgers}} = \dfrac{5}{16}$ pound per hamburger

22. $\dfrac{-10 \text{ pounds}}{30 \text{ days}} = -\dfrac{1}{3}$ pound per day

23. $\dfrac{570{,}000 \text{ people}}{47 \text{ sq mi}} \approx 12{,}128$ people per sq mi, or

about 12,100 people per sq mi

24. $\dfrac{\frac{2}{3} \text{ summer}}{\$120} = \dfrac{1 \text{ summer}}{d \text{ dollars}}$

$\dfrac{2}{3}d = 120$

$\dfrac{3}{2} \cdot \dfrac{2}{3}d = \dfrac{3}{2} \cdot 120$

$d = \$180$

25. $\dfrac{-3 + 14 + -22 + -28 + -26 + 2}{6} = \dfrac{-63}{6} =$

-10.5

26. $\dfrac{-14° + -18° + -16° + -8° + -12° + -15° + -13°}{7}$

$= \dfrac{-96°}{7} \approx 13.7°$

27. $\dfrac{8}{40} = .2 = 20\%$

28. $\dfrac{10}{5} = 2 = 200\%$

29. $\dfrac{216}{365} \approx .59 \approx 59\%$

30. 1.3 (In 1987, they produced $98{,}000 - 22{,}000$
$= 76{,}000$ cars. Divide 98,000 by 76,000 and
round to the nearest tenth.)
1992 Edition: 1.2 (In 1989, they sold 47,000
$+ 9{,}000 = 56{,}000$ cars. Divide 56,000 by
47,000 and round to the nearest tenth.)

31. $\dfrac{2}{10} = \dfrac{1}{5}$

32. $\dfrac{m}{60}$ (1 hr $= 60$ min)

33. $\dfrac{b}{b + g}$ ($b + g$ represents all the students.)

34. $\dfrac{5}{10} = \dfrac{1}{10}$ (The numbers ending in 4 are 4, 14,

24, 34, and 44.)

35. $\dfrac{35 \text{ copies}}{2.5 \text{ minutes}} = \dfrac{500 \text{ copies}}{m \text{ minutes}}$

$35\,m = 1250$

$m = \dfrac{1250}{35}$

$m \approx 35.7$ min, or about 36 min

36. $\dfrac{6 \text{ people}}{1\frac{1}{3} \text{ cups}} = \dfrac{10 \text{ people}}{c \text{ cups}}$

$6c = 1\dfrac{1}{3} \cdot 10$

$6c = \dfrac{4}{3} \cdot 10$

$6c = \dfrac{40}{3}$

$\dfrac{1}{6} \cdot 6c = \dfrac{1}{6} \cdot \dfrac{40}{3}$

$c = \dfrac{40}{18}$

$c = \dfrac{20}{9}$

$\dfrac{20}{9}$ cups

$\left(\dfrac{20}{9} = 2\dfrac{2}{9}, \text{ so this is very close to } 2\dfrac{1}{4} \text{ cups}\right)$

37. $\dfrac{8 \text{ cans}}{\$3} = \dfrac{5 \text{ cans}}{d \text{ dollars}}$

$8d = 15$

$d = \dfrac{15}{8}$

$d = 1.875$

5 cans will cost $1.88.

38. Many possible answers. Sample: How much did her money change each day?

$\dfrac{^-\$200}{4 \text{ days}} = {}^-\$50$ per day

39. Many possible answers. Sample: How fast is the crew going up the road? $\dfrac{^-6 \text{ km}}{^-3 \text{ days}} = 2$ km per day

40. $\dfrac{AB}{EL} = \dfrac{CD}{IK}$

$\dfrac{80}{56} = \dfrac{45}{IK}$

$80 \cdot IK = 2520$

$IK = \dfrac{2520}{80}$

$IK = 31.5$

41. $\dfrac{5}{x} = \dfrac{13}{6.5}$ $\dfrac{12}{y} = \dfrac{13}{6.5}$

$13x = 32.5$ $13y = 78$

$x = \dfrac{32.5}{13}$ $y = 6$

$x = 2.5$

The other lengths are 2.5 and 6.

42.

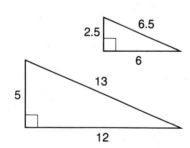

CHAPTER 12   COMBINING OPERATIONS

LESSON 12-1   (pp. 532-536)

1. **a.** the cost of 10 roses plus the cost of 1 rose
    b. $10 \cdot 3.75 + 1 \cdot 3.75$
    c. $10x + x$

2. **a.** $(45 + 25)w = 70w$
    b. Substitute a number for w.

3.

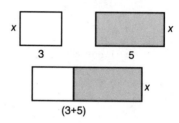

4. Distributive Property of Multiplication over Addition

5. Fred is correct. $6m - m = 6 \cdot m - 1 \cdot m$
    $= (6 - 1)m = 5m$
    (Check by substitution. For example, if
    $m = 10$, $6m - m = 6 \cdot 10 - 10 =$
    $60 - 10 = 50$. Fred's answer works because
    $5m = 5 \cdot 10 = 50$.)

6. $8x$ (Think: $3x + 5x = (3 + 5)x$)

7. $10y + 8$ (Think: $(4 + 6)y + 8$)

8. $6.9v$ (Think: $(2.4 + 3.5 + 1)v$)

9. $10b + 8$ **10.** $2v$

11. $5m$ **12.** $5.22t$

13. $30h + 40$ (Think: $(60 - 30)h + 40$)

14. Many possible answers.
    Sample: $15x - 3x = (15 - 3)x$

15. $3x + 2x$, or $5x$ cents

16. $68,000$ (Think: $(994 + 6) \cdot 68$)

17. $\$37.50$ (Think: $(12 - 2) \cdot \$3.75$)

18. subtracting $.01 \cdot 4$ or 4 cents

19. $40B + 15.5B + 24B$ or $79.5B$

20. $2x + 3x = 600$ **21.** $7y - y = 12.6$
    $\quad\;\; 5x = 600$ $\quad\;\; 6y = 12.6$
    $\quad\;\;\; x = \dfrac{600}{5}$ $\quad\;\;\; y = \dfrac{12.6}{6}$
    $\quad\;\;\; x = 120$ $\quad\;\;\; y = 2.1$

22. **a.** 3(2 multiplications and one addition)

b. 2(1 addition and 1 multiplication)

c. $(a + b)x$

23. Many possible answers. Samples: Does $3(4 + 5) = 3 \cdot 4 + 3 \cdot 5$? Yes, because $3(4 + 5) = 3 \cdot 9 = 27$, and $3 \cdot 4 + 3 \cdot 5 = 12 + 15 = 27$. Does $-2(8 + {}^{-}8) = -2 \cdot 8 + {}^{-}2 \cdot {}^{-}8$? Yes, because $-2(8 + {}^{-}8) = -2 \cdot 0 = 0$, and $-2 \cdot 8 + {}^{-}2 \cdot {}^{-}8 = -16 + 16 = 0$.

24. $180° - 55° = 25°$

25. **a.** $\frac{1}{3}$

b. $\dfrac{\frac{12}{5}}{3} = \frac{12}{5} \cdot \frac{1}{3} = \frac{12}{15} = \frac{4}{5}$

26. **a.** Many possible answers. The drawing should show two segments, $\overline{AB}$ and $\overline{BC}$ intersecting at B. AC is smallest in a drawing that shows $\overline{AB}$ with C on $\overline{AB}$ between A and B. AC is largest in a drawing that shows $\overline{AC}$ with B on $\overline{AC}$ between A and C.

b. smallest 15 $(AB - BC)$, largest 65 $(AB + BC)$

27. $\frac{2}{7}$

28. $\frac{21}{47}$

29. in lowest terms: $\frac{157}{200}$ (Multiply numerator and denominator of $\frac{3.14}{4}$ by 50.)

30.

LESSON 12-2 (pp. 537-540)

1. terminating

2. repeating

3. cannot tell

4. repeating

5. 3.04444 is finite, the rest are infinite.

6. **a.** $24.\overline{24}$

b.
$$\text{Let } x = .242424 \ldots$$
$$100x = 24.242424 \ldots$$
$$100x - 10x = 24.\overline{24} - .\overline{24}$$
$$99x = 24$$
$$x = \frac{24}{99} = \frac{8}{33}$$

7. $\frac{519}{99}$ or $\frac{173}{33}$ ($.\overline{24} = \frac{24}{99}$, from Question b, so $5.\overline{24} = 5\frac{24}{99} = \frac{519}{99}$. Or use $.\overline{24} = \frac{8}{33}$, then $5.\overline{24} = 5\frac{8}{33} = \frac{173}{33}$.)

8. Many possible answers. Sample: 4126 and 22 (Multiply 2063 and 11 by the same nonzero number.)

9.
$$\text{Let } x = 0.810810810 \ldots$$
$$1000x = 810.810810810 \ldots$$
$$1000x - x = 810.\overline{810} - .\overline{810}$$
$$999x = 810$$
$$x = \frac{810}{999} = \frac{30}{37}$$

10. **a.**
$$\text{Let } x = 0.2222 \ldots$$
$$10x = 2.2222 \ldots$$
$$10x - x = 2.\overline{2} - .\overline{2}$$
$$9x = 2$$
$$x = \frac{2}{9}$$

b. 9 marbles

c. 7 marbles

11.
$$\text{Let } x = 3.04050505 \ldots$$
$$100x = 304.050505 \ldots$$
$$100x - x = 304.05\overline{05} - 3.04\overline{05}$$
$$99x = 301.01$$
$$x = \frac{301.01}{99} = \frac{30,101}{9900}$$

12.
$$\text{Let } x = 58.8333 \ldots$$
$$10x = 588.333 \ldots$$
$$10x - x = 588.3\overline{3} - 58.8\overline{3}$$
$$9x = 529.5$$
$$x = \frac{529.5}{9} = \frac{5295}{90} = \frac{353}{6}$$

Many division problems are possible.
Samples: $353 \div 6$; $529.5 \div 9$

13. Many possible answers.
Sample: $58{,}833{,}333 \div 1{,}000{,}000$
$$\left(58.833333 = \frac{58.833333}{1} = \frac{58{,}833{,}333}{1{,}000{,}000}\right)$$

14.
$$\text{Let } x = 0.9999 \ldots$$
$$10x = 9.9999 \ldots$$
$$10x - x = 9.\overline{9} - \overline{9}$$
$$9x = 9$$
$$x = \frac{9}{9}$$
$$x = 1$$
$$\text{So } x = .\overline{9} = 1$$

15.
$$99.\overline{4}\% = .99\overline{4}$$
$$\text{Let } x = .994444 \ldots$$
$$10x = 9.94444 \ldots$$
$$10x - x = 9.94\overline{4} - .99\overline{4}$$
$$9x = 8.95$$
$$x = \frac{8.95}{9} = \frac{895}{900} = \frac{179}{180}$$

16. $4x + 3y + 2x + y + 0x + {}^-1y =$
$(4 + 2 + 0)x + (3 + 1 + {}^-1)y =$
$6x + 3y$

17.
$$10x - 1 = 30$$
$$10x + {}^-1 = 30$$
$$10x + {}^-1 + 1 = 30 + 1$$
$$10x = 31$$
$$x = \frac{31}{10} \text{ or } 3.1$$

18. 5300 ft (1 mi = 5280 ft)

19. $180° - 48\frac{2}{5}° = 180° - 48.4° = 131.6° =$
$131\frac{2}{5}°$

20. $x + 2x = 180°$ **21.** none
$$3x = 180°$$
$$x = \frac{180°}{3}$$
$$x = 60°$$

22.

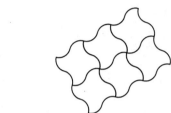

23.
$$\text{Let } x = 0.\overline{012345679}$$
$$100{,}000{,}000x = 1{,}234{,}567.9\overline{12345679}$$
$$100{,}000{,}000x - x = 1{,}234{,}567.9\overline{12345679}$$
$$- 0.\overline{012345679}$$
$$99{,}999{,}999x = 1{,}234{,}567.9$$
$$x = \frac{1{,}234{,}567.9}{99{,}999{,}999} = \frac{1}{81}$$

(Since you are told the numerator is 1, try dividing the numerator and denominator of $\frac{1234567.9}{99{,}999{,}999}$ by 1234567.9. It should divide evenly.)

24. a. $0.12121212 \ldots$
$+ 0.34534534 \ldots$
$\overline{0.46655746 \ldots} = 0.\overline{466557}$

b. $\text{Let } x = 0.\overline{466557}$
$$1{,}000{,}000x = 466557.\overline{466557}$$
$$1{,}000{,}000x - x = 466{,}557.\overline{466557}$$
$$- .\overline{466557}$$
$$999{,}999x = 466{,}557$$
$$x = \frac{466{,}557}{999{,}999} = \frac{1709}{3663}$$

$\Bigl($An alternate solution is to write each

repeating decimal as a simple fraction

and add. $0.\overline{12} = \frac{4}{33}$ and $0.\overline{345} = \frac{115}{333}$;

$\frac{4}{33} + \frac{115}{333} = \frac{5127}{10{,}989} = \frac{1709}{3663}\Bigr)$

1. 5 cookies $\cdot \dfrac{20¢}{\text{cookie}}$ + 4 browies $\cdot \dfrac{30¢}{\text{brownie}}$

    $= \$1.00 + \$1.20$

    $= \$2.20$

2. c cookies $\cdot \dfrac{20¢}{\text{cookie}}$ + b brownies $\cdot \dfrac{30¢}{\text{brownie}}$

    $= 20c + 30b$ cents

3. Many possible answers. Sample: $2m + 3n$

4. **a.** 4   **b.** 3

    c. It is already simplified.

5. **a.** 4   **b.** $5t$ and $2t$

    c. Several possible answers. Sample: $-4m$ and q;

    d. -4 **e.** 1

    f. $5t - 4m + 2t + q$

    $= 5t + 2t + -4m + q$

    $= (5 + 2)t + -4m + q$

    $= 7t - 4m + q$

6. $12a + 5a + 3b$

    $= (12 + 5)a + 3b$

    $= 17a + 3b$

    Sample check: Let $a = 2$ and $b = 3$.

    Then $12a + 5a + 3b =$

    $12 \cdot 2 + 5 \cdot 2 + 3 \cdot 3 = 43$,

    and $17a + 3b = 17 \cdot 2 + 3 \cdot 3 = 43$.

7. $-4x - y + y - 2$

    $= -4x + -y + y + -2$

    $= -4x + (-1 + 1)y + -2$

    $= -4x - 2$

    Sample check: Let $x = 5$ and $y = 10$. Then

    $-4x - y + y - 2 =$

    $-4 \cdot 5 - 10 + 10 - 2 = -22$,

    and $-4x - 2 = -4 \cdot 5 - 2 = -22$.

8. $3t - 3a - a - t$

    $= 3t + -t + -3a + -a$

    $= (3 + -1)t + (-3 + -1)a$

    $= 2t + -4a$

    $= 2t - 4a$

    Sample check: Let $t = 4$ and $a = 3$.

    Then $3t - 3a - a - t =$

    $3 \cdot 4 - 3 \cdot 3 - 3 - 4 = -4$,

    and $2t - 4a = 2 \cdot 4 - 4 \cdot 3 = -4$.

9. $-6 + 4v - 6 + -4v + v$

    $= 4v + -4v + v + -6 + -6$

    $= (4 + -4 + 1)v + -12$

    $= v - 12$

    Sample check: Let $v = 5$.

    Then $-6 + 4v - 6 + -4v + v =$

    $-6 + 4 \cdot 5 - 6 + -4 \cdot 5 + 5 = -7$,

    and $v - 12 = 5 - 12 = -7$.

10. already simplified

11. $3t - 6t + 9$

    $= 3t + -6t + 9$

    $= (3 + -6)t + 9$

    $= -3t + 9$

12. $3 - 6t + 9$

    $= -6t + 3 + 9$

    $= -6t + 12$

13. $3t + 6u - 9u - 12t$

    $= 3t + -12t + 6u + -9u$

    $= (3 + -12)t + (6 + -9)u$

    $= -9t + -3u$

    $= -9t - 3u$

14. $6L + 4M$ (A decagon has 10 sides.)

15. **a.** 4 ounces $\cdot 80\dfrac{\text{calories}}{\text{ounce}}$ + 1 bun $\cdot 200\dfrac{\text{calories}}{\text{bun}}$

    + 20 fries $\cdot 11\dfrac{\text{calories}}{\text{fry}}$ = 320 calories + 200 calories + 220 calories = 740 calories

    b. $520 + 11f$ calories

16. **a.** $6 \text{ Cs} \cdot 2\dfrac{\text{points}}{\text{C}} + 8 \text{ Bs} \cdot 3\dfrac{\text{points}}{\text{B}} +$

$5 \text{ As} \cdot 4\dfrac{\text{points}}{\text{A}}$

$= 12 \text{ points} + 24 \text{ points} + 20 \text{ points}$

$= 56 \text{ points}$

b. $2c + 3b + 4a$

17. $3x + 4y$

$= 3 \cdot \dfrac{1}{2} + 4 \cdot \dfrac{1}{3}$

$= \dfrac{3}{2} + \dfrac{4}{3}$

$= \dfrac{9}{6} + \dfrac{8}{6}$

$= \dfrac{17}{6}$

$= 2.8\overline{3}$

≈ 3

18. $(a + 2b) + (3a + 4b) + (5a + 6b)$

$= a + 3a + 5a + 2b + 4b + 6b$

$= (1 + 3 + 5)a + (2 + 4 + 6)b$

$= 9a + 12b$

19. $(3a + 5a)x$

$= ((3 + 5)a)x$

$= (8a)x$

$= 8ax$

20. $14x = \dfrac{2}{7}$

$\dfrac{1}{14} \cdot 14x = \dfrac{1}{14} \cdot \dfrac{2}{7}$

$x = \dfrac{2}{98}$

$x = \dfrac{1}{49}$

21. $\text{Let } x = 0.2\overline{3}$

$10x = 2.\overline{3}$

$10x - x = 2.\overline{3} - 0.2\overline{3}$

$9x = 2.1$

$x = \dfrac{2.1}{9} = \dfrac{21}{90} = \dfrac{7}{30}$

22. $\dfrac{a + b}{2}$

23. $\text{surface area} = 2 \cdot 3 \text{ ft} \cdot 1 \text{ ft} +$
$2 \cdot 3 \text{ ft} \cdot 1 \text{ ft} + 1 \text{ ft} \cdot 1 \text{ ft} = 13 \text{ ft}^2;$
$\text{volume} = 3 \text{ ft} \cdot 1 \text{ ft} \cdot 1 \text{ ft} = 3 \text{ ft}^3$

24. some points on the line: $(1, 6), (5, 2), (-3, 10)$

25.

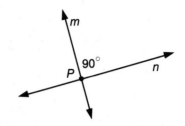

26. **a.** $n - 6$ **b.** $6 < n$

27. 61, 67

28.

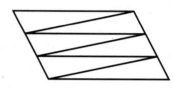

29. 40 (Think: $(10.2 - 0.2) \cdot 4 = 10 \cdot 4$)

30. $x + y$

31. 110 cubes (The staircase will be $\dfrac{25}{2.5}$, or

10 cubes high. So the total number of cubes,
since each step is 2 cubes wide, is: $2(1 + 2$
$+ 3 + \ldots + 10) = 2 \cdot 55 = 110.$)

LESSON 12-4 (pp. 546-550)

1. $3.29 \boxed{\times} \boxed{(}\boxed{853} \boxed{+} \boxed{268} \boxed{)} \boxed{=} \boxed{3688.09};$
$3.29 \boxed{\times} \boxed{853} \boxed{+} 3.29 \boxed{\times} \boxed{268} \boxed{=} \boxed{3688.09}$

2. **a.** the Distributive Property of Multiplication
over Addition

b. $x(a + b) = xa + xb$

3. $50(x + 4)$

$= 50 \cdot x + 50 \cdot 4$

$= 50x + 200$

Sample check: Let $x = 2.$

Then $50(x + 4) = 50(2 + 4) = 300,$

and $50x + 200 = 50 \cdot 2 + 200 = 300.$

4. $2(6 + 7n)$
$$= 2 \cdot 6 + 2 \cdot 7n$$
$$= 12 + 14n$$
Sample check: Let $n = 3$. Then $2(6 + 7n) =$
$2(6 + 7 \cdot 3) = 2 \cdot 27 = 54$, and $12 + 14n$
$= 12 + 14 \cdot 3 = 12 + 42 = 54$.

5. $a(b + 2c)$
$$= a \cdot b + a \cdot 2c$$
$$= ab + 2ac$$
Sample check: Let $a = 5$, $b = 6$, $c = 10$.
Then $a(b + 2c) = 5(6 + 2 \cdot 10) = 5 \cdot 26$
$= 130$, and $ab + 2ac = 5 \cdot 6 + 2 \cdot 5 \cdot 10$
$= 30 + 100 = 130$.

6. $5(100 + t + u)$
$$= 5 \cdot 100 + 5 \cdot t + 5 \cdot u$$
$$= 500 + 5t + 5u$$
Sample check: Let $t = 2$ and $u = 3$. Then
$5(100 + t + u) = 5(100 + 2 + 3) =$
$5 \cdot 105 = 525$, and $500 + 5t + 5u =$
$500 + 5 \cdot 2 + 5 \cdot 3 = 500 + 10 + 15$
$= 525$.

7. $3 \cdot \$29.95 = 3(\$30 - 5¢) =$
$3 \cdot \$30 - 3 \cdot 5¢ = \$90 - 15¢ = \$89.85$

8. $8 \cdot \$8.99 = 8(\$9 - 1¢) = 8 \cdot \$9 - 8 \cdot 1¢$
$= \$72 - 8¢ = \$71.92$

9. $a(b - c)$
$$= a \cdot b - a \cdot c$$
$$= ab - ac$$

10. $4(a - 5b)$
$$= 4 \cdot a - 4 \cdot 5b$$
$$= 4a - 20b$$

11. 58, 2 **12.** 60, 2

13. $732 \cdot 999,999,999,999,999$
$$= 732(1,000,000,000,000,000 - 1)$$
$$= 732 \cdot 1,000,000,000,000,000 - 732 \cdot 1$$
$$= 732,000,000,000,000,000 - 732$$
$$= 731,999,999,999,999,268$$

14. Add the cost of each part of one outfit; then
multiply by 3:
$3(\$69.95 + \$40.75 + \$15.50) = 3 \cdot \$126.20$
$= \$378.60$

15. $3(t + a + s)$ or $3t + 3a + 3s$ dollars

16. 8 ft (11 ft 3 in. + 7 ft 7 in. + 6 ft 2 in.) =
8 ft (24 ft 12 in.) = 8 ft (25 ft) = 200 ft²

17. $-2(3 + x) + 5(0.4x)$
$$= -2 \cdot 3 + -2 \cdot x + 5 \cdot 0.4x$$
$$= -6 + -2x + 2x$$
$$= -6 + (-2 + 2)x$$
$$= -6 + 0x$$
$$= -6$$

18. $\frac{1}{3}(3m + n) + \frac{1}{3}(3m - n)$
$$= \frac{1}{3} \cdot 3m + \frac{1}{3} \cdot n + \frac{1}{3} \cdot 3m - \frac{1}{3} \cdot n$$
$$= 1m + \frac{1}{3}n + 1m - \frac{1}{3}n$$
$$= 1m + 1m + \frac{1}{3}n - \frac{1}{3}n$$
$$= (1 + 1)m + \left(\frac{1}{3} - \frac{1}{3}\right)n$$
$$= 2m + 0n$$
$$= 2m$$

19. $4x + 72$
$$= 4 \cdot x + 4 \cdot 18$$
$$= 4(x + 18)$$

20. $16x - 8y + 56$
$$= 8 \cdot 2x - 8 \cdot y + 8 \cdot 7$$
$$= 8(2x - y + 7)$$

21. $100m + 81m + 64$
$$= (100 + 81)m + 64$$
$$= 181m + 64$$

22. $C + .5A$ dollars

23. square **24.** rhombus

25. rectangle **26.** parallelogram

27. a. $\dfrac{0.5 \text{ miles}}{4\frac{\text{miles}}{\text{hour}}} + \dfrac{1 \text{ mile}}{4\frac{\text{miles}}{\text{hour}}} = 0.125 \text{ hr} + .25 \text{ hr} =$

0.375 or $\frac{3}{8}$ hr, or 22.5 min

b. 6 minutes or .1 hr (Time for shortcut:
$\dfrac{1.1 \text{ miles}}{4\frac{\text{miles}}{\text{hour}}} = 0.275 \text{ hr or } 16.5 \text{ min})$

28. a. about 6.7%

(volume $= 20$ cm $\cdot$ 15 cm $\cdot$ 10 cm $=$

3000 cm³; $\frac{200}{3000} = .0\overline{6} \approx 6.7\%$)

b. 3000 cm³ − 200 cm³ = 2800 cm³

29. $1 - (2 - (3 - (4 - (5 - 6)))) = -3;$

$1 - (2 - (3 - (4 - (5 - (6 - 7))))) = 4$

30. $ac + ad + bc + bd$ (Add the areas of the 4 smaller rectangles.)

LESSON 12-5 (pp. 551-555)

1. $35s$

2. a. $-3x$ or $-9x$

b.
$$3x + 2 = 9x + 5$$
$$-9x + 3x + 2 = -9x + 9x + 5$$
$$-6x + 2 = 5$$
$$-6x + 2 + -2 = 5 + -2$$
$$-6x = 3$$
$$-\tfrac{1}{6} \cdot -6x = -\tfrac{1}{6} \cdot 3$$
$$x = -\tfrac{1}{2}$$

3.
$$B + 14 = 3B$$
$$-B + B + 14 = -B + 3B$$
$$14 = 2B$$
$$\tfrac{14}{2} = B$$
$$7 = B$$

He is 7 years old.

4.
$$4 - y = 6y - 8$$
$$4 - y + y = 6y - 8 + y$$
$$4 = 7y - 8$$
$$4 + 8 = 7y - 8 + 8$$
$$12 = 7y$$
$$\tfrac{12}{7} = y$$

check: $4 - y = 4 - \frac{12}{7} = \frac{28}{7} - \frac{12}{7} = \frac{16}{7}$,

and $6y - 8 = 6 \cdot \frac{12}{7} - 8 = \frac{72}{7} - \frac{56}{7} = \frac{16}{7}$

5.
$$2(n - 4) = 3n$$
$$2n - 8 = 3n$$
$$-2n + 2n - 8 = -2n + 3n$$
$$-8 = n$$

check: $2(n - 4) = 2(-8 - 4) = 2(-12) =$
-24, and $3n = 3 \cdot -8 = -24$

6.
$$\frac{t - 2}{4} = \frac{t - 6}{12}$$
$$12(t - 2) = 4(t - 6)$$
$$12t - 24 = 4t - 24$$
$$-4t + 12t - 24 = -4t + 4t - 24$$
$$8t - 24 = -24$$
$$8t - 24 + 24 = -24 + 24$$
$$8t = 0$$
$$t = \tfrac{0}{8}$$
$$t = 0$$

check: $\frac{t - 2}{4} = \frac{0 - 2}{4} = -\tfrac{1}{2}$, and $\frac{t - 6}{12} =$

$\frac{0 - 6}{12} = -\tfrac{1}{2}$

7.
$$0.6m + 5.4 = -1.3 + 2.6m$$
$$-0.6m + 0.6m + 5.4 = -0.6m + -1.3 + 2.6m$$
$$5.4 = -1.3 + 2m$$
$$1.3 + 5.4 = 1.3 + -1.3 + 2m$$
$$6.7 = 2m$$
$$\tfrac{6.7}{2} = m$$
$$3.35 = m$$

check: $0.6m + 5.4 = 0.6 \cdot 3.35 + 5.4 =$
$2.01 + 5.4 = 7.41$, and -1.3 to $2.6m = -1.3$
$+ 2.6 \cdot 3.35 = -1.3 + 8.71 = -7.41$

8.
$$2n = 500 + 6n$$
$$-6n + 2n = -6n + 500 + 6n$$
$$-4n = 500$$
$$-\tfrac{1}{4} \cdot -4n = -\tfrac{1}{4} \cdot 500$$
$$n = -125$$

9. **a.** $1000 + 200n$

   b. $750 + 250n$

   c.
$$1000 + 200n = 750 + 250n$$
$$1000 + 200n + {}^-200n = 750 + 250n + {}^-200n$$
$$1000 = 750 + 50n$$
$$^-750 + 1000 = {}^-750 + 750 + 50n$$
$$250 = 50n$$
$$\frac{250}{50} = n$$
$$5 = n$$

   5 months

10.
$$11p + 5(p - 1) = 9p - 12$$
$$11p + 5p - 5 = 9p - 12$$
$$16p - 5 = 9p - 12$$
$$^-9p + 16p - 5 = {}^-9p + 9p - 12$$
$$7p - 5 = {}^-12$$
$$7p - 5 + 5 = {}^-12 + 5$$
$$7p = {}^-7$$
$$p = \frac{{}^-7}{7}$$
$$p = {}^-1$$
check: $11p + 5(p - 1) = 11 \cdot {}^-1 + 5({}^-1 - 1) = {}^-11 + {}^-10 = {}^-21$, and $9p - 12 = 9 \cdot {}^-1 - 12 = {}^-9 - 12 = {}^-21$

11.
$$^-n + 4 - 5n + 6 = 21 + 3n$$
$$^-6n + 10 = 21 + 3n$$
$$^-6n + 10 + {}^-3n = 21 + 3n + {}^-3n$$
$$^-9n + 10 = 21$$
$$^-9n + 10 + {}^-10 = 21 + {}^-10$$
$$^-9n = 11$$
$$-\frac{1}{9} \cdot {}^-9n = -\frac{1}{9} \cdot 11$$
$$n = -\frac{11}{9}$$

check: $^-n + 4 - 5n + 6 = {}^-\left(-\frac{11}{9}\right) + 4 -$

$5 \cdot {}^-\frac{11}{9} + 6 = \frac{11}{9} + 4 - {}^-\frac{55}{9} + 6 = \frac{11}{9} +$

$\frac{36}{9} + \frac{55}{9} + \frac{54}{9} = \frac{156}{9}$, and $21 + 3n = 21 +$

$3 \cdot {}^-\frac{11}{9} = 21 + {}^-\frac{33}{9} = \frac{189}{9} + {}^-\frac{33}{9} = \frac{156}{9}$

12.
$$4x + 36 = 10x$$
$$^-4x + 4x + 36 = {}^-4x + 10x$$
$$36 = 6x$$
$$\frac{36}{6} = x$$
$$6 = x$$
$m \angle N = 4x + 36 = 4 \cdot 6 + 36 = 60°;$

$m \angle P = 10x = 10 \cdot 6 = 60°;$

$m \angle I = 180° - (60° + 60°) = 60°$

13.
$$F = \frac{5}{9}(F - 32)$$
$$F = \frac{5}{9} \cdot F - \frac{160}{9}$$
$$-\frac{5}{9}F + F = {}^-\frac{5}{9}F + \frac{5}{9}F - \frac{160}{9}$$
$$\frac{4}{9}F = -\frac{160}{9}$$
$$\frac{9}{4} \cdot \frac{4}{9}F = \frac{9}{4} \cdot {}^-\frac{160}{9}$$
$$F = {}^-40$$
$$^-40°F = {}^-40°C$$

14. **a.** Step 3 (He should have added 1 to both sides.)

   b.
$$5x - 1 = 2x + 8$$
$$^-2x + 5x - 1 = {}^-2x + 2x + 8$$
$$3x - 1 = 8$$
$$3x - 1 + 1 = 8 + 1$$
$$3x = 9$$
$$x = \frac{9}{3}$$
$$x = 3$$

15. $16(b + s + 12)$ or $16b + 16s + 192$ dollars

16. x cm $(4.4$ cm $+ 2.6$ cm $+ 2.1$ cm$) =$
x cm $\cdot 9.1$ cm $= 9.1x$ cm^2

17. $0.92 = \frac{92}{100} = \frac{23}{25}$

18. $4.\overline{3} = 4\frac{1}{3} = \frac{13}{3}$

19.
$$\text{Let } x = 6.\overline{36}$$
$$100x = 636.\overline{36}$$
$$100x - x = 636.\overline{36} - 6.\overline{36}$$
$$99x = 630$$
$$x = \frac{630}{99} = \frac{70}{11}$$

20.

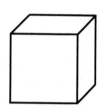

21. $1.3y + {}^-4z - y - {}^-2.7z + 8$
$= 1.3y + {}^-y + {}^-4z + 2.7z + 18$
$= (1.3 + {}^-1)y + ({}^-4 + 2.7)z + 18$
$= .3y + {}^-1.3z + 18$
$= .3y - 1.3z + 18$

22. some points on the line: (2, 2), ($^-4$, 8), (5, $^-1$)

23. **a.** 2,160,000
b. 2.16×10^6 (Write 2.16. The decimal point must move 6 places to the right to get 2,160,000, so the exponent of 10 is 6.)

24. BOOK

25. 295% of 2,160,000 = 2.95 · 2,160,000 = 6,372,000 farms

26. **a.** $^-5$ ($4x + 7 = 4 \cdot {}^-5 + 7 =$ $^-20 + 7 = {}^-13$, and $2x - 3 =$ $2 \cdot {}^-5 - 3 = {}^-10 - 3 = {}^-13$)
b. 8 ($5x - 7 = 5 \cdot 8 - 7 = 40 - 7 = 33$, and $3x + 9 = 3 \cdot 8 + 9 = 24 + 9 = 33$)

LESSON 12-6 (pp. 556-561)

1. $c = 20w + 5$

2. $c = 20 \cdot 6 + 5 = 120 + 5 = 125$ cents = $1.25

3. $c = 20 \cdot 3 + 5 = 60 + 5 = 65$ cents
(2.4 ounces is rounded up to 3 ounces.)

4.
$$45 = 20w + 5$$
$$45 + {}^-5 = 20w + {}^-5$$
$$40 = 20w$$
$$\frac{40}{20} = w$$
$$2 = w$$
letters weighing over 1 oz but not over 2 oz

5. $1.85

6. Divide by 100.

7. A table makes it easy to find the rates and easy to understand.

8. A graph takes the least space, allows for any values, and can be used by a computer.

9. Graphing pictures the rates and shows changes over time.

10. $c = 5 \cdot w = 5 \cdot 2 = 10\text{¢}$

11. $c = 5 \cdot w = 5 \cdot 10 = 50\text{¢}$ (9.2 ounces is rounded up to 10 ounces.)

12. 7 (Read the graph: A 3-oz letter in 1975 cost 35¢. In 1965, 35¢ is the cost of a 7-oz letter.)

13. **a.** 5¢ **b.** 13¢ **c.** 25¢

14. 11¢ (Check the formula: $c = 11w + 2$)

15. Many possible answers. Samples: (4, 0), (2, $^-4$)

16. sample points: (0, 5), (1, 2), (2, $^-1$)

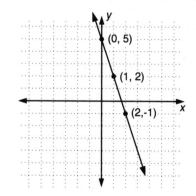

17. a. sample points: $(0, -4)$, $(6, 0)$, $(3, -2)$

(For $x = 0$, solve the equation $2 \cdot 0 - 3y = 12$: $y = -4$. For $x = 6$, solve the equation $2 \cdot 6 - 3y = 12$: $y = 0$. For $x = 3$, solve the equation $2 \cdot 3 - 3y = 12$: $y = -2$.)

b.

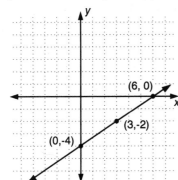

1992 Edition only:

c. $(3, -2)$

18. (a) (Some of the points on the line are $(0, -10)$, $(2, 0)$, and $(3, 5)$)

19. a.

weeks from now (w)	number of packages left (L)
1	388
2	376
3	364
4	352
5	340
6	328

b. The pairs $(1, 388)$, $(2, 376)$, and so on (from the table in part **a**), lie on the same line.

c.
$$0 = 400 - 12w$$
$$-400 + 0 = -400 + 400 - 12w$$
$$-400 = -12w$$
$$\frac{-400}{-12} = w$$
$$33\tfrac{1}{3} = w, \text{ or } w = 33.\overline{3}$$

d. In about 33 weeks the paper will be used up.

20. a. $y = 11x + 2$

b. Change the program as follows:

```
20 FOR X = 1 TO 100
30 Y = ⁻3 * X + 5
```

21.
$$11 - 2y = 8y + 5$$
$$11 - 2y + 2y = 8y + 5 + 2y$$
$$11 = 10y + 5$$
$$11 + {-5} = 10y + 5 + {-5}$$
$$6 = 10y$$
$$\frac{6}{10} = y$$
$$\frac{3}{5} = y, \text{ or } y = .6$$

check: $11 - 2y = 11 - 2 \cdot .6 = 11 - 1.2 = 9.8$, and $8y + 5 = 8 \cdot .6 + 5 = 4.8 + 5 = 9.8$

22.
$$3(5n + 22) = 5n + 6 + 19n$$
$$15n + 66 = 24n + 6$$
$$-24n + 15n + 66 = -24n + 24n + 6$$
$$-9n + 66 = 60$$
$$-9n + 66 + {-66} = 6 + {-66}$$
$$-9n = -60$$
$$n = \frac{-60}{-9} = \frac{60}{9} = \frac{20}{3}$$

check: $3(5n + 22) = 3(5 \cdot \frac{20}{3} + 22) =$
$3\left(\frac{100}{3} + \frac{66}{3}\right) = 3\left(\frac{166}{3}\right) = 166$, and
$5n + 6 + 19n = 5 \cdot \frac{20}{3} + 6 + 19 \cdot \frac{20}{3} =$
$\frac{100}{3} + \frac{18}{3} + \frac{380}{3} = \frac{498}{3} = 166$

23.
$$\frac{x - 9}{2} = \frac{x + 4}{3}$$
$$3(x - 9) = 2(x + 4)$$
$$3x - 27 = 2x + 8$$
$$-2x + 3x - 27 = 2x + 2x + 8$$
$$x - 27 = 8$$
$$x - 27 + 27 = 8 + 27$$
$$x = 35$$

check: $\frac{x - 9}{2} = \frac{35 - 9}{2} = \frac{26}{2} = 13$, and
$\frac{x + 4}{3} = \frac{35 + 4}{3} = \frac{39}{3} = 13$

24. 1 = the whole salad. After Alvin ate $\frac{1}{4}$, $1 - \frac{1}{4}$
remained. Betty ate $\frac{1}{2}\left(1 - \frac{1}{4}\right)$. Together they
ate $\frac{1}{4} + \frac{1}{2}\left(1 - \frac{1}{4}\right)$. The remaining amount is
$1 - \left(\frac{1}{4} + \frac{1}{2}\left(1 - \frac{1}{4}\right)\right)$.

Simplify $1 - \left(\frac{1}{4} + \frac{1}{2}\left(1 - \frac{1}{4}\right)\right)$

$= 1 - \left(\frac{1}{4} + \frac{1}{2}\left(\frac{4}{4} - \frac{1}{4}\right)\right)$

$= 1 - \left(\frac{1}{4} + \frac{1}{2} \cdot \frac{3}{4}\right)$

$= 1 - \left(\frac{1}{4} + \frac{3}{8}\right)$

$= 1 - \left(\frac{2}{8} + \frac{3}{8}\right)$

$= 1 - \frac{5}{8}$

$= \frac{8}{8} - \frac{5}{8}$

$= \frac{3}{8}$

$\frac{3}{8}$ of the salad remains

25. $\frac{1}{2}P + \frac{3}{4}Q$ cups

26. $\$.22(65\%$ of $18,000)$
$= \$.22(.65 \cdot 18,000)$
$= \$.22(11,700)$
$= \$2574$

27. **a.** -8
b. $-5 - {}^-3 = -5 + 3 = -2$
c. 15 **d.** $\frac{5}{3}$ or $1.\overline{6}$

28. $\frac{42}{5} = \frac{7x}{10}$
$35x = 420$
$x = \frac{420}{35}$
$x = 12$

29. $33°$ (m $\angle DBC = 180° - 130° = 50°$;
m $\angle BDC = 180° - 83° = 97°$; m $\angle BCD =$
$180° - (50° + 97°) = 180° - 147° = 33°$)

30. **a.** 5 **b.** 2 **c.** 0
d.

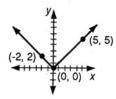

e. Sample points: $(3, 3)$, $(1, 1)$, $(6, 6)$, $(-3, 3)$,
$(-1, 1)$, $(-4.5, 4.5)$, $(-5, 5)$
f. a right angle

*31. *1992 Edition only:* Answers will vary.
*32. *1992 Edition only:* Intersection point is
$\left(\frac{-3}{2}, \frac{-15}{2}\right)$

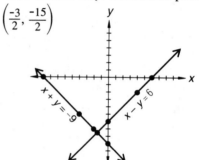

CHAPTER 12 PROGRESS SELF-TEST   (p. 563)

1. $m - 3m$
$= (1 - 3)m$
$= -2m$

2. $4x + 1 + 3x$
$= 4x + 3x + 1$
$= (4 + 3)x + 1$
$= 7x + 1$

3. $7m - 2n - 4m + n$
$= 7m + {}^-4m + {}^-2n + n$
$= (7 + {}^-4)m + (-2 + 1)n$
$= 3m + {}^-1n$
$= 3m - n$

4. For any numbers a, b, and x, $ax + bx =$
$(a + b)x$.

5.
$$1 - 9x = 13 + 3x$$
$$1 - 9x + 9x = 13 + 3x + 9x$$
$$1 = 13 + 12x$$
$$-13 + 1 = -13 + 13 + 12x$$
$$-12 = 12x$$
$$\frac{-12}{12} = x$$
$$-1 = x$$

6.
$$2(y - 3) = 12y$$
$$2y - 6 = 12y$$
$$-2y + 2y - 6 = -2y + 12y$$
$$-6 = 10y$$
$$\frac{-6}{10} = y$$
$$-\frac{3}{5} = y, \text{ or } y = -.6$$

7.
$$\frac{2t + 7}{4} = \frac{t - 8}{5}$$
$$5(2t + 7) = 4(t - 8)$$
$$10t + 35 = 4t - 32$$
$$-4t + 10t + 35 = -4t + 4t - 32$$
$$6t + 35 = -32$$
$$6t + 35 + -35 = -32 + -35$$
$$6t = -67$$
$$t = \frac{-67}{6}, \text{ or } t = -11.1\overline{6}$$

8.
$$0.2m + 6 = -m + 2 + 0.4m$$
$$0.2m + 6 = -0.6m + 2$$
$$0.6m + 0.2m + 6 = 0.6m + -0.6m + 2$$
$$0.8m + 6 = 2$$
$$0.8m + 6 + -6 = 2 + -6$$
$$0.8m = -4$$
$$\frac{1}{0.8} \cdot 0.8m = \frac{1}{0.8} \cdot -4$$
$$m = -5$$

9.
$$A + 7 = 1.5A$$
$$-A + A + 7 = 1.5A + -A$$
$$7 = .5A$$
$$\frac{1}{.5} \cdot 7 = \frac{1}{.5} \cdot .5A$$
$$14 = A$$

Lee is 14 years old.

10. T books $\cdot \dfrac{\$3.95}{\text{book}} + F$ books $\cdot \dfrac{\$4.95}{\text{book}} +$

V books $\cdot \dfrac{\$5.95}{\text{book}} =$

$\$3.95T + \$4.95F + \$5.95V$

11. $p = b + b + 40 + b + b + 40 =$
$4b + 80$

12. $500H + 11F$ calories (The hamburgers have $H \cdot 4 \cdot 80$ calories, or $320H$ calories. The buns have $180H$ calories. The french fries have $11F$ calories. The total is $320H + 180H + 11F = 500H + 11F$ calories.)

13.
$$5 \cdot 3 - 2y = 10$$
$$15 - 2y = 10$$
$$-15 + 15 - 2y = -15 + 10$$
$$-2y = -5$$
$$y = \frac{-5}{-2}$$
$$y = \frac{5}{2} \text{ or } 2.5$$

The second coordinate is 2.5.

14. Many possible answers. Samples: $(2, 4)$, $(10, 28)$, $(3, 7)$. (When $x = 2$, $y = 3 \cdot 2 - 2 = 4$. When $x = 10$, $y = 3 \cdot 10 - 2 = 28$. When $x = 3$, $y = 3 \cdot 3 - 2 = 7$.)

15.

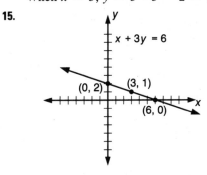

16.
$$\text{Let } x = 0.\overline{81}.$$
$$100x = 81.\overline{81}$$
$$100x - x = 81.\overline{81} - 0.\overline{81}$$
$$99x = 81$$
$$x = \frac{81}{99} = \frac{9}{11}$$

17.
$$\text{Let } x = 1.02\overline{8}$$
$$10x = 10.28\overline{8}$$
$$10x - x = 10.28\overline{8} - 1.02\overline{8}$$
$$9x = 9.26$$
$$x = \frac{9.26}{9} = \frac{926}{900} = \frac{463}{450}$$

18. $49 \cdot 7 = (50 - 1) \cdot 7 = 50 \cdot 7 - 1 \cdot 7 =$
$350 - 7 = 343$

19. from Line 3 to Line 4

20. $A = w(1.5 + .75 + .3) = w(2.55) = 2.55w$

CHAPTER 12 REVIEW (pp. 564-565)

1. $2v + 8v$
$= (2 + 8)v$
$= 10v$

2. $5x - x - 2x$
$= (5 - 1 - 2)x$
$= 2x$

3. $13a + 4b + 7a$
$= 13a + 7a + 4b$
$= (13 + 7)a + 4b$
$= 20a + 4b$

4. $-9 + 5m + 2 - 3m + m$
$= 5m - 3m + m - 9 + 2$
$= (5 - 3 + 1)m - 7$
$= 3m - 7$

5. $-6r + 3t - 8t + 7 - 8r$
$= -6r - 8r + 3t - 8t + 7$
$= (-6 - 8)r + (3 - 8)t + 7$
$= -14r - 5t + 7$

6. $m(1 + n) - m$
$= m \cdot 1 + mn - m$
$= m + mn - m$
$= mn$

7. $6(a - b + 2c)$
$= 6 \cdot a - 6 \cdot b + 6 \cdot 2c$
$= 6a - 6b + 12c$

8.
$$\text{Let } x = 5.\overline{7}$$
$$10x = 57.\overline{7}$$
$$10x - x = 57.\overline{7} - 5.\overline{7}$$
$$9x = 52$$
$$x = \frac{52}{9}$$

9.
$$\text{Let } x = 0.89\overline{2}$$
$$10x = 8.92\overline{2}$$
$$10x - x = 8.92\overline{2} - 0.89\overline{2}$$
$$9x = 8.03$$
$$x = \frac{8.03}{9} = \frac{803}{900}$$

10.
$$\text{Let } x = 6.\overline{54}$$
$$100x = 654.\overline{54}$$
$$100x - x = 654.\overline{54} - 6.\overline{54}$$
$$99x = 648$$
$$x = \frac{648}{99} = \frac{72}{11}$$

11.
$$\text{Let } x = 0.\overline{393}$$
$$1000x = 393.\overline{393}$$
$$1000x - x = 393.\overline{393} - 0.\overline{393}$$
$$999x = 393$$
$$x = \frac{393}{999} = \frac{131}{333}$$

12.
$$15x + 8 = 7x + 32$$
$$-7x + 15x + 8 = -7x + 7x + 32$$
$$8x + 8 = 32$$
$$8x + 8 + -8 = 32 + -8$$
$$8x = 24$$
$$x = \frac{24}{8}$$
$$x = 3$$
check: $15x + 8 = 15 \cdot 3 + 8 = 45 + 8$
$= 53$, and $7x + 32 = 7 \cdot 3 + 32 =$
$21 + 32 = 53$

13.
$$2 - 35m = 10m + 19 - 6m$$
$$2 - 35m = 4m + 19$$
$$2 - 35m + -4m = -4m + 4m + 19$$
$$2 + -39m = 19$$
$$-2 + 2 + -39m = -2 + 19$$
$$-39m = 17$$
$$-\frac{1}{39} \cdot -39m = -\frac{1}{39} \cdot 17$$
$$m = -\frac{17}{39}$$

check: $2 - 35m = 2 - 35 \cdot -\frac{17}{39} = 2 + \frac{595}{39}$

$= \frac{78}{39} + \frac{595}{39} = \frac{673}{39}$, and $10m + 19 - 6m =$

$10 \cdot -\frac{17}{39} + 19 - 6 \cdot -\frac{-17}{39} = -\frac{170}{39} + \frac{741}{39} +$

$\frac{102}{39} = \frac{673}{39}$

14.
$$\frac{E - 9}{6} = \frac{3E + 5}{3}$$
$$3(E - 9) = 6(3E + 5)$$
$$3E - 27 = 18E + 30$$
$$-3E + 3E - 27 = -3E + 18E + 30$$
$$-27 = 15E + 30$$
$$-27 + -30 = 15E + 30 + -30$$
$$-57 = 15E$$
$$\frac{-57}{15} = E$$
$$-\frac{19}{5} = E, \text{ or } E = -3.8$$

check: $\frac{E - 9}{6} = \frac{-3.8 - 9}{6} = \frac{-12.8}{6} =$

$-2.1\overline{3}$, and $\frac{3E + 5}{3} = \frac{3 \cdot -3.8 + 5}{3} =$

$\frac{-6.4}{3} = -2.1\overline{3}$

15.
$$7(y - 3) = 2y + 9 + 6y$$
$$7y - 21 = 8y + 9$$
$$-7y + 7y - 21 = -7y + 8y + 9$$
$$-21 = y + 9$$
$$-21 + -9 = y + 9 + -9$$
$$-30 = y$$
check: $7(y - 3) = 7(-30 - 3) = 7 \cdot -33 =$
-231, and $2y + 9 + 6y = 2 \cdot -30 + 9 +$
$6 \cdot -30 = -60 + 9 + -180 = -231$

16. from Line 2 to Line 3

17. $\$19.95 \cdot 4 = (\$20 - \$.05)4 =$
$\$20 \cdot 4 - \$.05 \cdot 4 = \$80 - \$.20 = \$79.80$

18. $5 \cdot 39 + 5 \cdot 39 = (5 + 5)39 = 10 \cdot 39 =$
390

19. T tablespoons $\cdot \dfrac{100 \text{ calories}}{\text{tablespoon}} +$

P pieces $\cdot \dfrac{70 \text{ calories}}{\text{piece}} = 100T + 70P$ calories

20. $7.99r + 4.95$ dollars
1992 Edition: $7.99c + 12.95$ dollars

21. $11E + 12T$

22.
$$E + 10 = 2.5E$$
$$-E + E + 10 = -E + 2.5E$$
$$10 = 1.5E$$
$$\frac{1}{1.5} \cdot 10 = \frac{1}{1.5} \cdot 1.5E$$
$$6.\overline{6} = E$$
Elijah is $6.\overline{6}$ years, or 6 years and 8 months old

23.
$$5 + \frac{2}{3}n = 4 + \frac{3}{4}n$$
$$5 + \frac{2}{3}n + -\frac{2}{3}n = 4 + \frac{3}{4}n + -\frac{2}{3}n$$
$$5 = 4 + \frac{9}{12}n + \frac{-8}{12}n$$
$$5 = 4 + \frac{1}{12}n$$
$$-4 + 5 = -4 + 4 + \frac{1}{12}n$$
$$1 = \frac{1}{12}n$$
$$12 \cdot 1 = 12 \cdot \frac{1}{12}n$$
$$12 = n$$

24. $x \cdot 20 + x \cdot 5 = 25x$
(or $25x = x \cdot 20 + x \cdot 5$)

25.

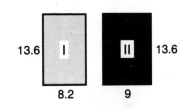

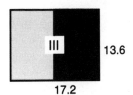

Area I + Area II = Area III
$8.2 \cdot 13.6 + 9 \cdot 13.6 = (8.2 + 9) \cdot 13.6$

26. Many possible answers. Samples: (1, −1), (2, 3), (3, 7)

(When $x = 1$, $y = 4 \cdot 1 - 5 = -1$.
When $x = 2$, $y = 4 \cdot 2 - 5 = 3$.
When $x = 3$, $y = 4 \cdot 3 - 5 = 7$.)

27. Many possible answers. Samples: (5, 0), (0, 2), (10, −2)

(When $x = 5$, $2 \cdot 5 + 5y = 10$. Solve for y: $y = 0$. When $x = 0$, $2 \cdot 0 + 5y = 10$. Solve for y: $y = 2$. When $x = 10$, $2 \cdot 10 + 5y = 10$. Solve for y: $y = -2$.)

28.

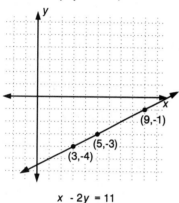

$x - 2y = 11$

29.

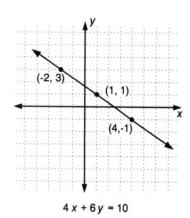

$4x + 6y = 10$

LESSON 13-1 (pp. 568-572)

1. A triangle is made up of three line segments. A triangular region consists of the space inside the three segments (and the triangle itself).

2. triangular region, triangle

3. 40 mm and 9 mm

4. 41 mm

5. $A = \frac{1}{2}ab$

$= \frac{1}{2} \cdot 40 \text{ mm} \cdot 9 \text{ mm}$

$= 180 \text{ mm}^2$

6. $p = 9 \text{ mm} + 40 \text{ mm} + 41 \text{ mm} = 90 \text{ mm}$

7. legs 8 and 15; hypotenuse 17;

area $= \frac{1}{2} \cdot 8 \cdot 15 = 60$ square units;

perimeter $= 8 + 15 + 17 = 40$ units

8. 157.5 square units (area of larger triangle $=$ $\frac{1}{2} \cdot 20 \cdot 21 = 210$; area of smaller triangle $=$ $\frac{1}{2} \cdot 10 \cdot 10.5 = 52.5$; $210 - 52.5 =$ 157.5 square units)

9. $\frac{1}{2}ab$

10. 146.5 square feet (area of triangle $=$ $\frac{1}{2} \cdot 13 \text{ ft} \cdot 25 \text{ ft} = 162.5 \text{ ft}^2$; area of square $= 4 \text{ ft} \cdot 4 \text{ ft} = 16 \text{ ft}^2$; $162.5 \text{ ft}^2 - 16 \text{ ft}^2 = 146.5 \text{ ft}^2$)

11. **a.** $A = \frac{1}{2} \cdot 6 \cdot h = 3h$

b. $A = \frac{1}{2} \cdot 6 \cdot h = 3h$

12. $A = \frac{1}{2} \cdot 20 \text{ in.} \cdot 30 \text{ in.} = 300 \text{ in.}^2$

13. 48 square inches (length of longer leg of yellow triangle $= \frac{2}{5} \cdot 30$ in. $= 12$ in.; length of shorter leg of yellow triangle $= \frac{2}{5} \cdot 20$ in. $= 8$ in.; area of yellow triangle $= \frac{1}{2} \cdot 12$ in. $\cdot 8$ in. $= 48$ in.^{2})

14. 40 square units (area of $\triangle QST = \frac{1}{2} \cdot 10 \cdot 19 = 95$ square units; area of $\triangle QRT = \frac{1}{2} \cdot 10 \cdot 11 = 55$ square units; area of $\triangle RST = 95 - 55 = 40$ square units)

15. $48 = \frac{1}{2} \cdot 6 \cdot x$

$48 = 3x$

$\frac{48}{3} = x$

$16 = x$

The other leg is 16 cm.

16. **a.** Make a right angle with a 1-in. segment and a 2-in. segment. Then draw the hypotenuse of the right triangle.

b. $A = \frac{1}{2} \cdot 1$ in. $\cdot 2$ in. $= 1$ in.^{2}

c. $2\frac{2}{8}$ in. or $2\frac{1}{4}$ in.

17. 8.64 square units (area of $\triangle ELA = \frac{1}{2} \cdot 6 \cdot 8 = 24$ square units; area of $\triangle EFA = \frac{1}{2} \cdot 4.8 \cdot 6.4 = 15.36$ square units; area of $\triangle ELF = 24 - 15.36 = 8.64$ square units)

18. $\frac{1}{9}$

19. $\left(\frac{1}{3}\,m\right)^3 = \frac{1}{3}\,m \cdot \frac{1}{3}\,m \cdot \frac{1}{3}\,m = \frac{1}{27}\,m^3$

20. $-\frac{8}{3}$

21. Let $x = 0.41\overline{6}$

$10x = 4.16\overline{6}$

$10x - x = 4.16\overline{6} - 0.41\overline{6}$

$9x = 3.75$

$x = \frac{3.75}{9} = \frac{375}{900} = \frac{5}{12}$

22. (c) (The first copy is 80% as large as the original. The second copy is 80% as large as the first, or 80% $\cdot$ 80% as large as the original. 80% $\cdot$ 80% $= .8 \cdot .8 = .64 = 64\%$)

23. $(a + b)(c + d) = ac + ad + bc + bd$

24. $11 - 5x = 511$

$-11 + 11 - 5x = -11 + 511$

$-5x = 500$

$-\frac{1}{5} \cdot -5x = -\frac{1}{5} \cdot 500$

$x = -100$

25. $a^2 + b^2$

$= 7^2 + 100^2$

$= 49 + 100$

$= 149$

26. **a.** 40%   **b.** about 35.8%

c. about 24.2%

(The width of each stripe is $\frac{1}{13} \cdot 1.3$ m $=$ .1 m. The area of each short stripe $= 1.1$ m $\cdot$ .1 m $= .11$ m^2, and the area of each long stripe $= 2$ m $\cdot$ .1 m $= .2$ m^2. So the area of red stripes $= 4 \cdot .11$ m$^2 + 3 \cdot .2$ m$^2 = 1.04$m.^{2} The area of the flag $= 2$ m $\cdot 1.3$ m $= 2.6$ m^2, so the percent that is red $= \frac{1.04}{2.6} = .4 = 40\%$. The area of white stripes $= 3 \cdot .11$ m$^2 + 3 \cdot .2$ m$^2 = .93$ m^2, so the percent that is white stripes $= \frac{.93}{2.6} \approx .358 \approx 35.8\%$. The area of the blue rectangle $= .9$ m $\cdot .7$ m $= .63$ m^2, so the percent that is the blue rectangle with stars $= \frac{.63}{2.6} \approx .242 \approx 24.2\%$.)

1. square root

2. square, square root

3. 2.5 is a square root of 6.25.

4. 3, -3

5. 9, -9

6. 2, -2

7. 5, -5

8. radical

9. 8

10. 1

11. -7

12. **a.** 17.320508

   b. Multiply it by itself.

   c. 17.32

13. 1.4142 . . . ≈ 1.414

14. (c)

15. **a.** 20 m   **b.** 20   **c.** -20

16. $\sqrt{8} \approx 2.82 \approx 2.8$

17. $\sqrt{25} + \sqrt{16}$
    $= 5 + 4$
    $= 9$

18. $\sqrt{25} - \sqrt{16}$
    $= 5 - 4$
    $= 1$

19. $\sqrt{25 + 16}$
    $= \sqrt{41}$
    ≈ 6.4031

20. $\sqrt{25} \cdot \sqrt{25}$
    $= 5 \cdot 5$
    $= 25$

21. $\sqrt{25 - 16}$
    $= \sqrt{9}$
    $= 3$

22. $\sqrt{5^2 + 4^2}$
    $= \sqrt{25 + 16}$
    $= \sqrt{41}$
    ≈ 6.4031

23. 7 and 8 ($7^2 = 49$, $8^2 = 64$)

24. 10 square units

25. $\sqrt{2}$ ($\sqrt{2} = 1.41421 \ldots$; $\frac{239}{169} = 1.41420 \ldots$)

26. **a.** 8 square units (It contains 4 whole squares and 8 half-squares.)

   b. $\sqrt{8}$ units ($\sqrt{8} \cdot \sqrt{8} = 8$)

27. 16.4

28. 16.9

29. 16.4, 16.5

30. 16

31. $A = \frac{1}{2} \cdot 24 \text{ m} \cdot 10 \text{ m} = 120 \text{ m}^2$

32. $A = 2\left(\frac{1}{2} \cdot 5 \cdot 28\right) = 140$ square units

33. **(a)** (Some points on the line are (0, -4), (2, 0), and (3, 2).)

34. $3x + 4y + 5x + 6y + 7x + 8y$
    $= 3x + 5x + 7x + 4y + 6y + 8y$
    $= (3 + 5 + 7)x + (4 + 6 + 8)y$
    $= 15x + 18y$

35. **(b)**

36. **a.** $\sqrt{1} = 1$; $\sqrt{2} \approx 1.414$, $\sqrt{3} \approx 1.732$, $\sqrt{4} = 2$, $\sqrt{5} = 2.236$, $\sqrt{6} \approx 2.449$, $\sqrt{7} \approx 2.646$, $\sqrt{8} \approx 2.828$, $\sqrt{9} = 3$, $\sqrt{10} \approx 3.162$, $\sqrt{11} \approx 3.317$, $\sqrt{12} \approx 3.464$, $\sqrt{13} \approx 3.606$, $\sqrt{14} \approx 3.742$, $\sqrt{15} \approx 3.873$

   b. $\sqrt{2} \cdot \sqrt{3} \approx 1.414 \cdot 1.732 \approx 2.449$; $\sqrt{6} \approx 2.449$

   c. $\sqrt{15}$ ($\sqrt{3} \cdot \sqrt{5} \approx 1.732 \cdot 2.236 \approx 3.873$; $\sqrt{15} \approx 3.873$)

   d. $\sqrt{a} \cdot \sqrt{b} = \sqrt{ab}$

37. **a.** Answers may vary depending on computer. Sample: 12.2474487

   b. Sample output:

   ```
    1   1
    2   1.41421356
    3   1.7320581
    4   2
    5   2.23606798
    6   2.44948974
    7   2.64575131
    8   2.82842713
    9   3
   10   3.16227766
   11   3.31662479
   12   3.46410162
   13   3.60555128
   14   3.74165739
   15   3.87298335
   ```

   c. Answers will vary.

LESSON 13-3 (pp. 579-583)

1. A theorem is a statement that follows logically from other statements known (or assumed) to be true.

2. (b)

3. If the legs of a right triangle have lengths a and b, and the hypotenuse has length c, then $a^2 + b^2 = c^2$.

Throughout the Solution Manual,
in the equations that arise from the Pythagorean
Theorem, only positive square roots are given.

4. **a.** $8^2 + 9^2 = y^2$
   b. $64 + 81 = y^2$
   $$145 = y^2$$
   $$\sqrt{145} = y$$

5. **a.** $x^2 + 8^2 = 10^2$
   b.
   $$x^2 + 64 = 100$$
   $$x^2 + 64 + {}^-64 = 100 + {}^-64$$
   $$x^2 = 36$$
   $$x = \sqrt{36}$$
   $$x = 6$$

6. **a.**

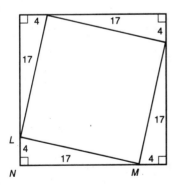

   b. $21 \cdot 21 = 441$

   c. $\frac{1}{2} \cdot 4 \cdot 17 = 34$

   d. $441 - 4 \cdot 34 = 441 - 136 = 305$
   e. $\sqrt{305}$

7.
$$3^2 = 1^2 + x^2$$
$$9 = 1 + x^2$$
$${}^-1 + 9 = {}^-1 + 1 + x^2$$
$$8 = x^2$$
$$\sqrt{8} = x$$
$\sqrt{8}$, or about 2.8 m

8. $6^2 + 7^2 = c^2$
$$36 + 49 = c^2$$
$$85 = c^2$$
$$\sqrt{85} = c$$
$$9.2 \approx c$$
9.2 inches

9. a right triangle

10. (b) (The third angle is a 90° angle.)

11. **a.** 9 km + 2 km = 11 km
    b. $9^2 + 2^2 = c^2$
    $$81 + 4 = c^2$$
    $$85 = c^2$$
    $$\sqrt{85} = c$$
    $\sqrt{85}$ or about 9.2 km
    c. about 11 − 9.2, or 1.8 km

12. $\sqrt{5}$ (The legs of the right triangle have lengths 1 and 2. $(CD)^2 = 1^2 + 2^2$, so $CD = \sqrt{5}$.)

13. **a.** about $13\frac{7}{8}$ or 13.9 in.

    b. $8.5^2 + 11^2 = c^2$
    $$72.25 + 121 = c^2$$
    $$193.25 = c^2$$
    $$\sqrt{193.25} = c$$
    $\sqrt{193.25}$ or about 13.9 in.

14. (b) (Use 2501 to compensate for there being no year 0: ${}^-572 + 2501 = 1929$)

15. $\sqrt{225 - 144}$
    $= \sqrt{81}$
    $= 9$

16. $\sqrt{2^2 + 3^2}$
    $= \sqrt{4 + 9}$
    $= \sqrt{13}$
    ≈ 3.6056

17. false ($\sqrt{9} + \sqrt{16} = 3 + 4 = 7$,
but $\sqrt{25} = 5$.)

18. **a.** 0

b. 0

19. 610 (Enter 2.5 $\boxed{y^x}$. 7 $\boxed{=}$)

20.
$$5000 = 50 + x - 25$$
$$5000 = 25 + x$$
$$^-25 + 5000 = ^-25 + 25 + x$$
$$4975 = x$$

21. 125 games $\cdot \dfrac{31\ \text{hits}}{40\ \text{games}} = 125 \cdot \dfrac{31}{40}$ hits $\approx$
97 hits

22. (a) (The order of the addends x and 1 was switched.)

23. $\dfrac{10\ \text{miles}}{35\ \frac{\text{miles}}{\text{hour}}} = \dfrac{10}{35}$ hour $= \dfrac{2}{7}$ hour

or about 17 minutes $\left(\dfrac{2}{7} \cdot 60 \approx 17\right)$

24. Many possible answers. Sample: A string half as long as another (having equal tension and diameter) sounds a note one octave higher than the other.

LESSON 13-4 (pp. 584-588)

1. $A = \dfrac{1}{2} \cdot hb$

$= \dfrac{1}{2} \cdot 24 \cdot 39$

$= 468$ square units

2. $A = \dfrac{1}{2} \cdot hb$

$= \dfrac{1}{2} \cdot 12 \cdot 14$

$= 84$ square units

3. **a.** $\overline{YA}$; **b.** $\overline{XB}$; **c.** $\overline{ZC}$

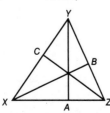

4. **a.** height **b.** base

5. Let b be the length of a side of a triangle with area A, and let h be the length of the altitude drawn to that side. Then $A = \dfrac{1}{2} \cdot hb$.

6. $A = \dfrac{1}{2} \cdot hb$

$= \dfrac{1}{2} \cdot 7 \cdot 6$

$= 21$ square units

7. **a.**
$$4^2 + (AD)^2 = 8^2$$
$$16 + (AD)^2 = 64$$
$$^-16 + 16 + (AD)^2 = ^-16 + 64$$
$$(AD)^2 = 48$$
$$AD = \sqrt{48}\ \text{cm, or}$$
$$\text{about } 6.9\ \text{cm}$$

b. $A = \dfrac{1}{2} \cdot hb$

$= \dfrac{1}{2} \cdot \sqrt{48} \cdot 8$

$= \dfrac{1}{2} \cdot 8 \cdot \sqrt{48}$

$= 4\sqrt{48}\ \text{cm}^2$, or about $27.7\ \text{cm}^2$

8.
$$A = \dfrac{1}{2} \cdot hb$$
$$300 = \dfrac{1}{2} \cdot h \cdot 40$$
$$300 = 20h$$
$$\dfrac{300}{20} = h$$
$$15\ \text{cm} = h$$

9. $A = \dfrac{1}{2} \cdot hb$

$= \dfrac{1}{2} \cdot 92 \cdot 230$

$= 10{,}580\ \text{m}^2$

10. 132 square units (area of $\triangle EAC =$

$\frac{1}{2} \cdot 12 \cdot 27 = 162$ square units;

area of $\triangle RAC = \frac{1}{2} \cdot 12.5 = 30$ square units;

area of $\triangle EAR = 162 - 30 = 132$ square units)

11. $3x + 14x + 2x + x = 20x = 20 \cdot 5.671 = 113.42$

12. $a(a + 2) = a \cdot a + a \cdot 2 = a^2 + 2a$

13. $$x - 0.4 = 3.02$$
$$x - 0.4 + 0.4 = 3.02 + 0.4$$
$$x = 3.42$$

14. $\frac{440}{-6} = -73.\overline{3} \approx -73$

15. $3\%, \frac{3}{10}, .\overline{3}, \sqrt{3}$ $(3\% = .03; \frac{3}{10} = .3 = .30,$
$.\overline{3} = .3333 \ldots ; \sqrt{3} \approx 1.732)$

16. $\frac{2}{5} + \frac{1}{3} + \frac{1}{4}$

$= \frac{24}{60} + \frac{20}{60} + \frac{15}{60}$

$= \frac{59}{60}$

17. $-4m = -4 \cdot -4 = 16$

18. three hundred forty-five and twenty-nine hundredths

19. $0.25 \sqrt{1454}$

$\approx 0.25 \cdot 38.13$

≈ 9.5325

≈ 10 seconds

20. 12 numbers (Multiply $4 \cdot 3$, or make a list: 12, 14, 16, 32, 34, 36, 52, 54, 56, 72, 74, 76.)

21. $\frac{0.46}{9.2} = \frac{46}{920} = \frac{1}{20}$ (Multiply numerator and

denominator of $\frac{0.46}{9.2}$ by 100; divide numerator

and denominator of $\frac{46}{920}$ by 46.)

22. 6 square inches (The length of the nearly horizontal segment is $3\frac{13}{16}$ in. The length of the altitude drawn to that side is $2\frac{15}{16}$ in. A $=$

$\frac{1}{2} \cdot hb = \frac{1}{2} \cdot 2\frac{15}{16} \cdot 3\frac{13}{16} = .5 \cdot 2.9375 \cdot 3.8125$

$= 5.5996 \ldots \approx 6)$

LESSON 13-5 (pp. 589-593)

1. Any polygon can be split up into triangles. By adding the areas of the triangles, you can get the area of the polygon.

2. Check if it has at least one pair of parallel sides.

3. false   4. true   5. false

6. true   7. false

8. **a.** 20 and 17

b. 22

c. $A = \frac{1}{2} \cdot h(b + B)$

$= \frac{1}{2} \cdot 22(20 + 17)$

$= 11 \cdot 37$

$= 407$ sq. units

9. **a.** Many possible answers. Sample:

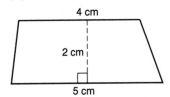
4 cm
2 cm
5 cm

b. $A = \frac{1}{2} \cdot h(b + B)$

$= \frac{1}{2} \cdot 2(4 + 5)$

$= 1 \cdot 9$

$= 9$ cm^2

10. $A = \frac{1}{2} \cdot h(b + B)$

11. The area of a trapezoid is one-half the product of its height and the sum of its bases.

12. Many possible answers. Sample:

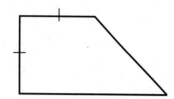

13. $A = \frac{1}{2} \cdot h(b + B)$

$= \frac{1}{2} \cdot 8(40 + 40)$

$= 4 \cdot 80$

$= 320$ square units

14. $A = \frac{1}{2} \cdot h(b + B)$

$\approx \frac{1}{2} \cdot 1100(900 + 1100)$

$\approx 550(2000)$

$\approx 1,100,000 \text{ km}^2$

15.
$A = \frac{1}{2} \cdot h(b + B)$

$60 = \frac{1}{2} \cdot 10(5 + B)$

$60 = \frac{1}{2}(50 + 10B)$

$60 = 25 + 5B$

$-25 + 60 = -25 + 25 + 5b$

$35 = 5B$

$\frac{35}{5} = B$

$7 \text{ m} = B$

16. figure, polygon, quadrilateral, trapezoid, parallelogram, rectangle, square

17. One example of an altitude is the dotted segment.

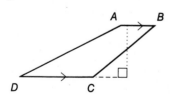

18. false (The sum of the lengths of only the legs of one triangle is one-half the perimeter of the rectangle.)

19. $A = \frac{1}{2} \cdot ab$

$= \frac{1}{2} \cdot 12 \cdot 16$

$= 96 \text{ ft}^2$

20. $0.5^2 + 1.2^2 = (AC)^2$

$0.25 + 1.44 = (AC)^2$

$1.69 = (AC)^2$

$\sqrt{1.69} = AC$

$1.3 = AC$

21. true $\left(\sqrt{\frac{1}{2}} = \sqrt{.5} \approx .707\right)$

22.
$2t - 5 = 9 + 8t$

$-2t + 2t - 5 = -2t + 9 + 8t$

$-5 = 6t + 9$

$-5 + -9 = 6t + 9 + -9$

$-14 = 6t$

$-\frac{14}{6} = t$

$-\frac{7}{3} = t$, or $t = -2.\overline{3}$

23.
$3(2u - 5) = 27$

$6u - 15 = 27$

$6u - 15 + 15 = 27 + 15$

$6u = 42$

$u = \frac{42}{6}$

$u = 7$

24. $2\frac{1}{3} + 3\frac{1}{4} + 4\frac{1}{5}$

$= 2 + \frac{1}{3} + 3 + \frac{1}{4} + 4 + \frac{1}{5}$

$= 9 + \frac{1}{3} + \frac{1}{4} + \frac{1}{5}$

$= 9 + \frac{20}{60} + \frac{15}{60} + \frac{12}{60}$

$= 9 + \frac{47}{60}$

$= 9\frac{47}{60}$

≈ 10

25. $A - \frac{2}{3}A = \frac{3}{3}A - \frac{2}{3}A = \left(\frac{3}{3} - \frac{2}{3}\right)A =$

$\frac{1}{3}A$ or $\frac{A}{3}$

26. Let $x = 8.\overline{2}$

$10x = 82.\overline{2}$

$10x - x = 82.\overline{2} - 8.\overline{2}$

$9x = 74$

$x = \frac{74}{9}$

27. **a.** Several possible answers. Sample: a
quadrilateral with no sides parallel;

b. Many possible answers. Sample:

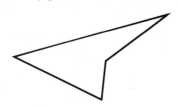

LESSON 13-6 (pp. 594-600)

1. A circle is the set of points at a certain
distance from a certain point.

2. diameter

3. circumference

4. $C = \pi d$

$\approx 3.14 \cdot 10$

≈ 31.4

≈ 31 cm

5. πs

6. $\frac{22}{7}$

7. **a.** estimate

b. 3.14

c. 3.14159

d. Answers may very depending on calculator.
Some calculators show 3.1415927.

*Throughout the Solution Manual, answers involving
estimations with π may vary slightly from your
answers depending on the approximation you used
for π.*

8. $C = \pi d$

$\approx \pi \cdot 7920$

$\approx 24{,}900$ mi

9. $\pi = \frac{C}{d}$ and $d = \frac{C}{\pi}$

10. A number is rational when it can be written as
a simple fraction.

11. A number is irrational when it cannot be
written as a simple fraction.

12. rational

13. irrational

14. rational

15. irrational

16. rational

17. rational

18. A real number is a number that can be written
as a decimal.

19. They are all real numbers.

20. yes (They are studied in higher mathematics
courses.)

21. $C = \pi d$

$= \pi \cdot 1.2$

$= 1.2\pi$

≈ 3.77 in.

22. $C = \pi d$

$= \pi \cdot 2r$

$= 2r\pi$

23. $C = 2r\pi$

$= 2 \cdot 12\pi$

$= 24\pi$

≈ 75 miles

24. $C = \pi d$

$50 = \pi d$

$\frac{50}{\pi} = d$

16 in. $\approx d$

25. $C = \pi d$

$\quad = \pi \cdot 24$

$\quad \approx 75.4$ in.

The bike goes about $10 \cdot 75.4$ or 754 inches (about 63 feet).

26. $\frac{355}{113}$ ($\frac{22}{7} = 3.1428571 \dots$; $\frac{355}{113} =$

$3.1415929 \dots$;$\pi = 3.1415926 \dots$)

27. $\sqrt{10}$ ($\sqrt{10} = 3.162277 \dots$)

28. $\pi + 1 \approx 3.14 + 1 \approx 4.14 \approx 4.1$

29. 162 square units (area of $\triangle OAB = \frac{1}{2} \cdot 6 \cdot 15$

$= 45$; area of $\triangle OBC = \frac{1}{2} \cdot 6 \cdot 7 = 21$; area

of $\triangle OCD = \frac{1}{2} \cdot 6 \cdot 12 = 36$; area of $\triangle ODA$

$= \frac{1}{2} \cdot 6 \cdot 20 = 60$; area of $ABCD = 45 +$

$21 + 36 + 60 = 162$)

30. $p = 15 + 7 + 12 + 20 = 54$

31. $\sqrt{841} - \sqrt{400}$

$\quad = 29 - 20$

$\quad = 9$

32. 156 square units (First find the length of the longer base, $B \cdot B = x + 8 + x$, where x is the length of the shorter leg of each right triangle. Solve the equation $13^2 = x^2 + 12^2$ to get $x = 5$. So $B = 5 + 8 + 5 = 18$.

The area of the trapezoid $= \frac{1}{2} \cdot h(b + B) =$

$\frac{1}{2} \cdot 12(8 + 18) = 6 \cdot 26 = 156$.)

33. $5\sqrt{3} \approx 5 \cdot 1.732 \approx 8.7 \approx 9$

34. $|2 - n|$

$\quad = |2 - 5|$

$\quad = |2 + -5|$

$\quad = |-3|$

$\quad = 3$

35. $9x^3 - 7x^2 + 12$

$\quad = 9 \cdot 6^3 - 7 \cdot 6^2 + 12$

$\quad = 9 \cdot 216 - 7 \cdot 36 + 12$

$\quad = 1944 - 252 + 12$

$\quad = 1704$

36. $\dfrac{m \text{ miles}}{20 \frac{\text{miles}}{\text{hour}}} = \dfrac{m}{20}$ hours

37. $\quad .6n = 30$

$\quad \frac{1}{.6} \cdot .6n = \frac{1}{.6} \cdot 30$

$\quad\quad\quad n = 500$

38. $\frac{6}{30} = .2 = 20\%$

39. a. $3\frac{1}{7} \approx 3.1428571$; $3\frac{10}{71} \approx 3.1408451$

b. Decimals had not yet been invented.

c. 74 or 75 years old

($-212 - -287 = -212 + 287 = 75$.

If he died in that part of 212 B.C. before his birthday, he was 74 years old.)

d. He was stabbed to death by a soldier while drawing a diagram in the sand.

40. a. Many possible answers. Sample: If 100 is put in the blank, the last line is

100   3.13207653

b. It adds the reciprocals of the squares from 1 to n, then takes the square root of 6 times this sum. As n gets larger and larger, the result gives a better and better approximation of π.

c. Many possible answers. Sample: If 1000 is put in the blank, the last line is

1000   3.14063806.

LESSON 13-7 (pp. 600-603)

1. $8^2 = 64$ square units

2. πr^2

3. $A = \pi r^2$

$\quad = \pi \cdot 4^2$

$\quad = 16\pi$

$\quad \approx 50$ square units

4. The square of Question 1 could completely cover the circle of Question 3.

5. $A = \frac{1}{2} \cdot \pi r^2$

$= \frac{1}{2} \cdot \pi \cdot 6^2$

$= 18\pi$ square units

6. A central angle is an angle with its vertex at the center of the circle.

7. sector   **8.** $90°$ **9.** $\frac{90°}{360°} = \frac{1}{4}$

10. $A = \frac{1}{4}\pi r^2$

$= \frac{1}{4}\pi \cdot 10^2$

$= 25\pi$ square units

11. $A = \pi r^2$

$= \pi \cdot 12.15^2$

$= 147.6225\pi$

≈ 463.77 mm^2

12. $\boxed{\pi}\ \boxed{\times}\ 50\ \boxed{x^2}\ \boxed{=}$

13. $\frac{50°}{360°} \cdot 180$ m$^2 = 25$ m^2

14. **a.** 0.3125π or about 0.98 in.^{2} (area of larger circle $= \pi \cdot .75^2 = .5625\pi$ in.; area of smaller circle $= \pi \cdot 5^2 = .25\pi$ in.^{2}; area of ring $= .5625\pi - .25\pi = .3125\pi$ ≈ 0.98 in.^{2}

b. the ring (area of smaller circle $= .25\pi$ in.^{2}; area of ring $= .3125\pi$ in.^{2})

15. **a.** $\frac{360°}{3} = 120°$

b. $A = \frac{120°}{360°} \cdot \pi r^2$

$= \frac{1}{3} \cdot \pi \cdot 7^2$

$= \frac{49\pi}{3}$

≈ 51.3 ft^2

16. $A = \frac{1}{8} \cdot \pi r^2$

$= \frac{1}{8} \cdot \pi \cdot 6^2$

$= \frac{9\pi}{2}$

$= 4.5\pi$

≈ 14.1 sq in.

14.1 sq in. $\cdot \dfrac{10\text{ calories}}{\text{sq in.}} = 141$ calories

17. $A = \frac{3}{4} \cdot \pi r^2$

$= \frac{3}{4} \cdot \pi \cdot 9^2$

$= \frac{243\pi}{4}$

$= 60.75\pi$

≈ 191 m^2

18. $C_1 = \pi d$ $C_2 = \pi d$

$= \pi \cdot 2 \cdot .5$ $= \pi \cdot 2 \cdot .75$

$= \pi \cdot 1$ $= \pi \cdot 1.5$

$= \pi$ $= 1.5\pi$

≈ 3.1 in. ≈ 4.7 in.

19.
$$a^2 + b^2 = c^2$$
$$14^2 + b^2 = 50^2$$
$$196 + b^2 = 2500$$
$$-196 + 196 + b^2 = -196 + 2500$$
$$b^2 = 2304$$
$$b = \sqrt{2304}$$
$$b = 48$$

20. $A = \frac{1}{2} \cdot hb$

$= \frac{1}{2} \cdot 60 \cdot 80$

$= 2400$ square units

21. A decimal represents an irrational number when it is infinite and does not repeat.

22. 100 years $\cdot \dfrac{0.01\text{ inch}}{\text{year}} = 1$ inch

23. $\dfrac{PR}{50} = \dfrac{40}{55}$

$55 \cdot PR = 2000$

$PR = \dfrac{2000}{55}$

$PR = \dfrac{400}{11} = 36.\overline{36}$

24. $5(x - y + 12) + 6(y + x - 8)$

$= 5x - 5y + 60 + 6y + 6x - 48$

$= 5x + 6x - 5y + 6y + 60 - 48$

$= (5 + 6)x + (-5 + 6)y + 12$

$= 11x + y + 12$

25. **a.** circle (Measure the diameter of the circle and the length of a side of the square. From these, calculate the approximate area of each figure.)

   b. no (Try various lengths, but keep the pair of string pieces equal in length for each experiment.)

LESSON 13-8 (pp. 604-608)

1. William Playfair in the late 1700s drew the first circle graphs.

2. pie graph

3. 180°

4. 75 people

5. $\dfrac{20}{80} = \dfrac{1}{4}$

6. India

7. $.20 = \dfrac{1}{5}$

8. false (The sum is 360°.)

9. **a.** $\dfrac{2}{10} = 20\%$

   b. $\dfrac{2}{10} \cdot 360° = 72°$

10. $\dfrac{3}{10} \cdot 360° = 108°$

11. $\dfrac{4}{10} \cdot 360° = 144°$

12. true (The area of the Colorado sector is $\dfrac{3}{10}$ of the area of the circle; the area of the Montana sector is $\dfrac{1}{10}$ of the area of the circle.)

13. **a.** 60 – 64   **b.** 20 – 29

   c. age 5

   d. 48.3 million (Combine the 2 sectors.)

14. **a.** $\dfrac{15}{50} = .3 = 30\%$

   b. $\dfrac{20 + 5}{50} = \dfrac{25}{50} = \dfrac{1}{2}$

   c.

Choice of Elective

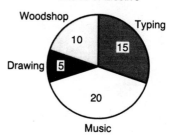

(Music sector: $\dfrac{20}{50} \cdot 360° = .4 \cdot 360° = 144°$; Woodshop sector: $\dfrac{10}{50} \cdot 360° = .2 \cdot 360° = 72°$; Drawing sector: $\dfrac{5}{50} \cdot 360° = .1 \cdot 360° = 36°$; Typing sector: $\dfrac{15}{50} \cdot 360° = .3 \cdot 360° = 108°$)

15. about 695 square feet (area of circle = $\pi r^2 = \pi \cdot 15^2 = 225\pi \approx 707$ ft²; area of square = $3.5^2 = 12.25$ ft²; surface area of water $\approx 707 - 12.25 \approx 695$ ft²)

16. (c) ($\dfrac{75}{8} = 9.375$, but $\dfrac{4}{.32} = 12.5$. In a and b, the numerator and denominator of the fraction on the left was multiplied by 3 to give the fraction on the right.)

17.
$$3.5x + 4 = 9x - 1$$
$$-3.5x + 3.5x + 4 = -3.5x + 9x - 1$$
$$4 = 5.5x - 1$$
$$4 + 1 = 5.5x - 1 + 1$$
$$5 = 5.5x$$
$$\frac{1}{5.5} \cdot 5 = \frac{1}{5.5} \cdot 5.5x$$
$$\frac{5}{5.5} = x$$
$$\frac{50}{55} = x, \text{ or } x = \frac{10}{11}$$

18.
$$.5^2 + 1^2 = (IB)^2$$
$$.25 + 1 = (IB)^2$$
$$1.25 = (IB)^2$$
$$\sqrt{1.25} = IB$$
$$1.1 \text{ in.} \approx IB$$

19.
$$A = \frac{1}{2} \cdot hb$$
$$= \frac{1}{2} \cdot .5 \cdot 2$$
$$= .5 \cdot .5 \cdot 2$$
$$= .5 \text{ in.}^2$$

20. 2.39×10^5 (In decimal form, the number is 239,000. Write 2.39. The decimal point must move 5 places to the right to get 239,000, so the exponent of 10 is 5.)

21. $3(5m - 6t - 4) = 3 \cdot 5m - 3 \cdot 6t - 3 \cdot 4$
$$= 15m - 18t - 12$$

22. $8.7(4.2 - r) + r = 8.7 \cdot 4.2 - 8.7r + r$
$$= 36.54 + (-8.7 + 1)r = 36.54 - 7.7r$$

23. $-23° + 14° = -9°$ turn

24. $4\pi(2)^2 = 4\pi \cdot 4 = 16\pi \approx 50.3$

25. a. 97 ($1985 - 1887 = 98$, but since he died in that part of 1985 before his birthday, he was 97.)

b. (1) Read the problem carefully. (2) Devise a plan. (3) Carry out the plan. (4) Check your work.

26. Answers will vary.

27. Computer activities will vary.

*28. *1992 Edition only:* Pie *a la mode* means pie topped with ice cream. The phrase *a la mode* generally means stylish or fashionable; thus it is related to the use of the word *mode* as in the lesson, for the most common appearance of an event makes that event in a sense in fashion.

LESSON 13-9 (pp. 609-612)

1. A sphere is the set of points in space at a certain distance from a certain point.

2. In a sphere of radius r and surface area S, $S = 4\pi r^2$.

3. $S = 4\pi r^2$
$$= 4\pi \cdot 12^2$$
$$= 4\pi \cdot 144$$
$$= 576\pi$$
$$\approx 1810 \text{ cm}^2$$

4. In a sphere of radius r and volume V, $V = \frac{4}{3}\pi r^3$.

5. $V = \frac{4}{3}\pi r^3$
$$= \frac{4}{3}\pi \cdot 12^3$$
$$= \frac{4}{3}\pi \cdot 1728$$
$$= 2304\pi$$
$$\approx 7238 \text{ cm}^3$$

6. Archimedes

7. $4 \boxed{\div} 3 \boxed{\times} \boxed{\pi} \boxed{\times} 7 \boxed{y^x} 3 \boxed{=}$

8. surface area

9. volume

10. surface area

11. volume

12. $S = 4\pi r^2$
$$= 4\pi \cdot 4.295^2$$
$$= 73.7881\pi$$
$$\approx 232 \text{ in.}^2$$

13. $V = \frac{4}{3}\pi r^3$
$$= \frac{4}{3}\pi \cdot 4.295^3$$
$$\approx 105.6\pi$$
$$\approx 332 \text{ in.}^3$$

14. a. $S = 4\pi r^2$
$$= 4\pi \cdot 1080^2$$
$$= 4,665,600\pi$$
$$\approx 15,000,000 \text{ mi}^2$$

b. $\dfrac{197,000,000}{15,000,000} \approx 13$ times

15. about 52% (volume of ball $= \frac{4}{3}\pi r^3 = \frac{4}{3}\pi \cdot 6^3$

$= 288\pi$; volume of box $= 12^3 = 1728$;

$\frac{288\pi}{1728} = \frac{\pi}{6} \approx .52 \approx 52\%$)

16.

Length of Time Adults Sleep

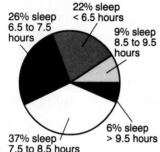

26% sleep 6.5 to 7.5 hours

22% sleep < 6.5 hours

9% sleep 8.5 to 9.5 hours

6% sleep > 9.5 hours

37% sleep 7.5 to 8.5 hours

(22% of 360° $= .22 \cdot 360° = 79.2°$;

26% of 360° $= .26 \cdot 36° = 93.6°$;

37% of 360° $= .37 \cdot 360° = 133.2°$;

9% of 360° $= .09 \cdot 360° = 32.4°$;

6% of 360° $= .06 \cdot 360° = 21.6°$)

17. $A = \pi r^2$

$= \pi \cdot 15^2$

$= 225\pi$

$\approx 707 \text{ mi}^2$

18. a. 29.4% of 197,000,000 =

$.294 \cdot 197,000,000 = 57,918,000 \approx$

58 million mi²

b. $\frac{3,540,000}{58,000,000} \approx .06 \approx 6\%$

c. USSR, Canada, China

19. Let r be the radius of the circle.

a. $A = \frac{1}{2} \cdot hb$

$= \frac{1}{2} \cdot r \cdot r$

$= \frac{1}{2}r^2$

b. $\frac{1}{2}r^2$ (Since $r^2 + r^2 = (AC)^2$, $AC = \sqrt{2r^2}$.

So area of smaller semicircle =

$\frac{1}{2}\pi \cdot \left(\frac{\sqrt{2r^2}}{2}\right)^2 = \frac{\pi}{2} \cdot \frac{2r^2}{4} = \frac{\pi r^2}{4}$.

Area of that part of smaller semicircle inside

larger circle $= \frac{1}{4}\pi r^2 - $ area of $\triangle ABC =$

$\frac{1}{4}\pi r^2 - \frac{1}{2}r^2 = \frac{\pi r^2}{4} - \frac{1}{2}r^2$.

So area of lune $= \frac{\pi r^2}{4} - \left(\frac{\pi r^2}{4} - \frac{1}{2}r^2\right) =$

$\frac{\pi r^2}{4} + \frac{-\pi r^2}{4} + \frac{1}{2}r^2 = \frac{1}{2}r^2$.)

c. They are equal. (You can verify this work with special cases.)

CHAPTER 13 PROGRESS SELF-TEST (p. 614)

1. $C = \pi d$

$= \pi\left(2 \cdot \frac{3}{8}\right)$

$= .75\pi$

$\approx 2.4 \text{ in.}$

2. $(\sqrt{3})^2 = 3$

3. $\sqrt{10}$

4. $\sqrt{30} + \sqrt{51} \approx 5.48 + 7.14 \approx 12.62 \approx 13$

5. $x^2 + 24^2 = 26^2$

$x^2 + 576 = 676$

$x^2 + 576 + ^-576 = 676 + ^-576$

$x^2 = 100$

$x = \sqrt{100}$

$x = 10$

6. $5^2 + 10^2 = (AB)^2$

$25 + 100 = (AB)^2$

$125 = (AB)^2$

$\sqrt{125} = AB$

7. $\sqrt{25}$ ($\sqrt{25} = 5$)

8. $A = \frac{1}{2} \cdot ab$

$= \frac{1}{2} \cdot 24 \cdot 7$

$= 84 \text{ cm}^2$

9. $A = \frac{1}{2} \cdot hb$

$\quad = \frac{1}{2} \cdot 30 \cdot 36$

$\quad = 540$ square units

10. $A = \frac{1}{2} \cdot h\,(b + B)$

$\quad = \frac{1}{2} \cdot 8(9 + 30)$

$\quad = 4 \cdot 39$

$\quad = 156$ square units

11. The legs are $\overline{AC}$ and $\overline{BC}$. The hypotenuse is $\overline{AB}$.

12.
$$A = \frac{1}{2} \cdot hb$$
$$400 = \frac{1}{2} \cdot 25 \cdot b$$
$$400 = \frac{25}{2}b$$
$$\frac{2}{25} \cdot 400 = \frac{2}{25} \cdot \frac{25}{2}b$$
$$32 \text{ in.} = b$$

13. quadrilateral

14. $C = \pi d$

$\quad = \pi \cdot 7$

$\quad \approx 22$ in.

15. $A = \pi r^2$

$\quad = \pi \cdot 16^2$

$\quad = 256\pi$ square units

16. A decimal represents an irrational number when it is infinite and nonrepeating.

17. $S = 4\pi r^2$

$\quad = 4\pi \cdot 12^2$

$\quad = 576\pi$

$\quad \approx 1810$ cm^2

18. $V = \frac{4}{3}\pi r^3$

$\quad = \frac{4}{3}\pi \cdot 9^3$

$\quad = \frac{4}{3}\pi \cdot 729$

$\quad = 972\pi$

$\quad \approx 3054$ cubic units

19. The total number of players is 48.

$\frac{10 \text{ cellos}}{48 \text{ players}} = 0.208\overline{3} \approx 20.8\%$

20. $A = \frac{m}{360} \cdot \pi r^2$

$\quad = \frac{60}{360} \cdot \pi \cdot 4^2$

$\quad = \frac{1}{6} \cdot \pi \cdot 16$

$\quad = \frac{8\pi}{3}$ cm^2

$\quad \approx 8.4$ cm^2

CHAPTER 13 REVIEW (pp. 615-616)

1. $A = \frac{1}{2} \cdot hb$

$\quad = \frac{1}{2} \cdot 12 \cdot 25$

$\quad = 150$ square units

2. $A = \frac{1}{2} \cdot ab$

$\quad = \frac{1}{2} \cdot 200 \cdot 210$

$\quad = 21,000$ cm^2

3. $A = \frac{1}{2} \cdot ab$

$\quad = \frac{1}{2} \cdot 8 \cdot 3$

$\quad = 12$ square units

4. $A = \frac{1}{2} \cdot hb$

$\quad = \frac{1}{2} \cdot 8 \cdot 12$

$\quad = 48$ square units

5. 8 and 9 ($8^2 = 64$ and $9^2 = 81$)

6. −1 and −2 ($\sqrt{3}$ is between 1 and 2, so −$\sqrt{3}$ is between −1 and −2.)

7. $\sqrt{144 + 256} = \sqrt{400} = 20$

8. 6 and −6

9. $3^2 + 8^2 = (BI)^2$

$\quad 9 + 64 = (BI)^2$

$\quad\quad\quad 73 = (BI)^2$

$\quad\quad \sqrt{73} = BI$

10.
$$(HA)^2 + 12^2 = 20^2$$
$$(HA)^2 + 144 = 400$$
$$(HA)^2 + 144 + \text{-}144 = 400 + \text{-}144$$
$$(HA)^2 = 256$$
$$HA = \sqrt{256}$$
$$HA = 16$$

11.
$$20^2 + 48^2 = c^2$$
$$400 + 2304 = c^2$$
$$2704 = c^2$$
$$\sqrt{2704} = c$$
$$52 = c$$

12.
$$1^2 + y^2 = 2^2$$
$$1 + y^2 = 4$$
$$\text{-}1 + 1 + y^2 = \text{-}1 + 4$$
$$y^2 = 3$$
$$y = \sqrt{3}$$

13. $A = \frac{1}{2} \cdot h\,(b + B)$

$\quad = \frac{1}{2} \cdot 120(60 + 350)$

$\quad = 60 \cdot 410$

$\quad = 24{,}600$ square units

14. $A = \frac{1}{2} \cdot h(b + B)$

$\quad = \frac{1}{2} \cdot 120(350 + 350)$

$\quad = 60 \cdot 700$

$\quad = 42{,}000$ square units

15. $A = \frac{1}{2} \cdot h(b + B)$

$\quad = \frac{1}{2} \cdot 120(60 + 110)$

$\quad = 60 \cdot 170$

$\quad = 10{,}200$ square units

16. $A = \frac{1}{2} \cdot h(b + B)$

17. $C = \pi d$

$\quad = \pi(2 \cdot 10)$

$\quad = 20\pi$ units

$\quad A = \pi r^2$

$\quad = \pi \cdot 10^2$

$\quad = 100\pi$ square units

18. $C = \pi d$

$\quad = \pi \cdot 2$

$\quad \approx 6$ m

19. $A = \frac{m}{360} \cdot \pi r^2$

$\quad = \frac{90}{360} \cdot \pi \cdot 10^2$

$\quad = \frac{1}{4} \cdot \pi \cdot 100$

$\quad = 25\pi$ square units

20. $A = \frac{m}{360} \cdot \pi r^2$

$\quad = \frac{100}{360} \cdot \pi \cdot 6^2$

$\quad = 10\pi$

$\quad \approx 31$ square units

21. $S = 4\pi r^2$

$\quad = 4\pi \cdot 5^2$

$\quad = 100\pi$ square units

22. $V = \frac{4}{3}\pi r^3$

$\quad = \frac{4}{3}\pi \cdot 4^3$

$\quad = \frac{256\pi}{3}$

$\quad \approx 268$ in.^{3}

23. all but π

24. all but $\sqrt{4}$ ($\sqrt{4} = 2$)

25. A decimal always represents a real number.

26. $A = \frac{1}{2} \cdot ab$

$\quad = \frac{1}{2} \cdot 8 \cdot 10.5$

$\quad = .5 \cdot 8 \cdot 10.5$

$\quad = 42$ in.^{2}

27. $A = \frac{1}{2} \cdot hb$

$= \frac{1}{2} \cdot 3 \cdot 1.8$

$= 2.7 \text{ m}^2$

28. $A = \pi r^2$

$= \pi \cdot 2^2$

$= 4\pi$

$\approx 13 \text{ mi}^2$

29. $S = 4\pi r^2$

$= 4\pi \cdot 10^2$

$= 400\pi$

$\approx 1257 \text{ cm}^2$

30. $A = \frac{1}{12}\pi r^2$

$= \frac{1}{12}\pi \cdot 9^2$

$= \frac{27\pi}{4}$

$\approx 21.2 \text{ in.}^2$

31. $C = \pi d$

$= \pi(2 \cdot 10)$

$= 20\pi$

$\approx 63 \text{ ft}$

32. $C = \pi d$

$= \pi(2 \cdot 150{,}000{,}000)$

$= 300{,}000{,}000\pi \text{ km}$

$\approx 942{,}000{,}000 \text{ km}$

33. $V = \frac{4}{3}\pi r^3$

$= \frac{4}{3}\pi \cdot 2^3$

$= \frac{32}{3}\pi$

$\approx 33.5 \text{ in.}^3$

34. $V = \frac{4}{3}\pi r^3$

$= \frac{4}{3}\pi \cdot 1.5^3$

$= 4.5\pi$

$\approx 14 \text{ cm}^3$

35. $\sqrt{50}$

36. $(\sqrt{4.9})^2 = 4.9$

37. $\sqrt{2}$ (Area of tilted square $= 2$, so length of side $= \sqrt{2}$ because $\sqrt{2} \cdot \sqrt{2} = 2$.)

38. $6 ($27 - ($5 + $4 + $2 + $10))$

39. $25\% = \frac{1}{4}$, and the sector for lunch has more than a quarter of the circle's area.

40.

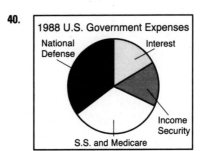

(Income Security: $\frac{125}{840} \cdot 360° \approx 53.6°$;

National Defense: $\frac{295}{840} \cdot 360° \approx 126.4°$;

Interest on national debt: $\frac{140}{840} \cdot 360° = 60°$;

S.S. and Medicare: $\frac{280}{840} \cdot 360° = 120°$)

1992 Edition:

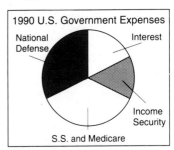

(Income Security: $\frac{137}{952} \cdot 360° \approx 52°$;

National Defense: $\frac{303}{952} \cdot 360° \approx 115°$;

Interest on national debt: $\frac{170}{952} \cdot 360° = 64°$;

S.S. and Medicare: $\frac{342}{952} \cdot 360° = 129°$)